**LEONARD MOSS, M.D.**
*Cornell University Medical College*

# MANAGEMENT STRESS

**ADDISON-WESLEY PUBLISHING COMPANY**

Reading, Massachusetts
Menlo Park, California • London
Amsterdam • Don Mills, Ontario • Sydney

This book is in the
Addison-Wesley Series on Occupational Stress

*Series Editor:* Dr. Alan A. McLean

**Library of Congress Cataloging in Publication Data**

Moss, Leonard, 1927–
    Management stress.

    (Addison-Wesley series on occupational stress; 5)
    Includes bibliographies and index.
    1.  Executives.   2.   Job stress.   I.   Title.
II.   Series.
HF5500.2.M67        658.4'07        80-22246
ISBN 0-201-05050-1

ISBN 0-201-05050-1

ABCDEFGHIJ-AL-89876543210

# FOREWORD

The vast literature concerned with the individual coping with work stress stems from many and diverse disciplines, primarily psychiatry, clinical and social psychology, sociology, cultural anthropology, and occupational and internal medicine, with significant contributions from such widely different fields as behavioral toxicology and personnel and management. While each discipline is concerned with so-called "psychosocial stressors," communication between the several disciplines has generally been the exception rather than the rule. Lawyers, for example, tend to communicate mainly with other lawyers about the issues that concern them. Union leaders tend to communicate most often with other union leaders. Clinical psychologists direct their communications to their colleagues, but use a different language from that used by many of the psychiatrists who are equally concerned. Even social psychologists and industrial sociologists sometimes find it difficult to exchange data. The transfer of useful data from one discipline to another has proven to be very difficult. "Some researchers go about rediscovering the known, with little deference to an existing literature or to determinable frontiers for contemporary research; and what consensus may be possible is *not adequately disseminated for beneficial application beyond home base.*"*

---

* Robert Rose, editorial, *Journal of Human Stress*, Vol. 3 No. 1, March 1977.

Communication across disciplines is not the only difficulty that students of job-related stress encounter. Transcultural communication is a problem too. Western physiologists, for instance, who are concerned with hormones in the brain, have difficulty communicating ·with their eastern European colleagues who prefer to speak in terms of "higher nervous function."

There is growing common concern. Theories and practices in each discipline are beginning to cross-pollinate other disciplines and to exert a positive influence toward understanding the stresses of the workplace and workers' reactions.

The many denominators of concern for an employee population under stress form the unifying theme of these volumes. As a field of study, occupational stress is beginning to gel. It is a subject of increasing interest not only to members of unions and management, but also to the health professionals who serve as their consultants. Increasingly, awareness and expertise are being focused on both theoretical and practical problem solving. The findings of social scientists have led to the enactment of legislation in the Scandinavian countries, for instance, where employers are now required, under certain circumstances, to provide meaningful work and appropriate job satisfaction with a minimum of occupational stress.

The authors of these books represent many points of view and a variety of disciplines. Each, however, is interested in the same basic thing—greater job satisfaction and greater productivity for each employee. The books were written independently with only broad guidelines and coordination by the editor. Each is a unique, professional statement summarizing an area closely related to the main theme. Each extracts from that area applications which seem logically based on currently available knowledge.

All of the authors treat, from differing perspectives, three key concepts: stress, stressor, and stress reactions. *Stress* defines a process or a system which includes not only the stressful event and the reaction to it, but all the intervening steps between. The *stressor* is a stressful event or stressful condition that produces a psychological or physical reaction in the individual that is usually unpleasant and sometimes produces symptoms of emotional or physiological disability. The *stress reaction* concerns the consequences of the stimulus provided by a stressor. It is, in other words, the response to a stressor, and it is generally unhealthy. Most often, such reactions may be defined in rather traditional psychological terms, ranging from mild situational anxiety and depression to serious emotional disability.

Many frames of reference are represented in this series. A psychoanalyst describes the phenomenon of occupational stress in executives. A sociologist reflects the concern with blue-collar workers. Health-care-delivery systems and the prevention of occupational stress reactions are covered by occupational physicians. Other authors focus on social support systems and on physiological aspects of stress reactions. All the authors are equally concerned with the reduction of unhealthy environmental social stimuli both in the world of work and in the other aspects of life that the world of work affects. In each instance, the authors are concerned with defining issues and with drawing the kinds of conclusions that will suggest constructive solutions.

The legal system, beginning with worker's compensation statutes and more recently augmented by the Occupational Safety and Health Act, deals directly with occupational stress reactions and will be the subject of one of the books in the series. That statute, which created both the Occupational Safety and Health Administration and the National Institute for Occupational Safety and Health, contains a specific directive mandating study of psychologically stressful factors in the work environment. We have seen criteria documents and standards for physical factors in the work environment. We may soon see standards developed to govern acceptable levels of psychological stressors at work such as already exist in Sweden and Norway; another significant area of concern for this series.

At the beginning of this series it is difficult to foresee all the pivotal areas of interest which should be covered. It is even more difficult to predict the authors who will be able and willing to confront the issues as they emerge in the next few years. In a rapidly changing technological, scientific, and legislative world, the challenge will be to bring contemporary knowledge about occupational stress to an audience of intelligent managers who can translate thoughts into constructive action.

Alan A. McLean, M.D.
Editor

# INTRODUCTION:
# A FRAMEWORK

The most valuable information about management stress comes from observations of how competent managers cope with conditions that challenge their accustomed career and life patterns. As a psychiatrist and consultant to a large corporation, I have had the opportunity to make such observations over many years, in many settings and circumstances.

My interest in management stress developed early in my practice when the corporation was undergoing far-reaching changes in structure and management policy. At that time a number of their managers were referred to me for relief of distress; to achieve perspective in an atmosphere of uncertainty and job insecurity; and for the resolution of personal crises associated with change. The in-depth interviews I conducted at that time resulted in my awareness that there are patterns in management stress and its relief.

Later, when I became consultant to the Corporate Medical Director on issues pertaining to stress reduction, I had the opportunity to observe "from the inside" how managers react to challenging conditions. I systematically collected information through designed studies of a broad spectrum of stressful conditions: how managers adjust to the challenging effects of such stressors as a new management team; the effects of an extraordinarily heavy workload as a result of the energy crisis; unanticipated changes in organizational structure; the stressfulness of working abroad, and various aspects of job change and job loss.

I found no significant difference in the content of confidential interviews held in my private office, and those that took place in the privacy of the manager's office. The issues discussed were the same—stress reactions, and career-related personal crises.

Observations of managers in different organizations at comparable levels dealing with comparable stressful circumstances, confirm the impression that the reactions are characteristic of managers under stress and *not* those of vulnerable individuals with special adjustment difficulties.

When I was asked to write the volume on management stress for the Addison-Wesley Series on Occupational Stress, I accepted because my base of information appeared to be adequate for such an undertaking. But organizing this information proved to be much more difficult than I had originally anticipated.

Constructing an appropriate outline of management stressors presented the greatest problem. Contributions of experts in the fields of organizational behavior, psychology, sociology, and medical epidemiology are quoted here to support the framework presented in this volume. This framework uses the manager's characteristic experiences with stress and career-related personal problems as building blocks.

Managerial stressors are categorized according to source:

- management's control of authority and accepted modes of behavior.

- the interpersonal dynamics of hierarchical organizations.

- career development patterns.

- changes in the harmony between the manager and the organization that result when the individual and the organization develop along divergent pathways.

- changing social and cultural values.

Coping strategies are presented in general terms as principles or guidelines, rather than as specific prescriptions or *how to's*. This approach relies on the creative intelligence of the reader to abstract from the material presented, what has personal relevance, and to use it to meet personal needs.

I have confidence in this perspective. It has been demonstrated on innumerable occasions in my clinical experience, that armed with realistic self-awareness, well-motivated individuals will use their creative intelligence to find solutions to their problems—solutions that could not have been formulated or prescribed for them by anyone else.

Coping strategies are not described in detail because readers are likely to have vastly different needs. Young managers are interested in the problems of making the transition from solo performers to positions of leadership. Older managers are concerned about preserving their positions of leadership in an atmosphere of shrinking opportunities. Managers whose work environment is stable are not likely to be concerned with preservation of the harmony between the individual and the job during periods of changing organizational structure and practices. But managers undergoing such change will probably look for help with their immediate pressing problems. Strategies are presented to help the manager and the manager's family think through solutions to personal crises and to offer managers suggestions for appropriate supports to the coping efforts of others.

Models are presented to clarify coping principles. *The Executive's Map of Management Stress* (page 246) can be used as a guide to self-assessment and to the thinking through of current personal and career adjustment issues. *A Personal Stress Counseling Program* (page 240) sets forth suggestions for providing personal, confidential exchanges of ideas, advice, and feedback with professionals knowledgeable about the pressures of a manager's work and roles.

The stress process model serves as an integrating concept. It should help to define the effects of stressors, to chart the modifying influences of social supports and individual differences, and to point to strategies to reduce distress and to enhance effective coping. Thus, the concept of stress as a process provides a useful framework for the consideration of the sources and consequences of management stress.

# ACKNOWLEDGMENTS

I would like to thank my close and valued friends and esteemed colleagues, Dr. Preston Munter, Dr. Bernard Riess, Dr. Harry Sinclaire and Dr. Alan McLean with whom it has been my good fortune over a span of twenty years, to exchange ideas and observations about how to help managers cope with stress. Several of the concepts and portions of the illustrative material that appear in this book are a direct outgrowth of these exchanges and the stimulating discussions they provoked. Alan McLean deserves special thanks for his advice, encouragement, and sound judgment in his role as editor of this series.

My many friends in the "large corporation," to which I am a consultant, deserve a special expression of gratitude. During hundreds of hours of interviews they informed me of the problems and pressures of the manager's work and roles and told me all they could about management stress. I have chosen not to identify the "large corporation" because I do not wish the reader to conclude that the material used to describe managers and their problems comes from this one source. In fact, it comes from many sources, and each illustrative interview is a composite drawn from a number of parallel situations.

Many persons contributed greatly to the writing of this book. Dr. Leon Warshaw's blend of encouragement and constructive criticism helped to focus the early chapters. Judith Kurzweil and Carl

x    Acknowledgments

Long supplied much of the literature on organizational dynamics. To Camille Strano, Olive Harrielal and Joan DiGangi goes my special appreciation for their enthusiastic cooperation in the preparation of the manuscript. To my daughter Vanessa and my son William my gratitude and affection for their "personal support" as I labored to complete the task.

My wife Ruth is not only a support, she is a partner in the effort. Her perspective, judgment and editorial skill were invaluable to the preparation of the manuscript.

*New York, New York*                                                    L. M.


*August 1980*

# CONTENTS

# 1

# THE NEED TO KNOW ABOUT STRESS

Signs of stress are widespread among managers and executives today, and so are the adverse effects of stress on their well-being, effectiveness, and health.

In recent years there has been a profound increase in such traditional signs of tension as:

- worry about making job decisions.
- feelings of insecurity.
- dissatisfaction with job advancement.
- sleeping and drinking problems.

Tension is evident throughout the ranks of management. Different groups of managers evidence tensions in distinct ways and for characteristic reasons. Hard-driving managers, age thirty-five or under, in their present positions only a short while, are prone to periods of stress during which they become restless, irritable, and unable to relax (Kiev and Kohn, 1979).

The effects of stress on health are also increasing. Coronary heart disease (CHD) has been linked to such factors as work pressure, heavy work load, and the responsibility for managing people. The incidence of CHD increases with age, of course. But as the average age of managers is dropping, the incidence of CHD among younger individuals is climbing, indicating that stress factors in the management role are taking their toll on the health of even younger executives (*Business Week*, November 15, 1976).

As women become executives they fall victim to heart disease, ulcers, alcoholism, and other ills traditionally associated with male executives. The health profile of the female executive is becoming more like that of the striving businessman and less like that of other women (both working and nonworking).

Feelings of job insecurity preoccupy middle-aged executives in mid or late career. Many face radical career shifts prompted by the evaporation of goals and opportunities in an ever-narrowing organizational hierarchy, as well as by the trend toward the hiring of younger managers and the forced early retirement of older managers. The problems of executives in mid or late career raise complex issues of human-resource management for business organizations.

Often the impact of management stress is transmitted to the executive's family, which leads to crises in the executive's personal life. Decisions traditionally imposed by the organization, such as the role of the executive's spouse, where the family will live, what its life style will be, are more and more being called into question. The family now demands that their interests be given a higher priority in the planning of an executive's career.

It would thus appear that anyone in a managerial role will go through peaks of extraordinary stress and periodic personal crises during the course of a career in an organizational setting. The problem is not that managers themselves have some special vulnerability to stressful or changing conditions. Rather, the pressures and dynamics of the management process and contemporary trends both internal and external to organizational life reinforce existing pressures or create new ones.

Personnel practitioners must understand the dynamics of stress in order to help others cope with it. Top level executives must understand the dynamics of stress to manage organizational change. Every manager must have a strategy to cope with the personal crises that result from the interaction of work environment stresses and the stresses of personal life.

More and more employers are responding to the threat of increasing management stress by initiating a wide variety of programs designed to help employees maintain their health and neutralize those stress responses that predispose to illness. Stress management usually includes physical fitness programs, training in relaxation techniques, and even advice in the use of leisure time.

It is unusual, however, to find an employer-initiated program designed to provide insights into how to anticipate and cope with stress at the source (e.g. the ever narrowing opportunities available to executives in a hierarchical structure that dooms even competent individuals to disappointment or midcareer crises). Even more unusual are organization-supported programs to resolve career-related *personal* crises, such as the complications that arise from a spouse's refusal to transfer because of established roots in the community, or conflicting career or personal interests.

In the final analysis managers or executives bear the responsibility for formulating a personal coping strategy that fits their individual needs. They must update and renegotiate this strategy as the needs of career and family life change.

Every manager, and anyone planning to become a manager, should know as much as possible about the sources and dynamics of management stress. Knowing what to anticipate and how to prepare for it helps the manager to achieve the benefits of successful coping (confidence, competence, security, and personal growth), to minimize the disabling consequences of stress (work or personal maladjustment, precipitation of a wide range of chronic illnesses), and to deal effectively with the usual strains that accompany the stress process.

## THE STRESS PROCESS

Stress reflects the ordinary pressures of day-to-day living as well as the extraordinary pressures that confront each of us from time to time. Stress is not necessarily harmful. Some degree of stress is normal and is in fact necessary for day-to-day functioning. Some stress tends to keep us mentally and physically alert and stable.

Some challenge is essential in the manager's working life. Managers and executives seek a high level of intrinsic gratification in their jobs, gratification based on the use of competence and experience, or the application of skills. Challenge and pressure act as stimuli leading to the satisfaction of accomplishment. As in other areas of life, work has its ordinary and extraordinary pressures. Coping with the ordinary pressures of the management process should require no special strategies other than those supplied through regular personnel support systems, or those learned through training, experience, and on-going management education. In the discussion of management stress presented here, the concept of a stressor as an *extraordinary pressure* rather than an ordinary stimulus is preferred.

Thus, a *management stressor* is defined as:

1   any objective condition or any change in the work environ-
    ment that is perceived as potentially harmful, threatening,
    challenging, or frustrating; or
2   any set of circumstances related to work that requires change
    in the individual's on-going life pattern.

The modern concept of stress links stressors and the reactions
that follow in a dynamic sequence of conditions illustrated in Fig.
1.1.*

• the impact of environmental stress from all sources (stressors)
  poses a threat to the individual.

• mediating factors such as social support systems (context) influence the individual's perception of stressors and so serve to
  modify their impact.

• the individual's adaptive coping capacity and other characteristics (vulnerability) influence how the individual deals with
  the perceived threat.

• stress responses (strain, stress reactions) that accompany the
  coping process are experienced as distressing and may trigger
  illness.

• the consequences of this process (confidence, sense of mastery,
  illness, maladjustment) become evident over time.

Stressors are thus linked to their consequences. Different stressors
require different actions to cope with these consequences.

### SOURCES OF MANAGEMENT STRESS

Managers are likely to feel the impact of stress from many different sources:

---

* Various investigators (Cobb, 1974) (Rahe, 1974) (House & Wells, 1978)
(McLean, 1979) have developed research models of the stress process that
present essentially the same elements in slightly different dynamic relationships determined by the purposes the model is designed to serve. The model
used here was originally adapted to study the effect of psychosocial and work
environment stressors in situations where entry into a new work setting also
required significant change in life patterns and circumstances.

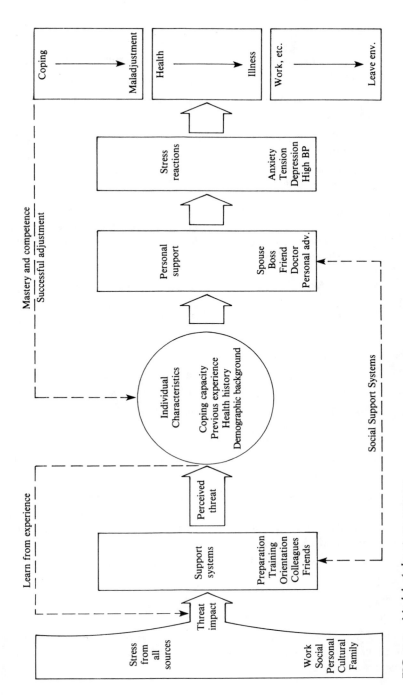

FIG. 1.1 *Model of the stress process.*

5

- the pressures and dynamics of the management process itself.
- the accelerating pace of change in business life today.
- new social values that are challenging established organizational practices.
- pressures from the manager's personal life such as family and social goals and responsibilities.
- the changes in self-image, perspective, and capacities that accompany growth and development during adult life.

Each source of stress is illustrated here using commonly occurring events in the life of managers and executives. The impact of these experiences can best be understood in terms of the following characteristics of stressful life events:

1   Any change, especially when rapid, generates stress.
2   Difficult conditions to which an individual has been accustomed for a long time are less disturbing than more favorable conditions that are unfamiliar.
3   Novelty enhances the impact of stressful events.
4   Unanticipated or unpredictable events evoke a sense of helplessness or uncertainty, which magnifies the stress reaction.
5   Events over which an individual has no control, undesired events, or events that represent a loss of something or someone valued or important are perceived as particularly stressful.
6   Stress from all environments to which an individual is exposed seems to have a cumulative effect.
7   Numerous stressors operating simultaneously or in sequence have greater impact than stressors that occur singly. Behavioral capabilities tend to drop dramatically with even a mild degree of overloading.
8   Anyone can be overwhelmed by stressors of sufficient magnitude.

Observations of actual situations involving managers and their problems are used here to highlight peaks of stress and personal crises. The reader is encouraged to identify with and worry about whatever strikes a responsive chord as we review the sources and consequences of stress.

Organizational and personal coping strategies described throughout and summarized in chapters 11 and 13 will help the reader think through and resolve the problems and worries aroused by earlier chapters.

## REASONS TO WORRY ABOUT STRESS

A word of explanation about why the reader is encouraged to worry. It is a well-known characteristic of the way managers deal with career or personal crises that problems are either denied or buried under a heavy workload (often the main reason for such activity) until things have reached an impasse.

### Examples

By the time the manager finally hears what his wife has been telling him for years—that when he brings work home night after night she perceives this as a loss of interest in her—he can be assured that her interests have turned elsewhere. Managers who begin to worry about their careers as they "approach fifty and obsolescence" can be sure that they have already missed the boat because the average age at which people at their level are promoted to the next level of management is forty-five. They should have been looking for career alternatives five years before when their skills were more marketable and their "high potential" badges were just beginning to tarnish.

Factors in the interpersonal dynamics of most organizations tend to delay the recognition of career problems and personal crises until it may be too late to do anything constructive to resolve them.

### To illustrate:

- the distractability and lack of concentration that accompany worry about personal problems are often mistaken by managers as loss of competence.

- reluctance to relocate because of personal or family objections to the move may never be expressed because managers view this reluctance as a sign of poor motivation or disloyalty, sure indications that they will never be offered such an opportunity again.

- anger at the way they are treated by superiors, or anger at being asked to do something contrary to personal values is often suppressed for fear of retaliation. Suppressed anger leads to apathy, depression, and loss of drive. There is nothing more alarming to managers than a loss of drive, which is seen as a sign of approaching obsolescence, being all washed up, or a has been.

• feelings of apprehension and a desire to call for help in response to unexpected contingencies or emergencies may be considered by managers to be signs of weakness or dependence.

Fears of exposing these negative qualities lead to suppression of emotion, depression, and subsequent poor performance. A vicious cycle of defensiveness and compromised effectiveness is thus established with the result that the conflicts that led to the downhill cycle are not discovered until it may be too late.

Special conditions are often necessary to help managers or executives break through intense preoccupation with productivity, profitability, and advancement, to focus on personal considerations. Employer-endorsed programs may be required to heighten managers' awareness of characteristic career and related personal problems. Awareness, a sense of involvement with the problem, allowing themselves to perceive the full impact of stressful life events or conflicts even though this perception may provoke tension, alarm, depression, or uncertainty are all necessary to stimulate coping behavior. The ability to become aware of relevant problems as they develop and to worry about them constructively is a valuable personality asset.

But worry does not necessarily promote constructive thinking through of problems. In fact, anxiety has a confusing and paralyzing effect often leading to counterproductive or self-defeating behavior. Worrying about relevant issues can only be effective if there is hope, some indication that coping is possible, and a concept of how to go about it.

Hope does not necessarily have to take the form of assurance that the problem can actually be resolved satisfactorily. What is essential is the knowledge that it is possible to take constructive action, to initiate a coping strategy that may succeed if followed through to a conclusion. Personal and organizational coping strategies are presented here to demonstrate that something *can* be done about stress and to point the way to thinking through *what* can be done.

## REASONS FOR OPTIMISM

Happily, there is cause for hope. Several new developments indicate that coping strategies that address relevant issues and fit individual needs can significantly reduce the undesirable consequences of management stress. The most important of these new developments is the growing awareness that the *supportive context* in which the coping process takes place has a crucial influence on the outcome of that process. In other words, managers' efforts to deal with stress are more likely to succeed if they expect approval and support in those efforts from others directly involved. Conversely, chances are greater that coping will fail if others are, or are thought to be, disapproving or nonsupportive.

The dissonance between what managers would like to do out of self-interest, and what those same managers think the organization approves of, can have a stifling effect on the creative use of initiative. The organization can help to resolve such problems by means of supportive measures that clarify what to expect, exactly where managers stand at present, and what is in prospect for the future as far as that can be foreseen.

Such clarification need not come only from formal performance appraisals or meetings with top management during which they "tell it the way it is." Active involvement of managers and executives in planning, problem solving, and policy making is a most effective way to help managers cope with stress at the source. In an organizational setting, coping should be a team effort with managers and management each playing appropriate roles and bearing distinct, although different, responsibilities for the outcome.

People often take for granted a connection exists between the success of their efforts to cope with stressful life events and support or lack of support from others. Scientific evidence now suggests how, why, and under what conditions social support reduces the perception of stress and protects against its illness-producing consequences.* For example, social support reduces known occupational stresses such as role conflict and ambiguity, job dissatisfaction, and low occupational self-esteem. It also mitigates the effect of potentially stressful objective situations such as a boring job, heavy workloads, and unemployment. A positive relationship was found

---

* A complete summary of data on social support systems appears in James House's book in this series.

between perceived work overload and increase in coronary heart disease risk factors, particularly for workers who had low social support from others both at work and at home (House and Wells, 1978).

Chapter 12 considers in detail what is meant by social support systems; how support is related to occupational stress, health, and safety; and the functioning of relevant support systems in managers' working and personal environments. What gives cause for optimism, is the prospect that appropriate social support can be developed that will contribute substantially to the reduction of occupational stress from any source. If we bear in mind that stress from all environments to which an individual is exposed seems to have a cumulative effect, and that it is the *total impact* of stress that contributes to the precipitation of illness and other adverse effects, then support systems that reduce stress from any one source may modify the effect of other stressors that may otherwise be beyond our control.

Thus, providing managers or executives with the opportunity to resolve personal crises, particularly if career pressures contributed to the development of those crises, will strengthen their ability to withstand pressures within the organization. And, resolution of stress from sources within the organization will have a beneficial effect on conflicts and concerns that arise from the manager's personal life.

The positive value of organizational support for individual coping efforts was graphically demonstrated to me from my very first clinical contacts with managers and their dependents who were going through career-related personal crises. When I first entered the private practice of psychiatry and psychoanalysis years ago, I began a clinical association with a multinational corporation, which has continued to the present. Early on it became apparent to me that patients referred through the company's medical department made significantly greater progress in treatment than similar patients referred from other sources. The contrast was so remarkable I reviewed my records to find the reasons for this.

Actually, the explanation was not difficult to find. Patients who did well were referred by physicians (occupational physicians included) who supported their seeking psychiatric consultation, viewed it as a potentially constructive move, and were prepared to cooperate in implementing the recommendations developed from such consultations. Patients referred by supportive occupational physicians for brief counseling for problems in living, for acute personal crises, or for longer-term treatment came with positive expectations and assurances of approval. As a result the goals of therapy were much more easily accomplished. Occasionally, relief from emotional distress was evident even before the initial therapeutic interview.

By contrast, the group that did much less well was referred by physicians who said, in essence, "We've tried everything including psychotropic medication and nothing has worked. I can't think of anything else to do for you. You might as well see a shrink." For these patients, referral to a psychiatrist for help with the resolution of commonly occurring problems of daily life was taken as an indication that they were failures, hopelessly untreatable, and perhaps seriously mentally ill. With such an attitude about themselves and the nonsupportive manner in which they were referred, it is not difficult to understand why treatment outcome tended to match their expectations.

Anticipation of lack of management support was another source of poor outcome of counseling with managers and their families referred for characteristic problems stemming from career-related personal crises (depression, alcoholism, marital difficulties, infidelity, divorce, maladjusted teen-aged children). "What's the good of my realizing all of this. Nothing will change. It's frustrating to raise painful issues if they aren't going to do anything about it at the office."

As will be shown in the review of the relationship between social support and health, it has been established through scientifically controlled studies that patients who are well supported tend to remain in treatment of all types, not just psychotherapy. They follow recommendations, require less medication, and consequently experience an acceleration of recovery compared to patients who are less well supported or who are socially isolated (Cobb, 1976). Support referred to in these studies comes from nonmedical sources such as family, employers, and coworkers.

Recent interest in strategies to *manage organizational change* is another development that promises to make a substantial contribution toward controlling the rising incidence and prevalence of management stress and its consequences. The purpose of this planning approach to new organizational structure and practices, job redesign, or relocation is twofold: to assure that the new structure will fit market, environmental, and personnel requirements and minimize the human cost of changing conditions.

To control management stress when organizational change is contemplated, it is essential that the managers and executives involved be given the opportunity, through management-sponsored programs, to communicate with the initiators of change and thereby gain an understanding of what is to be changed, the anticipated benefits, and how this change is to be accomplished. If managers are convinced of the necessity for change they will participate more willingly even if they themselves are adversely affected by it. Otherwise, many overt and subtle forms of resistance to change or dependence on old practices, aspirations, and relationships may complicate the change process for both manager and management.

Even for managers who participate willingly, change involves some measure of painful loss as familar and valued habits and relationships are relinquished for the new, uncertain, or unknown. Preparation for change should include an opportunity to mourn the old and accommodate to the new. Participation and involvement before the fact provide the manager with an opportunity to start the mourning process before the loss has actually occurred. Thus the costly effect of depression and lowered effectiveness that inevitably accompany adaptation to organizational change can be reduced.

A further reason for optimism about the manager's ability to cope successfully with stress is that in the appropriate receptive setting *managers can be creative* about finding suitable solutions and strategies for their own troubled circumstances. The appropriate setting is one in which confidentiality is assured, one that has the explicit or implicit approval of management, but one in which management does not necessarily participate.

These impressions come from study of stress factors among approximately 100 members of upper management in a large corporation. The opportunity for the study developed from a review of experience with the health of employees at a headquarters following a major reorganization. The reorganization encompassed the merger of several companies, the replacement of a loose paternalistic management style with management by objectives, and firing and hiring from the outside for the first time. What attracted the attention of the medical department was the dramatic rise in the incidence of depression, tension, and anxiety states immediately after the announcement of the intention to reorganize. Physical responses such as rise in blood pressure and illnesses such as peptic ulcer began to show the same dramatic increase after a lag of about six months. In the opinion of the medical director there was a need for a study of stress factors to be used to design stress reduction programs, inasmuch as the proper function of a medical department in industry is to prevent illness as well as treat it. Although we tend to take health maintenance programs and their stress management components for granted these days it was a relatively advanced idea for its time about 10 to 15 years ago.

The study began with a series of stress interviews that I conducted. The interviews began with a description of the circumstances that led to my becoming consultant to the medical department. I then said I was interested in exploring the sources of stress in the lives of executives. The results of these inquiries would be used to formulate health maintenance and illness prevention programs. Generally, I had the opportunity to say little more than that before the executive broke in with enthusiasm, "Stress! Let me tell you about stress," and for the next hour and a half described what was most stressful for himself or herself (almost exclusively himself at that time). Occasionally there was a pause to question whether the interview was confidential before proceeding. Of course it was. Usually confidentiality was taken for granted.

At the end of the interview most participants volunteered that they had "enjoyed it" and hadn't realized they felt so strongly about the issues raised. Further, they had never before thought of the useful and often creative ideas they discovered through their own free associations to what stress meant to them and their total life situation.

Some executives realized that they had viable alternatives should the level of stress become unbearable, or should the fallout effect on their families seriously intensify existing problems. Others realized alternatives should be developed. Some became aware of their resistance to even the thought of leaving the company and doing something else, because they had become dependent on their present situation. Others became hopeful that with some thought they could challenge that locked-in feeling.

It may seem as if thoughts of leaving the organization were prevalent during these interviews. In fact those who were most loyal and most committed to their present job situations did, indeed, have viable alternatives but chose to remain where they were because that present situation provided the brightest prospects.

The experience was useful because it brought relief from distress (often denied or suppressed), which in turn released constructive personal problem-solving capacities or greater self-assurance in personal decisions or choices. Often relief resulted from the realization that previously unvoiced concerns were "normal" consequences of the peaks of stress and the personal crisis all managers and executives are likely to experience because of the complex interplay between organizational life and other life roles.

Interest in stimulating their own job enrichment program, determination to improve communications, greater concern for the welfare of their dependents, relief at the exposure of interpersonal conflicts at work, or a sense of satisfaction that they were coping well were other sentiments expressed during these interviews.

Certainly the interviews indicated that there is an important need for managers to have the opportunity to (1) explore their personal reactions to organizational life, (2) discuss confidentially in a nonbusiness setting those aspects of life they find most stressful:

- relationships with superiors or subordinates.
- the impact of work pressure transmitted downward from the top.
- problems with too much or too little responsibility.
- the impact of business on family life or vice versa.
- worries about future career prospects.
- their depressed or dissatisfied spouses.
- troubled adolescent children.
- almost anything else that occupied the center of their concerns.

### PRINCIPLES FOR COPING STRATEGIES

The foregoing executive stress study as well as other experiences as an outside observer in clinical practice and an inside consultant on various aspects of management stress and organizational change provided me with the basis for the following principles in organizing the discussion of management stress:

1   Anyone in a managerial or executive role will go through peaks of extraordinary stress and periodic personal crises during a career in an organizational setting.

2   These peaks of stress and personal crises are rarely related to the pressures and dynamics of the work environment alone, but most often result from the interaction of organizational factors and other important influences:

- competing personal, family, or social interests, goals and responsibilities, and/or
- changes in capacity, perspective, and self-image that accompany growth and development during adult life.

3   A strategy to cope with personal crises is essential for every manager and executive. To be effective, personal coping strategies must be suited to individual needs and take into account the interaction of many different themes in the manager's total life sphere.

4   In an organizational setting, coping becomes a team effort with managers and management each playing appropriate roles and bearing distinct, although different, responsibilities for the outcome.

5   Stress management programs initiated by the organization cannot be relied upon for solutions to career-related personal problems. Individual and organizational interests often differ and may even conflict. The individual manager or executive is ultimately responsible for formulating personal coping strategies.

6   Elements essential to both individual and management strategies to cope with stress include:

- personal health maintenance.
- realistic anticipation of and appropriate preparation for stressful career and life events.
- the opportunity to ventilate relevant concerns under timely and appropriate circumstances, which may lead to the discovery of constructive and often creative personal perspectives.

7   Different stressors require different actions. Executives responsible for both personal and organizational coping strategies will find a conceptual map of the area of management stress a useful guide to the accurate diagnosis of sources of stress and the planning of appropriate interventions.

## REFERENCES

*Business Week* (1976). The corporate woman: Stress has no gender. (November 15, 1976) 73–76.

*Business Week* (1979). Executive stress may not be all bad. (April 30, 1979) 96–103.

Cobb, S. (1974). A model for life events and their consequences. In B. S. Dohrenwend and B. P. Dohrenwend (Eds.) *Stressful Life Events.* New York: Wiley.

Cobb, S. (1976). Social support as a moderator of life stress. *Psychosomatic Medicine* **38** (5):300–314.

House, J. S., and J. A. Wells (1978). Occupational stress, social support and health. In A. McLean (Ed.) *Reducing Occupational Stress.* Cincinnati: National Institute for Occupational Safety and Health. HEW (NIOSH) Publication No. 78–140.

Kiev, A., and V. Kohn (1979). *Executive Stress.* An AMA Survey Report. New York: American Management Association.

McLean, A. A. (1979). *Work Stress.* Reading, Mass.: Addison-Wesley.

Rahe, R. H. (1974). The pathway between subjects' recent life changes and their near-future illness reports: Representative results and methodological issues. In B. S. Dohrenwend and B. P. Dohrenwend (Eds.) *Stressful Life Events.* New York: Wiley.

# 2
# THE POPULATION
# AT RISK

It is important to define the individuals for whom the framework for management stress is being prepared—the population at risk. Business school graduates who spend three years in a training assignment with a large corporation, then decide the managerial role does not suit their entrepreneurial spirit and seek careers in other areas are not the focus here. A commitment to the manager's role was never made. Managerial work and the manager's role is not for everyone.

The concern here is with persons who choose to become managers and then executives because of a perceived compatibility with the organization and with the manager's role in that organization. Subsequent fluctuations in the harmony between the individual and the organization are certainly very much our concern.

Stressfulness is in the eye of the beholder. If a situation is not perceived as challenging (threatening, dangerous, harmful, frustrating) by the person involved, then the stress process will not be initiated. Thus, a manager experienced in dealing with what distinguishes managerial work—fragmentation of tasks, frequent interruptions, the need to respond to communications from a wide variety of sources, frequently and quickly shifting moods, lack of free time for reflection, predetermined interpersonal, informational and decisional roles—will perceive these as ordinary pressures and not feel especially stressed. Rather, the *absence* of daily pressures and challenges when there is not enough to do, or when the job does not provide sufficient complexity to be interesting, has been shown to be stressful because of the *absence* of challenge. Thus the *population at risk* can be defined as those individuals who perform managerial work, function in managerial roles, and have made the commitment to such work because of a perceived compatibility between personal interests and what the job provides or promises to provide.

This chapter describes the characteristics of managerial work and the manager's working roles. Cultural differences in these roles are illustrated to emphasize that we are referring to the United States management process throughout, unless otherwise indicated.

## CHARACTERISTICS OF MANAGERIAL WORK

Studies of how managers spend their time show remarkable similarities at all levels of the hierarchy from foremen to middle and senior managers, to chief executives. Characteristics of what Henry Mintzberg (1973) refers to as "the most demanding of jobs in this high tension environment" that is, managerial work, are summarized, followed by his outline of the ten obligatory managerial roles. Work and roles taken together provide a composite picture of how a manager or executive must function. Mintzberg's propositions about the characteristics of managerial work are:

1  Managers feel compelled to perform a great quantity of work at an unrelenting pace. They have little free time, rarely take breaks, and their minds are on their jobs during much of the free time they have.

2  Activities are characterized by brevity, variety, and interruptions with the trivial interspersed with the consequential. Superficiality is an occupational hazard of the manager's job.

3  The manager lives with the continuing awareness of what else must be done.

4  The pressure of the job does not encourage the development of a planner, but of an adaptive information manipulator who favors live action—the current, the specific, the well defined, the nonroutine. Current information is favored (gossip, hearsay, speculation); routine reports are not.

5  Verbal and written contacts are the manager's work. Most time is spent in verbal contact; mail receives cursory treatment although it must be processed regularly. Managers generate less mail than they receive, most of it necessary response to input mail.

6   The informal media of the telephone and unscheduled meetings are used for brief contacts when parties are known to each other and when information or requests must be transmitted quickly.

7   The scheduled meeting consumes more of the manager's time than any other communication media. Discussion at the beginning and end of each scheduled meeting is of special interest and frequently involves the flow of important information.

8   Generally little time is spent in open-ended touring that provides the manager with the opportunity to observe informally without prearrangement.

9   The manager may be likened to the neck of an hourglass, standing between the organization (or local work group) and a network of outside contacts (including other affiliated work groups). These external contacts consume from one-third to one-half of the manager's contact time. Nonline relationships are a significant and complex component of the manager's job.

10   Subordinates generally consume one-third to one-half of the manager's contact time, most often for the purpose of making requests, exchanging information, or planning strategy.

11   The manager spends relatively little time with supervisors (or directors in the case of the chief executive)—generally about 10 percent.

The manager's job reflects a blend of duties and rights. Although superficial study of managers' activities suggests that they often control little of what they do, closer analysis indicates that managers can exert control in important ways. Managers are responsible for many initial commitments. These in turn lead to a set of ongoing activities and obligations. Managers can take advantage of these obligations by exercising leadership, extracting information, and in many other ways.

### THE MANAGER'S WORKING ROLES

The manager's formal authority and status give rise to interpersonal roles (figurehead, liaison, leader), which then give rise to informational roles (monitor, disseminator, spokesman), which in turn enable the manager to perform decisional roles (entrepreneur, disturbance handler, resource allocator, negotiator). Each of these ten roles can be summarized as follows:

**1** Figurehead—This is the simplest of managerial roles. As the symbolic head of the organization the manager is obligated to carry out a number of social, inspirational, legal, and ceremonial duties.

**2** Leader—This role identifies the manager's relationship with subordinates and pervades virtually all activities in which subordinates are involved. The manager motivates, activates, hires, trains, promotes, fires, and exerts power over subordinates.

**3** Liaison—Managers spend considerable time developing a network of contacts outside their immediate organizational unit, contacts during which information and favors are traded for mutual benefit. The manager's "unique access to all subordinates and to special outside contacts (many of them nerve centers of their own organizations) enable the manager to develop a powerful data base of external and internal information. In effect, the manager is the organization's generalist with the best store of non-routine information" (Mintzberg, 1973, p. 97).

**4** Monitor—Through a personally developed information-gathering system that includes liaisons, contacts, and subordinates trained to bypass their superiors, the manager continually seeks and receives current, tangible, nondocumented information on internal operations, external events, ideas, and trends. The manager uses this information to build up a general understanding of his milieu for decision making.

**5** Disseminator—Influencers direct their statements of preference to the manager who then assimilates, integrates and interprets them and transmits this information on the organizational value system to subordinates. The manager sends external information into the organization and internal information from one subordinate to another.

**6** Spokesman—The manager transmits information to outsiders on the organization's plans, policies, actions, results, and serves outsiders as the expert in the field in which the organization operates. In this capacity the manager with the necessary information, authority, and control must take full responsibility for the organization's strategy-making system and policies.

**7** Entrepreneur—The manager initiates and designs much of the controlled change in the organization, searches for problems and opportunities, initiates improvement projects, and either delegates or assumes responsibility for their design. At any one time senior managers appear to maintain supervision over a large inventory of improvement projects in various stages of planning, development, or completion.

**8** Disturbance Handler—The manager is responsible for taking corrective action when the organization is faced with important and often unexpected disturbances (conflicts between subordinates, conflicts between organizational units, consequences of insensitive "poor" managers, the inevitable unanticipated consequences of innovative "good" management).

**9** Resource Allocator—The manager allocates organizational resources (money, manpower, reputation), sets priorities, establishes the basic work system, decides what will be done, by whom, and what structure will be used. "These are difficult choices—time is limited, yet the issues are complex and subordinates' proposals cannot be dismissed lightly. In some cases the manager decides on the proposer rather than the proposal" (p. 99).

**10** Negotiator—The manager takes charge participating as figurehead, spokesman, or resource allocator when the organization unit must engage in important negotiations with other units.

## CULTURAL DIFFERENCES IN MANAGERIAL ROLES

It often comes as a shock to find that what one group perceives as the best and only way to do things (that is, ideas, beliefs, aspirations, interpersonal relationships, ideas about working, leisure, status, what individuals strive for) can be organized in totally different ways by different groups who think *theirs* are the best and only ways to do things.

We often fail to realize that what the individual wants from a job may differ from one work culture to the next. We must remind ourselves that the description of managerial work and roles with which we are familiar, and the sources of stress that derive from organizational structure and practices that define the manager's functions, are determined by the United States life style. This life style, in the view of sociologists, is based on competitiveness and individualism. It is important to contrast the United States style with another based on different cultural norms. It is important to learn how different groups organize themselves in very different ways to accomplish the same goals of organizational efficiency, and in the case of business, to achieve productivity, profitability, and viability in the competitive world market.

### Career development

The Anglo-American management system gives rise to two major clusters of potential career development stressors:

1 lack of job security: fear of redundancy, obsolescence, or early retirement.

2 status incongruity: underpromotion or overpromotion, frustration at having reached one's career ceiling.

Anxieties about making mid-career and late-career changes are numerous and varied, as are the barriers to employing older managers (ages forty-five to sixty-five): feeling locked into pension systems; so-called overqualification; the need for credentials and certificates; the anxieties and frustrations of the struggle to achieve; the fear of inability to learn anything new at that age; the fear that one is not employable or will not be hired elsewhere.

In the United States to date, older managers and organizations have failed to anticipate and plan for ways to absorb a mobile, changing population of older experienced executives. By contrast, the Japanese management system is based on lifetime employment. (Drucker, 1971). The system includes maximum income security for younger managers while they still have dependent children, and in many instances, parents who are also dependents. The older manager (fifty-five is the official retirement age) receives less income security; as at that age, the need to feel useful and wanted in the status of "temporary employee" (status after fifty-five) is greater than the need for financial security.

The Japanese system is described here by listing a series of characteristics of the career development process. Managers are referred to as "he." Women are rare among managers, are almost always considered temporary rather than permanent employees, and are therefore excluded from benefits.

1 Hiring—The only way to get into a company's management is to enter from the University and work up from within. Hiring from the outside and into upper-level positions is practically unknown.

2   Career Progression—The newly hired manager knows he will have a job until retirement (age fifty-five) no matter how poorly he performs.

•   Until age forty-five the manager will be promoted and paid by seniority only. There is no performance appraisal, as a manager can neither be rewarded for performance nor penalized for nonperformance.

•   For the first twenty to twenty-five years the emphasis is on conforming, doing what he is being asked to do, showing proper respect and deference. It is "unthinkable" for a young manager to ask for a transfer or to quit and go elsewhere. It is "almost unheard of" to take a job with another company except with the expressed permission of the previous employer.

•   Personnel people make personnel decisions, often without consulting the manager to whom a subordinate is to be assigned.

•   Every young manager knows he is expected to help his colleagues look good rather than to stand out by himself by brilliance or aggressiveness.

3   Age forty-five—At age forty-five a small group of candidates is selected to enter the ranks of top management, where they may stay without the retirement age requirement. The rest remain in management until age fifty-five when retirement is compulsory. Between ages forty-five to fifty-five the manager will receive, at best, one more promotion.

•   Outstanding men, too specialized for top management, are transferred to top management of smaller organizational units where they can remain in office for an indefinite period of time. They may become "godfathers" to younger managers.

4   Age fifty-five—At age fifty-five the manager is given a severance bonus of two years salary and changes status from a permanent to a temporary employee who is not laid off as long as there is work for him to do.

### Godfather system

Drucker contrasts the Japanese system for developing young managers with the management process in the West: "Perhaps the greatest single complaint of young people in the large organization today is that there is nobody who listens to them, nobody who tries to find out who they are and what they are doing, nobody who acts as a senior counselor" (p. 139). Drucker sees the absence of such genuine contact as an important reason for the heavy turnover among young people in the West. Both young people and senior management need better communication links.

In the Japanese system care and feeding of their young managers is the first responsibility of top management. This responsibility is carried out largely by an informal network of senior middle managers who act as "godfathers." For the first ten years of a young manager's career the godfather sees him fairly regularly, is available for advice and counsel, helps informally with promotions and other career progression problems, and even administers discipline if necessary. Personnel people quietly consult the godfather before they make a move involving a young manager.

The managerial godfathers are men who are not likely to build factions of their own or play internal politics. They have already been passed over for top management spots in their own organizations and know that at age fifty-five they will be transferred to the top management of a subsidiary or an affiliate.

The strength of the Japanese system is that the godfather function is not a separate job, nor a personnel function entrusted to specialists, but is discharged by experienced, respected, and successful managers.

### Decision making

Drucker claims that in the United States brilliant reports of task force leaders and planners often do not get beyond the planning stage, or may be resisted, sabotaged, or delayed because of the length of time it takes to "sell" them within the organization.

Decision making in Japanese organizations is said to be by consensus. A proposed decision is debated throughout the organization until there is agreement that the appropriate central issues have been defined. Only then do Japanese organizations enter the action stage. Since everyone is included in the debate, the process is lengthy. Once the process has taken place, however, action is said to proceed rapidly as everyone has been presold on the decision.

### Training

Management education in United States organizations emphasizes training of younger managers for advancement. Little training is offered to longer service employees.

In Japan, continuous training is a regular part of every job until retirement. A manager is expected to train either at company or personal initiative for every job at his level. In this sense training is focused on performance rather than on promotion. The manager may or may not be required to perform these different jobs.

According to Drucker this method makes it possible to introduce new products or machines through the usual training network and achieve greater acceptance and less resistance to change than is found under other systems.

### Comment

The ways in which Japanese managers relate to each other, in contrast to the management process in the United States, may or may not have an effect on the bottom line. That is not of concern here. But the ways in which managers organize their personal relationships may have an effect on their ability to cope with managerial stress, on their health, well-being, and perhaps their effectiveness in performing managerial functions as defined by their work culture. Certainly the way managers are treated is perceived by them as a reflection of how human resources are valued by the organization.

Drucker's article is not summarized for the purpose of evaluating which system is better. The systems in Japan and the United States have evolved from different cultures and must be evaluated primarily in the context of the cultural values from which they emerged. The Japanese system is presented to illustrate that there are different ways of doing things; to help us think more broadly about our own accustomed practices (which we automatically tend to regard as the best); and to help us examine the unspoken assumptions on which our management structure, practices, and the dynamics of the manager's interpersonal relationships are based.

Rapid changes in cultural and social values are forcing us to rethink many of our business assumptions and practices. The rethinking process itself, and the changes that stem from this—some by trial and error, others by regulation and legislation—will act as a source of management stress for some time to come. To prepare for this process of reexamination of basic values (a process that is now proceeding at a rapidly accelerating pace) it is necessary (1) to become accustomed to questioning assumptions; (2) to make the process of thinking through change a more familiar one; (3) to reduce the "culture shock" and the resultant resistance to change that comes when a decision is made to change an element in our work culture that has become automatic, not because of its inherent efficiency, but because of the sense of security and familiarity it provides.

## MANAGERIAL GOALS

If cultural differences lead to significant variation in managerial roles, do these differences similarly influence what managers in different cultures want from their jobs? David Sirota and J. Michael Greenwood (1971) surveyed thousands of individuals at various levels employed in 25 countries by a large international corporation. They found that:

- Although national or cultural differences can be identified there is considerable similarity in the goals of all employees. Advancement, earnings, training, challenge, and some degree of autonomy are predominant goals which apply to work around the world.

- Differences among nations are relatively small, but it is possible to identify country "clusters" within which goals are nearly identical. For example, managers in the Anglo-American cluster score high on goals pertaining to individual achievement and low on the desire for security. In the Northern European cluster managers are less oriented to getting ahead and to recognition and more oriented toward job accomplishment; people are concerned about a friendly and efficient working environment and place considerable emphasis on their jobs not interfering with their personal lives.

*Japan shows a rather unique pattern in that many of the goals which ordinarily relate to one another do not seem to do so in this case. For example, while the Japanese are higher than others in their desire for earnings opportunities, their desire for advancement is relatively low. They are second highest on challenge, but are lowest on autonomy. The one internally consistent pattern for their nation relates to the immediate department environment; the Japanese place relatively strong*

*emphasis on working in a friendly and efficient department
and on having good physical working conditions.*

SIROTA AND GREENWOOD, 1971, p. 60

## Comment

These data suggest that although challenge and training are universally important work goals, how people get along with each other (social support system) and other social values reflected in the organization of work and work roles can vary widely across cultures.

The emphasis on quality-of-life issues in the Northern European countries is evident in managers' concern that their jobs must not interfere with their personal lives. In the United States managers also make an effort to keep personal life separate from work life, but the traditional idea that the "loyal" manager in the United States should place the organization first, and personal life second, is a concept that is currently under attack.

The role of a "friendly and efficient department" as a source of stress reduction will be discussed in detail. But here, too, the concept of the social atmosphere of the work environment, so important and characteristic an element in the Japanese management process, is not yet valued as highly in the United States or respected as a potential source of organizational strength.

## THE WORK SETTING

The managers' work, roles, and goals, as well as the influence of culture on these roles and goals have already been described. The settings in which these roles are performed vary widely even within the same organization. A manager may pass through a variety of settings on the way up the organizational ladder—a district sales office, manager of a manufacturing plant, a regional headquarters, a foreign affiliate, and a staff position at corporate headquarters. Does the setting change the managers' roles and functions, or do the similarities of managerial work, and therefore of managerial stressors, overshadow differences in work setting? To answer this question we must observe managers in action, in their natural habitat, where roles, functions, and cultural differences come together.

The following interview describes the work day of a manager and the manager's attitudes about his work. The interview is actually a composite of many such interviews with managers performing different functions in the same work setting. The essential points made are accurate. Details referring to the individuals and the setting are altered somewhat to preserve confidentiality and disguise the origins of this information.

## INTERVIEW 1 – Stranded Offshore

This interview took place not in an office but on the outside deck of an offshore oil production platform in the middle of the North Sea. I was there with a small group of social scientists to study the human stress aspects of offshore living and working conditions. A large proportion of the accidents that take place in complex man–machine systems are known to be caused directly or indirectly by human error, which in turn may be related to stress reactions. This issue has attracted a great deal of attention in the North Sea where at any one time from 200 to over 1200 individuals may work on a single giant production platform.

The aim of the study was to develop programs to assure that the health and safety of those working and living offshore would not be adversely affected by human behavior under stress.

Ian Gibbs, the thirty-eight-year-old platform manager with long experience, allowed me to follow him through his routine working day. It started at 6 A.M. During that day he

• responded to a number of emergency alarms and supervised the extinguishing of several small fires.

• answered inquiries from supervisors on shore about present and projected production schedules, providing input for their future planning assumptions. They urged him to speed up production. He argued that they were producing as fast as they could. He then called in his group of offshore managers and urged them to speed up production. They argued that they were working as fast as they could given the adverse weather conditions affecting offshore supply and maintenance. A technical discussion ensued, the net result of which was to call a manager at an onshore base and urge him to speed up the delivery of a necessary part to a necessary machine that was responsible for the shutdown of one of the wells.

• acted as referee in sensitive disputes among various factions of the multinational workforce. One group threatened not to work for another group whose supervisors displayed offensively authoritarian attitudes toward subordinates.

• met with representatives of various levels of workers and discussed why the food was so bad, why the theatre chairs were always broken, why the television controls never worked, and particularly why the phone connections to shore were not increased in number. All these issues seemed to relate to covert morale problems rather than to the actual practical problems caused by these inconveniences.

• found a worker who volunteered to be dropped from a helicopter in a basket to the mooring structure several miles away to check on the hose coupling point where tankers hook up to receive the crude oil produced on the platform.

• held a wrap-up meeting of managers before dinner.

• made rounds of the entire platform after dinner and did his paperwork until about 10 P.M.

It was clear to me that all personnel respected Ian, felt safe in his hands because of his excellent performance record in emergencies and unexpected contingencies. His fire-fighting team had a great *esprit de corps* that motivated rapid responses to alarms— a source of great reassurance to the remainder of the men working on the platform at the time.

Ian himself seemed to enjoy a sense of his own competence as well as the respect and admiration he received from others. To me, he appeared the model of a model offshore manager.

Having been impressed with his assurance I was surprised when he came to me very late that evening and asked if we could talk about something that was distressing him. "Let's go outside, it's the only place on the crowded platform we can be alone when we talk." When we began to talk that February evening in the middle of the North Sea I realized the same conversation could just as well have taken place at corporate headquarters.

He was concerned about what kind of career development program was open to him with his highly specialized background. "In a few years I won't be able to take the rigors of this job anymore. It's for younger men with quick reaction time and plenty of energy. Where can I go from here after managing one of the largest and most complex installations of its kind? Do I have a future onshore? Right now I'm worried that in just a few years I will become obsolete."

"Another problem is the work cycle, fourteen days offshore, fourteen days at home. I'm away from home so often my wife and two children have become accustomed to making decisions and planning without me. When I am home they are at school.

"My wife is talking about taking a job now that the children are older and require less attention. She is beginning to resent my being away so much and then having to change the family routine when I'm home. I don't know what the figures are but there are an awful lot of divorces among offshore workers and I really don't want that to happen to me.

"Sometimes my wife and I argue when I'm about to leave home for a tour of duty. It's on my mind when I come out here so I don't get into the job for a few days. That's actually dangerous because the workplace can change during the fourteen days onshore, a piece of equipment is down for repairs, new wells come on stream. I have to be able to concentrate when I first come out, I must learn the condition of that platform immediately.

"After two or three days I forget about family problems and get into the work, but it starts up again before I'm scheduled to go home. I don't sleep so well the last few nights.

"It's ironical—if there is an emergency offshore I'm not bothered by it at all. I know I can handle what comes up. I even feel good doing it. But what I'm really concerned about, as are the other managers, is if there is a family emergency when I'm out here, there is nothing I can do about it. I'm stranded offshore. That's why the group discussion today about being able to use telephones more than we are able to do now. We all feel it's very important to be able to contact our families as often as necessary when there is an emergency—onshore."

### Comment

The managers' work and roles offshore seem the same as those onshore, with the possible exception of the safety issue. Ian Gibbs as platform manager functioned as leader, liaison, monitor, disseminator, disturbance handler, resource allocator, negotiator, and so forth. His time was spent on a variety of tasks, dealing with superiors and subordinates, dealing with issues of varying degrees of importance with little free time to himself. In short, the manager's work and roles are similar in all settings.

Stressors also seem to be similar to those of managers in all settings. Ian's present career status is linked to concerns about his future; his work life is linked to his personal life. As has been found with other managerial functions involving safety factors, responsibility for people may be stressful, and the work itself may involve exposure to objectively dangerous conditions. But the greatest perceived stressor is his responsibility for his family and the limited control he has over his future, a future in which his relationship with his wife will more and more be determined by the restrictions and parameters of his career.

In summary, Ian's work life and personal life are linked. He perceives his family stressors as extraordinary pressures, but considers the daily safety problems as ordinary pressures. Ian feels adequate to the ordinary pressures, but he is concerned that he may not be able to control the extraordinary ones (career development, family relationships).

From this and many similar interviews it is clear that the true population at risk is the manager *plus* the manager's family.

### REFERENCES

Drucker, P. F. (1971). What we can learn from Japanese management. *Harvard Business Review* **71202**:110–122.

Mintzberg, H. (1973). *The Nature of Managerial Work.* New York: Harper & Row.

Sirota, D., and J. M. Greenwood (1971). *Understand Your Overseas Workforce.* **71110**:53–60.

# 3
# MANAGERIAL STRESSORS

If we explore what behavioral scientists and managers themselves perceive as sources of managerial stress, the outcome is surprising. Almost every conventional business practice is perceived as stressful under specific circumstances. The list below will be considered in detail in subsequent sections:

- the basic hierarchical structure of bureaucratic organizations.
- management style in the United States with its emphasis on productivity, striving, long working hours, individualism, competitiveness, and personal advancement.
- "management prerogatives" such as the right to unilaterally assign work or to control an individual's employability.
- practices such as management by objectives, performance appraisals, and career development programs if not designed or executed properly.
- the interpersonal aspects of the manager's role such as responsibility to and for others, the use of authority or power over others, rivalry with peers, and superior–subordinate relationships.
- the ambiguity with which work is assigned and results are measured.

Managerial stressors mean different things to different people. *Managers* concerned with survival in a power structure think of stressors as career events that threaten security or require important changes in ongoing life patterns. To managers, losing out on opportunities for advancement, being promoted beyond their level of competence, significant organizational changes (new top management, reorganization, merger, or takeover) are stressors.

*Top executives* responsibile for the health and survival of the organization think of stressors as events that expose them to interactions with external power structures that have different and often conflicting interests. These outside sources of power include customers, shareholders, creditors, governmental bodies on various levels, regulatory agencies, unions, and the public at large with its consumer advocacy and other special interest groups.

*Psychologists* interested in organizational behavior provide two definitions of stressors: (1) the pyramidal structure of bureaucratic organizations that exposes otherwise competent executives to obsolescence and defeat; (2) the mores within rigid hierarchical systems that tend to suppress much needed expressions of approval, support, and affection.

*Scientists* seeking to link variables in the work environment with indicators of cardiovascular and mental health identify as stressors such variables as: poor match of individual and environment; inadequate job content (too complex, not challenging enough); and work role stress (role conflict, role ambiguity, and work overload).

Scientific inquiry into the health consequences of organizational behavior is a relatively recent development, yet the flow of significant research findings is accelerating rapidly. Taken as a whole, scientific findings are interesting, provocative, promising, but rarely definitive. Correlations between stressors (work pressure) and their illness consequences (coronary heart disease) are of a relatively low order of magnitude, seldom accounting for more than 20 to 30 percent of the variance in outcome. Thus other factors, not identified in the research design, contribute 70 percent or more of the variance in coronary heart disease onset, job dissatisfaction, or whatever the outcome variables under investigation may be.

There is also uncertainty among scientists as to the proper emphasis for their research: whether to focus on the individual or the environment. It would seem that a study of work stress should investigate the impact of the environment on the person working within it. But researchers now agree that factors in the individual, rather than in the work environment, account for most of the variance in outcome (Kasl, 1978).

Methodological problems are likely to plague research for some time to come, unless scientists have an opportunity to observe the short-term and long-range outcomes of natural experiments that take place when groups of experienced managers cope with the challenging conditions to which they are exposed. To offer effective stress-reduction strategies, scientists consider it essential that they systematically observe such natural experiments. Unfortunately, such opportunities are infrequent. When these do occur, the ongoing monitoring of managers' and executives' stress responses is rarely a high priority. Instead top management is involved in coping with the challenging conditions that precipitated the natural experiment. So, it seems, it is left up to us to find a useful framework within which to describe managerial stressors and plan appropriate interventions.

I prefer to define managerial stressors as extraordinary pressures (peaks of stress and career-related personal crises) that occur from time to time, and to exclude the ordinary pressures in day-to-day work unless these reach the intensity or magnitude of an overload. Extraordinary pressures require special interventive action while ordinary pressures should be dealt with more or less routinely by the social support systems already in place within every organization.

It is my intention to include as relevant data, around which to build a framework for managerial stressors, only those extraordinary pressures that managers and executives themselves consider to be significant on the basis of their own experience.

## RELEVANT DATA

Relevant data can be collected from the following sources:

1   A consensus of what experienced executives consider significant sources of stress, collected by means of in-depth personal interviews.

2   Natural experiments in which the short- and long-term adaptation of managers and their dependents to changing conditions has been observed (merger, reorganization, relocation, expatriate assignment, rapidly changing social and economic conditions leading to peak workloads).

3    Observations of groups of individuals reacting to common stressful environmental changes (relocation of offices to a distant community); to similar stressful events in different organizations (managerial redundancy related to merger); and to stressors that characterize the organization in which they work (centralized management).

4    Observations of the characteristic fluctuations in compatability that develop as the relationship between the executive and the organization evolves over time.

5    Research findings of scientists from a variety of disciplines, linking variables in the work environment to indicators of job satisfaction, cardiovascular health, mental health, and other stress-related illness.

After I decided to use empirical data to define managerial stressors, I became concerned about the reliability of this information. The surveys are informal. There are no controls; the manager's own experience before an event serves more or less as a control. Subjective reporting is prone to error, although clinical, behavioral, and medical data tend to support subjective data in all the instances reported here. Certainly the personal crises and peaks of stress reported by executives and their dependents, from many different environments, are known to be significant by direct observation. But some scientists refer to data from in-depth interviews as soft data or intuition and not as the product of educated observation and judgment. Medical epidemiologists, for instance, insist that these connections stand the test of statistical significance before we draw valid conclusions and proceed to take interventive action on that basis.

To resolve this problem I sought professional help and consulted my close friend and colleague, Dr. Bernard Riess, a clinical psychologist with substantial experience in organizational and problem-solving training programs for top executives worldwide. I posed the question: "How can I be sure that the elements upon which I am planning to build a framework for management stress, namely, a consensus of the impressions of experienced executives, their spouses, my colleagues, and myself, are significant and not overly subjective, distorted or misleading?"

The answer came back immediately, as if my mentor were familiar with the problem. "Use the Eyeball Test of Significance! Collect all your data, lay it out in front of you and look at it carefully. If something pops out at you, hits you between the eyes as significant, it is!" So I will apply the "Eyeball Test of Significance," not once but twice. If a source of extraordinary pressure stands out as one of distinct importance to the executives surveyed through the various methods mentioned, *and* if this significance is confirmed through the clinical or organizational experience of colleagues, then I will assume it *is* a relevant observation and should be thought of as a managerial stressor.

The problem will be to connect these observations in a logical system that includes all significant stressors and perhaps will then reveal new connections among stressors and new interventions to cope with them.

## PRESSURES ON EXECUTIVES—GOOD OR BAD?

Before we go into the details of how to distinguish ordinary from extraordinary pressure, we must examine the controversy over whether the effect of pressure on executives is good or bad. This controversy is currently taking place in the executive suite, in the offices of management consultants, and, of course, in the professional and mass media. "Experts" are quoted to support the impressions of experienced managers and executives on both sides of the controversy. One side claims that pressure stimulates constructive action, therefore, efforts to reduce pressure on executives are either unnecessary or may be counterproductive. The other side claims that pressure is noxious (stressful), adversely influencing health, well-being, and effectiveness. Therefore, efforts to reduce pressure can preserve the productivity of key performers.

The influence of this debate on the attitudes of organizational decision makers can have considerable impact on the clarity, confidence, and determination of their approach to the relatively complicated problems involved in the design of organizational coping strategies. Furthermore, attitudes about pressure can have considerable influence on both individual and organizational coping style. Conventional executive coping style, based as it is on some unrealistic conceptions of the stress process, can serve as an obstacle, rather than as an aid, in dealing with managerial stressors.

Coping strategies, initiated by management and based on relatively superficial impressions of the effect of pressure on executives and how to cope with it, reflected in this controversy, are un-doubtedly well intentioned. There is, nevertheless, the ominous prospect that when executives who hold these impressions are in a position to make policy decisions, they will opt for strategies that address the wrong problems, misidentify the population at risk, or choose inappropriate programs.

## The debate

In the past, high-level executives were thought of as a select club of top dogs thriving on pressure, enjoying the use of power, happy with their status, and basking in admiration received from others. Top executives were viewed as having high opinions of themselves, confident in their points of view, flexible in their approach to life, not easily frustrated, and capable of handling intense pressure. If something went wrong, if an important venture did not work out as planned, these executives simply blamed others and moved them around on the organizational chess board. They did not feel per-sonally threatened. They were in complete control of their own circumstances.

Then along came the scientists with their research into coro-nary heart disease risk factors; the work-addicted coronary-prone personality; and new understandings of the illness consequences of stressful events, changes, and transitions. The opinions of ex-perts in the fields of medicine, psychiatry, psychology, and soci-ology and organizational behavior on the adverse effects of stress became translated into the popular belief that the pressure of high-level corporate positions inevitably leads to heart attacks, ulcers, alcoholism, or divorce. Consequently there was a need for stress management programs to maintain top executives in top working form. Executives became a protected species—too valuable to the organization to be exposed to the undesirable consequences of the newly discovered occupational hazard—*management stress.*

Soon, special programs began to flourish, in which coronary risk factors were attacked by measures to reduce smoking, blood pressure, obesity, and a sedentary way of life. The accumulation of daily tensions and anxieties was drained by relaxation tech-niques. Time-pressured striving was reduced by prolonged vaca-tions and other breaks in the usual daily work routine. Physical fitness and quality of life issues were emphasized to restore the top executive's sense of well-being. There are many positive claims for the value of stress management programs, such as improvement in work performance and creativity as a direct result of relaxation techniques (meditation), etc.

*Backlash*—But signs of disenchantment with such programs are also growing. "Executive stress may not be all bad" asserts a recent article on management in *Business Week* (April 30, 1979). "The happiness of hassles; they motivate, stimulate and provide the needed challenge" claims the caption under an accompanying cartoon, showing a smiling executive responding simultaneously to many urgent communications (phone calls taken, phone calls waiting, messages requiring a response, financial reports fresh from the adding machine, communications from subordinates waving important papers). Meanwhile, worried subordinates and harried secretaries surrounding the happy, hassled executive, appear to be frantic about the urgent issue each is handling. The article focuses an emerging reaction against the stress management techniques that have become so popular in recent years. Biofeedback and exercise techniques to reduce stress were specifically mentioned. Experts now believe that high-powered achievers thrive on pressure. Who are the experts? They are (1) physicians who staff preventive medical centers that guard the health of high-level executives, (2) chief executive officers of the corporations in question, and (3) stress management specialists—consultants to corporations on organizational development issues.

One expert, Dr. Reginald B. Cherry, Director of the Houstonian Preventive Medical Center in Houston is quoted as saying "Executives are often bored with these stress programs because they already know how to deal with stress." Charles E. Thompson, founder and director of professional services for the Thompson Medical Center in Chicago prefers such old solutions as changing jobs if the executive finds the job too stressful. Current antidotes to mounting stress (meditation and biofeedback) are dismissed as valueless by Thompson. "The successful executive learns very early to handle stress well. If a company has to reduce stress for an executive, it has the wrong executive."

Top executives are quoted to support the notion that many of them know how to take stress in stride.

- "The hours are tough on a typical person . . . (but) I don't think you can get to the top unless you can handle stress"—

John H. Vogel, Chairman of the National Bank of North America.

- "(I do) not particularly enjoy stress, (but) some degree of stress is a motivator. If the job's too soft, you lose your mental activity."—Roy A. Anderson, Chairman of Lockheed Corporation.

- "Stress is what you make of it, and that can be the difference between coping and collapsing."—John H. Zimmerman, Vice President of employee relations for Firestone Tire and Rubber Company.

- "Stress in the sense of challenge is important to getting a job done." Edmund T. Pratt, Jr., Chairman of Pfeizer, Inc.

Rosalind A. Forbes, a specialist in stress management and founder of Forbes Associates in New York City states, "High-powered executives need this stimulation that we call stress. They're adrenalin freaks. It becomes an asset for managers because it helps them to do a better job."

Experts are pitted against experts in this debate. Medical and social scientists find over forty interacting factors that may be sources of illness-precipitating management stress. Their solution is to reduce the stressfulness of the job and thereby increase executive effectiveness. Management consultants working close to or within management believe high-powered achievers thrive on pressure. Their solution is to fit the achiever to the high-pressured job.

However, evidence cited in the *Business Week* article indicates that experts on both sides of the issue may be right: the scientists for their observations of managerial stress among managers at all levels; and management consultants for accurate observations of the health of top level executives.

### The healthy top executive

Generally, the incidence of coronary heart disease increases with age, level of responsibility, and position in the organizational hierarchy. But there may be a different health profile at the very top of the pyramid. A 1974 study by the Metropolitan Life Insurance Co. found that *presidents and vice presidents of the 500 largest industrial companies had 40 percent fewer fatal heart attacks than middle managers of these companies.*

My own informal survey of the health of key executives in a large corporation tends to support the implications of the Metropolitan Life Insurance Co. study. It is my impression that high level executives responsible for the day-to-day efforts to insure the success, survival, and perpetuation of the organization tend to have fewer seriously incapacitating illnesses while on the job than other executives not so closely involved with operations at that level. Of course, retirement may come as a seriously stressful change for those accustomed to functioning at the helm of a large organization.

Thus, executives who are able to survive in the ranks of top management may have a health profile that is different from that of other managers. *The critical variable may be the extent to which the executive is able to exercise control of the job* rather than the survival of the fittest or the level achieved in the organizational hierarchy. In any case, top executives are not typical executives with regard to stress-related illness.

## THE TOP EXECUTIVE AS A ROLE MODEL

The formulation presented here links specific pressures inherent in the management process with adverse effects on executive health, well-being, and effectiveness. Some managers and executives using their own observations and experience (relevant data) question this formulation. Taking top executives in highly pressured jobs as role models or examples they argue that:

**1** *Pressure is not necessarily bad.* Challenge appears to motivate, stimulate, and catalyze constructive action. The *absence* of pressure is associated with dissatisfaction and reduced effectiveness.

**2** *Top executives appear to be a particularly healthy group.* Certainly their health profile does not indicate the need for special preventive stress-reduction programs. One does not observe among them the epidemic of stress-related illness that might be expected from research findings concerning the noxious consequences of intense striving, heavy workload, many responsibilities, and rapidly changing working conditions.

**3** *The usefulness of stress-management programs is difficult to evaluate for a relatively healthy executive population.* Research findings are not easily translated into techniques of predictable effectiveness. The value of techniques to increase fitness and relaxation, or to reduce coronary risk factors (heavy smoking, poor diet, sedentary life style) and thereby reduce the adverse effects of pressure on executives, is still unknown.

Attitudes toward the effect of pressure on executives can have far-reaching consequences. Those who view top executives in highly pressured jobs as a healthy, self-confident group will tend to generalize these observations to all managers and executives. When in a position to make policy decisions they will see no reason for special techniques to cope with management stress unless there is a clearly demonstrable need (widespread morale problems, significant increase in the incidence of coronary heart disease among key executives, high turnover). It will be difficult to sell them on preventive stress management and health maintenance programs. Aspiring young executives will be encouraged to model their coping style after that of high level executives who appear to be activated by challenge, not easily frustrated, and capable of handling great amounts of pressure. This attitude toward pressure, a coping style that thrives on challenge, is likely to be admired and emulated by younger executives and may become incorporated into the organization's characteristic personality or management style.

The danger of modeling their coping style after that of the high level executive is that aspiring young executives may be encouraged to strive for the impossible. The role of the top executive is uniquely different from the role of all other managers in that top executives are in a position to control their own circumstances, to choose their involvements. They have only subordinates and no superiors. Their ordinary work may involve intense pressure, but they also have maximum control over their own initiatives, a factor that may correlate with their apparent high level of health and confidence. For them, extraordinary pressure implies a lessening of control, as when they must respond to external initiatives or take on entirely new internal roles. Heavy workload in familiar roles is not as noxious as less intense involvement in new roles. Several conclusions can be drawn from the ongoing debate about whether pressure is all good or all bad:

1  What is good pressure for top executives may be bad pressure for other managers. Health maintenance and stress management programs should not be designed only for the needs of top executives.

2   Top managers are not appropriate models for the coping styles of executives at lower levels who do not have the same control over their own work requirements and initiatives.

3   All other managers who have both subordinates and superiors, who must translate often ambiguous demands into concretely measurable results, who must cope with peers (usually rivals), who must earn the respect of those below them while pleasing those above them—in short the 99.9 percent of the population at risk who have incomplete control over their circumstances—must find a role model more appropriate to their true situation than that of the top executive.

### Comment

The debate over the effectiveness of common health maintenance programs obscures the value of developing preventive strategies to cope with many aspects of organizational change. Executives in search of immediate strategies to cope with management stress are justifiably perplexed by the diverse attitudes about pressure and the many factors that have been identified as potential stressors. With the need to be concerned about such complexities, there is the danger that discriminating efforts to cope will become paralyzed or even ignored. This situation in turn leads to an exclusive reliance on techniques to reduce signs of tension and strain once these have surfaced (the wrong problem) by means of health maintenance programs (the wrong program) for top management only (the wrong population at risk).

Conceiving of the effect of pressures on executives as either all good or all bad is too superficial and inaccurate a construct upon which to develop individual and organizational strategies to cope with management stress. The distinction between ordinary and extraordinary pressure as it is perceived by the individual manager is much more useful in this regard.

### ORDINARY PRESSURE

Coping with the ordinary pressures in the day-to-day life of the manager or executive should require no special strategies other than those supplied by ordinary support systems that define what is expected of the individual and how the individual can effectively deal with the environment. These support systems may be 1) formal: such as orientation, training and development, management education programs, practices such as performance appraisals, departmental meetings, or 2) informal systems: such as interpersonal communication, sharing of common experiences and concerns, group affiliation, and cohesiveness.

The providers of such support (personnel practitioners, trainers, educators, superiors, colleagues, peers) constitute a social support system or network that supplies managers and executives during their ordinary day-to-day working life with:

- consistent feedback and communication about what is expected of them.
- support and assistance with tasks, and instructions in how to accomplish what is expected of them.
- evaluation of performance and appropriate rewards.
- definition of what is or is not potentially threatening, challenging, or harmful.
- protection against the deleterious effects of unfamiliarity and uncertainty.
- care, protection, comfort, and emotional assistance in times of need.

The distinction between ordinary and extraordinary pressures in the working life of the manager is not a mere semantic difference, but an issue of great practical importance in the planning of coping strategies. Ideal strategy is to improve the capability of the usual organizational support systems to anticipate and prepare for impending extraordinary pressures, and thereby reduce the perceived threat impact when stressors strike.

To illustrate, let us consider the problem of executives approaching age fifty-five who are not members of top management's policy-making group. They are entering the stressful period of trying to hold out until retirement while expecting opportunities for advancement to be limited. They fear that opportunities for similar employment outside the organization at that age are foreclosed; they feel vulnerable to "forced early retirement" should the organization choose to relocate, retrench, or reorganize, and they worry because inflation is progressing rapidly and they must work as long as possible before becoming resigned to a relatively fixed retirement income.

A program to help executives approaching age fifty-five who are holding out against retirement might include:

• management education that, in addition to preretirement preparation, prepares them for likely career crises such as midcareer changes.

• outplacement and second career training as part of regular career development programs; or training that prepares managers for new jobs within the organization. Such training should continue until retirement and thereby help prepare managers for preseparation and postseparation employment contingencies.

• redesign of late career progression to provide for more flexible use of the talents and experience of older managers and at the same time provide them with increased career options (for example, intraorganizational use as consultants or on special projects or task forces, part-time employment, use as community liaison, portable pensions).

Such preparation anticipates typical late career problems as well as the possibility that unexpected contingencies may appear to threaten established individual–organization compatibility. Should the organization decide to relocate, retrench, or reorganize, the impact on fifty-five-year-old managers will be more like that of an ordinary pressure as a result of this preparation rather than an extraordinary pressure threatening survival. *The long-service manager who is prepared by training and forethought to cope alone with the inevitable problems of late career is of inestimable help to management faced with an otherwise thorny separation problem.*

### Comment

Whenever possible it is desirable to anticipate the need for a stress management program to cope in advance with the issues raised by organizational change. When stress responses among executives have reached sufficient intensity to emerge as problems requiring special management intervention, initiating a stress reduction program is difficult. Special improvement programs take time to develop and "sell." Abruptly instituted programs lead to stress, resistance to something new, and opposition from those whose turf is most threatened. Thus the stress program creates its own stress as changes occur in accustomed practices, relationships, or areas of power.

Of course, unexpected, unwanted, or uncontrollable contingencies, often imposed by pressures from outside the organization, will always appear to executives as extraordinary pressures. Here too, regular organizational support systems can provide a buffer.

## EXTRAORDINARY PRESSURE

Impressions of how managers and executives distinguish ordinary from extraordinary pressures are presented here as a series of propositions about pressure in the managerial role. In general, extraordinary pressure refers to situations in which:

- work demands appear to be challenging in the extreme or even overwhelming.
- changing conditions are perceived as dangerous or harmful to job security.
- accustomed life patterns are threatened.
- the future is perceived as highly uncertain, unpredictable, uncontrollable, undesirable, or unknown.
- individuals feel conditions are unmanageable and that they are unable to cope.
- stress impact results in confusion, helplessness, or paralysis of effective action.

Of course, ordinary pressures can become extraordinary if they become intense, are unanticipated or unwanted, cannot be controlled, or when several pressures occur concurrently. There is probably a continuum from ordinary to extraordinary pressure. Ultimately, it is the judgment of experienced managers and executives that distinguishes the ordinary, expected, controllable pressures of day-to-day working life from the extraordinary pressures that confront them from time to time. The following propositions that distinguish ordinary from extraordinary pressure are derived from the judgment of experienced managers and executives.

1 *Daily Work and Roles*

- *Daily work and roles are viewed as ordinary pressures* even when they involve a heavy work load, long hours, considerable traveling and time away from home, involvement in many projects in different stages of completion, some ambiguity in the way work is assigned as well as in how their performance is regarded by superiors. It seems that when managers are doing what they expect to be doing, the perception is one of ordinary pressure even if the workload is intense, complex, or ambiguous.

• *Everyday struggle for control of their own work and for turf within the organization is seen as ordinary pressure* even if they are losing the struggle. Managers and executives expect to struggle for control or for areas of responsibility and authority with superiors, peers, and subordinates. Informal ways of getting around the formal hierarchical structure are common, sought after sources of satisfaction when successful. Control or pressure from above is "part of the game." So are the informal systems devised to circumvent the formal organizational structure.

• *Any threat to the control of their daily work by unexpected contingencies or developments outside the organization is seen as extraordinary pressure.* Managers expend a great deal of effort planning, budgeting, and defining objectives—all of which are means of controlling their regular work. Any external development that threatens this control is extraordinary pressure.

**2** *Office Politics*

• *Office politics (superior–subordinate relationships, interpersonal communications, informal systems for dissemination of information) is publicly described as ordinary pressure but privately considered as extraordinary and distressing.*

**3** *Leadership*

• *Top management's policies, plans, decisions, work assignments and performance demands are viewed as ordinary pressures* provided these are clearly stated and difficult, but not impossible, to achieve. Authority is granted as the prerogative of leadership. Any decision is better than no decision or an unclear decision, even when the decision taken may lead to difficulties in the manager's or executive's regular work. "At least we know where we stand."

• *Critical evaluation of the effectiveness of the leadership of an organizational unit is perceived as extraordinary pressure and is rarely expressed openly,* least of all directly to the leaders themselves. Top management is not expected to take kindly to criticism, or to requests from subordinates to share decision and policy making prerogatives. "If you don't like it, leave" and "Take it or leave it" are the leadership responses usually expected by subordinates.

• *The influence of leadership personality and style in shaping organizational personality, style and ethics is an ordinary pressure,* and accepted as a characteristic of organizational life. A distinct organizational personality provides much needed parameters within which managers and executives must function. Stability of organizational personality is reassuring and strengthens already established compatibilities between the individual and the organization.

• *Any change in accustomed organizationl personality, style, and ethics is perceived as extraordinary pressure* even if this change is for the better. "The devil you know is better than the devil you don't know."

4   *Organizational Change*

• *As a general rule the need to change an established procedure or practice is seen as an extraordinary pressure* unless the manager or executive is "sold" on the idea. Those who do not participate in planning the change, or who remain unconvinced of the need for it, are sold with difficulty. Those who are dependent on the status quo for reasons of security are most resistant to the change. A threat to the status quo is perceived by them as a threat to survival in the organization. Anything old is less threatening than something new.

• *Major organizational change of any type and for any reason is considered extraordinary pressure.* There is an element of uncertainty in any change that disrupts established role relationships, formal and informal communications systems, the existing power structure, or ordinary patterns of daily work. Uncertainty is the greatest stressor of all.

• *Any threat to established individual–organization compatibility is perceived as extraordinary pressure* even when that threat results from a desired change (promotion to new functional responsibilities) rather than an unwanted one (the need to learn radically new systems installed to replace familiar systems that have become obsolete).

5   *Career Development*

• *Early career work assignments are viewed as opportunities on the way up, therefore as the ordinary pressures of becoming a suc-*

*cessful executive*—even when these assignments involve intense striving to establish a track record of accomplishment, rotational assignments of short duration, and mobility required to take advantage of promotional opportunities. In fact it is considered extraordinary pressure when the young aspiring executive is *not* required to strive or compete, or does *not* receive rotational assignments of short duration.

- *Career development issues arising during midcareer or beyond the midforties are seen as extraordinary pressures—part of a declining career cycle* (that is, midcareer changes, second careers, late-career insecurities, the threat of forced early retirement). There seems to be an unspoken agreement between managers and management that career development programs should be made available to younger managers on the way up at the expense of older managers whose midcareer and late-career needs are virtually ignored.

6   *Personal Factors*

- *All family influences on managers' careers are viewed as extraordinary pressures.* This influence seems to reflect an intense and all-absorbing involvement of managers in their daily work of meeting planned objectives, achieving required results, and traveling a desired promotional route. Any influences from family and personal obligations that threaten to disturb these patterns of daily work are viewed as extraordinary pressures.

- *Changes in perspective as a result of the personal midlife transition (late thirties to midforties) were rarely mentioned as a source of pressure by managers and executives interviewed.* However, the new sense of their own individuality and their place in the world that results from this transition may often redefine the individual–organization compatibility established during an earlier period in the manager's life cycle. The disharmony that may result can in its turn become an extraordinary pressure.

### Comment

These propositions related to pressures in the managerial role indicate to me that managers tend to accept as ordinary pressures several potentially harmful aspects of that role. These aspects include:

- strong emphasis on competitive striving for productivity and individual advancement.

- the employer's unilateral control of the managers' employ-ability and career progression.
- a view of personal distress from any source, including work, as the private concern of the individual and not the respon-sibility or concern of the organization.
- the profound influence of organizational life on the life style of managers and their families.

There is a remarkable contrast between the manager's relatively benign view of these managerial stressors and their known con-sequences as indicated by research findings and evidence contrib-uted by experts in organizational behavior.

The noxious effect on health of competitive striving for pro-ductivity and advancement is particularly apparent when the man-ager is required to meet unilaterally imposed or inappropriate pro-duction standards, or when the effect of striving is not modified by the satisfaction of achievement. (See Chapter 5, The Striving-Satisfaction Balance). Yet managers accept a heavy workload as a matter of course and complain only when productivity suffers. Unfortunately, the noxious effects on health of heavy workload are likely to appear before performance suffers.

Conventional career development programs fail to sustain individual–organization compatibility throughout the managers' careers, as indicated by the high incidence of midcareer and late-career problems; managers boxed into middle-management roles with dim prospects for advancement or new horizons; managers who are locked into unrewarding jobs to protect accumulated ben-efits; and common concerns about forced early retirement. Career development needs continue throughout managers' careers, and even beyond, into retirement or separation from the organization for other reasons. Yet managers philosophically accept these com-mon career progression problems as unchangeable.

Organizational mores and style define career-related personal distress as the private concern of the individual rather than a concern of the organization, and encourage the misperception of emotional distress as an indication of weakness. A distress compo-nent inevitably accompanies the process of dealing with stressors from any source. Yet managers persist in defining all distress as personal, private, something to deny or conceal, but certainly noth-ing to be brought to the attention of the organization for remedy.

Aspects of the managerial role affect managers' personal and family life style in a fundamental way. Managers and their families are continuously affected by the consequences of heavy work pressure, of demands for the individual's complete attention to and absorption in the details of managerial work and roles, of mobility and other career progression requirements, of management's control of the manager's employability and economic survival. Yet managers see the impact of the job on their personal life as ordinary pressure and the impact of personal life on job performance as extraordinary pressure.

It is my impression that these aspects of managerial roles are accepted as "ordinary pressures" because the individual has no power to control or change them, and not because these pressures pose few threats, challenges, or frustrations. To assure continuing compatibility with the organization, managers learn to "live with" as "part of the game," then come to expect, and eventually seek to reinforce or perpetuate, the very stressors that may ultimately operate against their best interests.

Coping with managerial stressors involves fundamental changes in the system, or in job or career design, or organizational mores, which in turn requires policy decisions. These changes cannot be accomplished by individual action alone because the individual lacks the authority and influence to do so. Organizational coping strategies revolve around constructive and creative personnel policies that free the individual from organization-imposed rigidities and thereby enable managers, as individuals, to assume as much responsibility as possible for coping with the impact of managerial stressors.

## REFERENCES

*Business Week* (1979). Executive stress may not be all bad. April 30, 1979: 96–103.

Kasl, S. V. (1978). Epidemiological contributions to the study of work stress. In C. L. Cooper and R. Payne (eds.) *Stress at Work*. Chichester, England: Wiley.

# 4

# CONTROLLED FROM ABOVE

An organization's style of control, striving, and coping is determined by the policies and practices (both explicit and implicit) of top management. If organizational style acts as a stressor, organizational decisions made by top management are required to remedy the situation. Thus, top executives must become aware of how, why, and when their policies, decisions, attitudes and management style affect the intensity of managerial stressors in their organization. They must also become aware of their effect on organizational cohesion and the social support systems that play such a critical role in modifying the impact of managerial stressors.

Since top executives have a profound influence on the intensity of management stress in the organizations they lead, it follows that they also have a profound influence on managers' style of coping with that stress. This influence is exerted through their roles as leaders, decision makers, guardians of the organization's competitive health and survival, influencers of organizational personality, and as role models for younger executives.

Experienced managers and executives expect to be controlled from above. They accept as prerogatives of top management distribution of authority, responsibility, and accountability, and have learned to adapt to these prerogatives as a circumstance of their day-to-day working lives. But in return for their acceptance of and adaptation to being controlled from above, they expect a good deal. They expect top executives to be effective leaders: to formulate strategies and policies that clearly define organizational purposes, goals, and objectives. They expect their leaders to demonstrate competence in competing in the external world, in coping with it, and in leading their organizations to adaptive achievement (Levinson, 1976.) As the organization changes to meet competitve needs and threats to survival, top management is expected to maintain an internal equilibrium.

Furthermore, subordinates expect top management to achieve these results efficiently. They expect adequate definition of tasks, adequate guidance and direction, adequate functional policies and practices, and adequate compensation in the form of financial reward, fringe benefits, work satisfaction, and the fulfillment of basic psychological requirements of work. These requirements include opportunities for employees to continually develop their capacities, to have an effect on their fate, and to determine their life direction.

Inevitably leaders become models for other managers. Their leadership type affects the organizational personality—that collection of characteristic attitudes and ways of working and interacting, and the supportive social relationships and cohesiveness that give an organization its distinctive and unique qualities.

Leadership attitudes and style will determine whether the ordinary pressures of top management's prerogatives become extraordinary pressures. Depending on how authority, responsibility, and accountability are applied throughout the organization, and depending on how mores, behavioral attitudes, and social support characteristics of the organizational personality develop, these prerogatives can become serious managerial stressors adversely affecting:

- managers' much needed sense of control of their own work initiatives.
- the delicate balance between striving (work pressure) and satisfaction that can affect the managers' health and well being.
- the effectiveness of the prevailing executive style of coping with managerial stressors and personal distress.

Particularly pertinent are top executive attitudes toward:

- the intensity of work pressure, striving, expressions of aggression, competition and rivalry, and the delegation of authority.
- expressions of affection, concern and support in an organizational setting, and the responsibility of top management for career-related human relationship problems.

But top management involvement in human relationship problems is generally not given high priority unless a clearly definable need appears. This need usually takes the form of an acute emergency when the time for applying preventive measures has passed.

> *In most organizations human relationship problems are dealt with as an afterthought, an added burden to the organization which is incidental to its central thrust. They are, therefore, most frequently dealt with by a buying-off process as in fringe benefits; by a game-playing process, as in many kinds of organizational development activities; or by simple abandonment, as in leaving employee requirements solely to the bargaining table.*
>
> (LEVINSON, 1976, p. 77)

This chapter and the two that follow discuss the potential sources of management stress that are caused by control from above—by the policies, decisions, and management style of top executives.

## MANAGER IN CONTROL

Managers feel most comfortable when they can act on their own initiatives and control their own work, which they attempt to do through planning, budgeting, assigning objectives, and then involving themselves in an intense effort to meet these planned objectives, achieve required results, and travel a desired promotional route as a reward for effective performance. The stressfulness of this effort depends in part on the cooperation between managers and their superiors. Managers feel more in control (therefore less stressed) if:

- objectives are arrived at by mutual agreement with superiors.
- plans and budget include the input and involvement of those who are responsible for carrying them out.
- managers are given sufficient authority to achieve the results expected by superiors.
- managers have the power to choose the team they must depend on to carry out these objectives.

Assuming optimal conditions in these areas there is still considerable controversy over the extent to which managers can reasonably expect to control their work initiatives or the way in which this control is expressed. Given the impact of organizational dynamics on a manager's work and roles, is the manager *in control* like Peter Drucker's super conductor of a symphony orchestra or *controlled* like Sune Carlson's puppet in a puppet show?

According to Drucker:

> *One analogy is the conductor of a symphony orchestra, through whose effort, vision and leadership individual instrumental parts that are so much noise by themselves become the living whole of music. But the conductor has the composer's score; he is only interpreter. The manager is both composer and conductor.*

> (DRUCKER, 1954, pp. 341–342)

But according to Carlson's systematic study of managers:

> *Before we made the study, I always thought of a chief executive as the conductor of an orchestra, standing aloof on his platform. Now I am in some respects inclined to see him as the puppet in a puppet show with hundreds of people pulling the strings and forcing him to act in one way or another.*

> (CARLSON, 1951, p. 52)

In fact, managers appear to be in active control of a relatively small proportion of daily activities. Categorizing verbal activities according to active or passive involvement Mintzberg (1973) found that managers were ostensibly passive in 42 percent of such involvements (ceremonial activities, involvements where requests are made of the manager); more active in 31 percent (strategy, negotiation, informing, touring, and requests made by the manager); and neither active nor passive in 27 percent of all involvements (review, scheduling, external board work).

Some studies of the work of chief executives argue that even they spend most of their time *reacting*. Their priorities are set, not by the relative importance of a task, but by the relative necessity for the chief executive do it—to attend meetings set up by others, answer more mail than is initiated, and respond to requests of others rather than make requests of others.

Mintzberg concludes, however, that managers or chief executives are to be depicted as conductors or puppets depending on how their own affairs are managed. Managers or executives are able to make the initial decisions that in turn define many of their own long-term commitments. These decisions include initiating a project that, once underway, may demand time for years to come, or developing information channels that will provide a flow of information without the need for day-to-day control. Control is exerted through crucial decisions. These are usually made shortly after the manager assumes office and must be "lived with" from then on. Control can also be exerted by the judicious use of those activities in which managers or executives *must be* involved, that is, by turning problems into opportunities, by exploiting new ideas in the solution of these problems.

The ability to make the initial decisions that determine long-term commitments, and the ability to take advantage of obligatory activities and use them for their own needs most clearly distinguish successful and unsuccessful managers:

> *All managers appear to be puppets. Some decide who will pull the strings and how, and they then take advantage of each move that they are forced to make. Others, unable to exploit this high tension environment, are swallowed up by this most demanding of jobs.*

(MINTZBERG, 1973, p. 51)

Thus, managers develop techniques to exercise initiatives and control in an organizational setting. These techniques define the managerial function as experienced managers expect to perform that function from day to day. Pressures that arise within this familiar, expected, accustomed high-tension context are perceived as ordinary pressures.

## PRESSURE FLOWS DOWNWARD

Extraordinary pressures may arise from time to time that affect the ability of managers to act on their own initiatives and control their own work in the accustomed way. The following interview indicates the kind of problems that may develop when a manager is compelled by circumstances to respond to initiatives originating from external sources. It describes the pressures eminating from the executive suite during a period of national economic recession accompanied for the first time by increasing unemployment among managers in the United States. The views expressed represent a

consensus of experienced executives interviewed at that time as part
of a broad survey to explore executive stress factors.

## INTERVIEW 2 – Pressured from Above

Jim Powell was the general manager of a small plastics factory in
Pennsylvania until nine months prior to this interview when he
was promoted to a staff position in the New York office. There he
reports to a divisional Vice President on the Executive Committee.
The interview began with Jim's declaration that he was under
intense pressure.

"This company has a highly centralized management style.
Most decisions, even small ones, are made at the top. Members of
the Executive Committee must have accurate supporting material so
they are sufficiently familiar with the issues and can form the best
possible judgments. With a clear view from the top they are in the
best position to guide the company through troubled times like
business in general is going through now. Accurate information
requires good staff work and that's where I come in. I manage the
staff work.

"Since I came here, I haven't had more than a moment for
my family. They are still in the old house. I'm waiting for time to
look for a house near here so my family can join me. It's lonely
living in a hotel during the week. It's also hard commuting such a
long distance over the weekend, when I can get away, that is, when
there isn't some super top priority emergency for-immediate-
attention assignment that breaks on a Friday afternoon and requires
a report for decision at the Ex Com meeting Monday morning."

At this point I thought I had learned what Jim Powell considered to be stressful about his job—the intense work load under
severe time pressure, and the loneliness and dislocation caused by
separation from his family. I was surprised, therefore, when he
continued: "My greatest source of tension comes from not being
clear about exactly what is required of me because of the time
pressure we are under. As top man at my plant I could see the
whole picture clearly. Here, I don't always have a clear picture
of what the issues are, what information to collect, or what it will
be used for. Some of the assignments are vague, ambiguous. Often
I don't have the time to ask for clarification or my boss is not available to give it. As a result, my staff and I are often uncertain about
what is required. We try to cover all bases, to make each report as

complete as possible. The fear is enormous that something important will slip between the cracks just because we don't know about
it. We compensate by trying to do everything, which occasionally
turns out to be an enormous waste of time.

"Even so, it really isn't the pressure of such unusually intense
staff work or these special emergency projects that gets to me. It's
that I can't find the time to do my own job, to meet my own objectives for the year. All this emergency work is extra. I'm very concerned that at the end of the year they'll tell me I haven't met my
objectives—that they will forget or overlook the fact that I was
pulled away from my own work so many times to take care of their
top priority emergency assignments.

"In my old job as head of the plastics factory I could control
my own work, respond to my own initiatives rather than to initiatives or pressure from others. I could do my own planning and feel
sure that I had taken all factors into consideration, that nothing
slipped between the cracks. I didn't have anyone sitting on top
of me to please, day by day, memo by memo, rush special assignment by rush special assignment. I could afford to take a few risks.
Everything wasn't so critical, so exposed to view. And if I made a
mistake it wasn't a potential catastrophy. Now I fear a mistake
because of the possible consequences it might have."

At this point in the interview I expected an expression of dissatisfaction, frustration, distress, and lowered morale. Once again
I was surprised when Jim continued in such an enthusiastic vein.
"But on balance this is a great job and a great place to work. The
guy at the top is a genius. The Ex Com is getting us through the
recession in good shape. We haven't had the layoffs experienced
by other companies. My staff and I have confidence that the information we feed up to the top will be used constructively. We all
feel part of a team that's winning a tough battle. It's exciting. It's
all worth it."

Then came the note of caution. "I just hope this pace doesn't
continue for too much longer. I have my personal life to put in
order. My family doesn't have the same sense of excitement I
do. They have a sense of inconvenience and uncertainty. One
highly pressured week goes by like a day for me, like a month for
those waiting for something different to happen.

"I can foresee two types of problems developing in the near
future. As an organization, we're taut, stretched thin, brittle in the

sense that any new and important pressures may overload us. One more big pressure and something will have to give.

"And my family is already giving off signals of impatience. I hope my wife does what she has always done, that is put my work first and allow her schedule to be determined by what I have to do to get ahead in my career. That's the way she felt when we made the decision to take this promotion and come to New York. I hope she doesn't sour on the deal."

### Comment

The ordinary pressures of Jim Powell's managerial role were heightened by the need to put aside his usual work and respond instead to previously unanticipated, therefore unplanned for, initiatives of the Executive Committee. Most stressful was his inability to control his own work under circumstances in which he anticipated being held accountable for this work. Heightening this stress was the pressure from ambiguous communications and uncertainty about what is required of him. These pressures were brought about by emergency conditions and severe time pressure that made the usual problems of communication and delegation of authority more complicated.

Confidence that his superiors would use his work wisely and well, and enthusiasm about the outcome of this intense effort or "exciting action" modified his perception of stress and greatly reduced its potentially damaging consequences. Confidence in his superiors—a form of social support in the work environment—was the most important element in maintaining the management of this particular organization at an effective level of functioning and at a high level of morale and job satisfaction. The importance of a balance between work pressure and job satisfaction in reducing the undesirable consequences of work stress was graphically demonstrated in these interviews as was the role of confidence in superiors.

Solutions to the brittleness of a taut centralized management vulnerable to additional pressures might be:

• *Short term*—add manpower to accomplish objectives that may otherwise "slip between the cracks."

• *Long range*—review manpower needs in view of the expected consequences of the interaction between centralized management style and anticipated future emergencies.

• *Support systems*—provide some indication from superiors as to how performance will be judged under present emergency circumstances. By means of an explicit policy statement from above, indicate that superiors are aware of their subordinates' concerns about conflicting priorities, and that performance appraisals will take into account the possibility that previously assigned objectives may not be met as a result of conflicting priorities.

Potential problems posed by the family's reaction to the manager's "exciting action" (work overload, time pressure, emergency deadlines) were generally not addressed in this case. The assumption was made that family needs could be given a lesser priority than organizational needs, at least during the period of acute emergency. But with time family needs would have to be addressed or new sources of stress would be likely to develop.

One wonders what the outcome might have been if, during this period of emergency, important family problems had developed requiring Jim Powell's time and attention and distracting him from his primary objective of providing staff work for the Ex Com. How receptive would the organization have been to these "extraordinary pressures" of the manager's personal life? How confident was Jim Powell that he could have taken time to deal with a career-related personal crisis without jeopardizing his career? What would have happened if the adjustment of his wife or children, or financial complications arising from the delayed relocation of his family, or any other effect of the stressful situation on the family became a top priority assignment "for immediate attention"?

Once again the true population at risk is the manager and the manager's family. The impact of managerial stressors is felt both in and outside the workplace. The manager's stress responses and distress at work are likely to be more easily recognized by the organization. It is precisely for this reason that managers tend to suppress their reactions to stress while at work, but express their distress at home. Of course, this places even greater strain on family relationships during periods of intense pressure at work.

Some feedback system is necessary to inform top management's policy makers when stress responses arising from managerial stressors are being felt primarily at home or outside the workplace. It is the manager who must come forward and declare that personal complications stemming from stressors within the organization are becoming too intense, and that organizationally initiated changes are required to cope with them. Top management attitudes and organizational social support systems can go a long way toward creating an atmosphere that encourages such feedback. Constructive use of this type of input will strengthen both the individual's and the organization's resistance to the impact of management stress.

A feedback system to provide periodic and timely reports on the levels and sources of management stress (both at work and in the manager's personal life) is presented in Chapter 14.

In summary, the sense of control managers have over their work is determined by many factors: (1) the way in which authority, responsibility, and accountability are distributed by top management, (2) the manager's ability to plan objectives, take risks, and control results, (3) the success with which managers make decisions that determine long-term commitments, or take advantage of obligatory activities and use them for personal needs, (4) the opportunity for involvement and work satisfaction, and (5) the opportunity to develop their capacities, to have an effect on their fate, and to determine their life direction.

Put another way, managers will feel in control if, while functioning within the confines of managerial work and roles, opportunity is provided to effectively cope with the demands, responsibilities, and aspirations of work and personal and family life without irresolvable conflicts arising between these spheres.

### REFERENCES

Carlson, S. (1951). *Executive Behaviour: A Study of Work Load and the Working Methods of Managing Directors.* Stockholm: Strömbergs.

Drucker, P. F. (1954). *The Practice of Management.* New York: Harper & Row.

Levinson, H. (1976). *Psychological Man.* Cambridge, Mass.: The Levinson Institute.

Mintzberg, H. (1973). *The Nature of Managerial Work.* New York: Harper & Row.

# 5
# THE STRIVING-
# SATISFACTION
# BALANCE

For the purposes of this discussion, the term *striving* includes all efforts to satisfy those personal and organizational pressures that emphasize competitiveness, individualism, challenge, productivity, and personal achievement. The striving executive is thus, hard driving, responsible, and achievement oriented. These qualities are valuable assets to any organization. But they are also sources of risk—the risk of coronary heart disease (CHD) and other serious health problems.

Studies relate CHD and the dynamics of the management process (Cooper and Crump, 1978). Evidence links the greater incidence of CHD to higher occupational levels; greater responsibility for people; more intense work pressure; ambiguous job requirements; conflicting job demands or the need to do what is uncongenial to the individual. Taken as a whole, there is no evidence to suggest that factors in the management process *cause* CHD. But it would appear that stressful life events (including work stressors) serve as precipitating elements in influencing the timing or onset of myocardial infarction or sudden cardiac death.

Kasl (1978) suggests that three distinct factors are involved:

- a relevant personality predisposition.
- the demands of a particular work setting.
- the behavior and other reactions that are precipitated when demands activate predisposition.

Recent statistical studies indicate that individuals with a compulsion to overwork and engage in a struggle against the clock are three times more likely to develop some form of coronary heart disease than individuals with a more easygoing life style, free from a sense of striving and time urgency. Among younger men the figures are even more striking. Hard-driving men ages thirty-nine to forty-nine are 6.5 times more likely to develop some form of coronary heart disease than a matched control group of men with a more relaxed life style (Rosenman, Friedman, & Strauss, 1966). As much as 50 percent of top management and 39 percent of middle management may fall into the coronary-prone life style category based on their responses to a question about how often they work excessively and put in many discretionary hours per week.*

*Stress factors in the management role are taking their toll on the health of younger executives.* Dr. John P. McCann, medical board chairman of the New York-based Life Extension Institute stated in an interview reported in *Business Week*:

> Top executives are among the healthiest people in America. In a sense, they're champion athletes. These people make it in part because they are able to survive stress and, after they've made it, new challenges become stimuli rather than stress. It's the thirty-five-year-old comer who's still in the same spot at forty who feels a tension he cannot dissipate. He's your likeliest candidate for an executive disease.
>
> (BUSINESS WEEK, November 15, 1976)

Stress seems to know no gender The health profile of the female executive is becoming more like that of the striving businessman. Dr. McCann predicts that Life Extension's own records will produce firm statistical proof of this phenomenon within five years. According to Dr. Charles Winterhalter, medical director of Pitney-Bowes in Stamford, Connecticut:

> Women are getting coronaries as never before, but I can't say whether it's because they have been thrown into business situations with the same pressures as the men or whether some of

---

* Managers surveyed are members of the American Management Associations. About half the group (1,422) was chosen on a random basis from all members who hold the title of vice president, secretary, or treasurer (top management). The others (1,237) were selected on a random sample basis from all members who have the title of manager (middle management). (Kiev and Kohn, 1979).

*it is due to the life style that goes along with the situation, with smoking and drinking and other things.*

(BUSINESS WEEK, November 15, 1976)

Some observers point to the pressure to promote women as a factor contributing to their increased vulnerability to stress-related conditions. Many women in nonmanagerial jobs are suddenly promoted to posts with executive responsibility but without appropriate background or training. Once in that position, a woman may suffer from isolation or lack of social support as the only female executive among many males. A woman's effort to outdo her male counterparts by "acting tough" often leads to self-esteem and role problems, ending in depression.

There are differing views of the incidence of stress-related illness among the female managers and executives of the future. Some observers believe that as more women enter executive ranks with appropriate background, training, and experience for such roles, they will have less "executive illness" because women are thought to have higher psychological and physical endurance for stress.

Others (and I include myself in this group) implicate competitive pressures as contributors to the health problems of managers of both sexes. Women now entering the ranks of management are as aggressive and striving as young male managers. Women are spurred on by the growing number of successful women chief executive officers who provide role models. As women become as striving and competitive as young ambitious men have been, they will suffer a similar incidence of CHD and other consequences of striving and managerial stress.

Relevant data indicates that *job satisfaction is a buffer against the adverse effects of striving.* Top management is quick to point out (and research scientists agree) that managerial work is, of necessity very pressured at times, but that these pressures are more than compensated for by the satisfaction of accomplishment. Work "underload," boredom, monotonous or meaningless work can cause as much discomfort or suffering as a high level of activity or excessive striving.

The problem for management is that the same conditions that are linked to stress are also directly linked to job satisfaction. It is a paradox that a factor that is a major source of satisfaction can, at the same time, increase an individual's risk of CHD. Thus, top management faces a serious dilemma—how to preserve the constructive aspects of work pressure and striving (high productivity, personal satisfaction) and at the same time control the deleterious effects of pressured striving on health (Cooper and Crump, 1978).

## THE BURNOUT SYNDROME

Coronary heart disease is the most widely studied consequence of excessive or unbalanced striving, but other effects of pressured striving on the managers' well-being, effectiveness, and health are much more common. The syndrome of "burnout" is used more and more frequently these days to describe the adverse effects of working conditions where pressures are unavoidable and sources of satisfaction are unavailable.

Symptoms of individual burnout are listed in Table 5.1. Organizational burnout is considered in Chapter 7.

Persons prone to burnout have strong needs for approval and heightened expectations of themselves. They rely on work as a primary means of enhancing their self-concept. They overcommit their time and energy to work, at the expense of those outside activities that would normally provide them with enjoyment, satisfaction, and support. When organizational factors lead to the frustration of fewer rewards for increased labors, these individuals are spurred on to work even more intensely in the hope of regaining lost satisfactions. Sources of support and satisfaction external to the work situation are neglected. Any increase in pressure produces a vicious cycle.

### Coping techniques

Many techniques have been proposed to cope with the stressfulness of striving. Techniques within the control of the individual include:

- maintaining personal fitness.
- increasing respect for leisure time.
- reducing workload.
- not taking on too much work or behaving as if the individual had an unlimited capacity to cope with stressful conditions.

- cognitive coping—an analysis of stress-producing situations to decide what is worth worrying about and what is not.
- delegating workload—not carrying the entire load alone.
- establishing daily goals and setting priorities to accomplish the most important objectives.

But these techniques can only go so far in reducing the *"coronary proneness" of the work setting.* A determined effort by personnel practitioners and those responsible for career development pathways and job design is required to supplement the individual's constructive efforts. Management must do what the individual alone cannot do—reduce the coronary proneness built into work organization and practices.

TABLE 5.1   *Symptoms of individual burnout.*

1.  Early stages
    a.  Work Performance
        - Efficiency declines
        - Initiative dampens
        - Interest in work diminishes
        - Progressively less able to maintain work performance in times of stress
    b.  Physical Condition
        - Feels exhausted, fatigued, physically run-down
        - Headaches
        - Gastrointestinal disturbances
        - Weight loss
        - Sleeplessness
        - Shortness of breath
    c.  Behavioral Symptoms
        - Changing or dampened moods
        - Quickness to anger and increasing irritability
        - Diminished frustration tolerance
        - Suspiciousness
        - Feelings of helplessness
        - Increased levels of risk taking
2.  Later stages
    a.  Attempts at self-medication (tranquilizers, alcohol)
    b.  Increasing rigidity (thinking becomes closed, attitudes become inflexible, negativistic or cynical)
    c.  Abilities of self, coworkers, and organization are questioned
    d.  Time spent working increases, productivity declines dramatically.

Striving and satisfaction are both psychosocial factors very much affected by the mores and attitudes within an organization. Achieving a balance between striving and satisfaction is the joint responsibility of the individual and the organizaton.

## ATTITUDES TOWARD STRIVING

### Stress as an "asset"

Seasoned, level headed, experienced managers tend to accept an environment of heavy workload, time pressure, and unrealistic deadlines. Rather than make an effort to change the environment they adapt by regarding stress as an asset, according to the authors of the AMA poll.

> *Many survey participants view stress as a challenge and an opportunity for personal growth rather than as an obstacle. These people thrive on situations in which there is pressure, competition, tension, and risk; they feel exhilarated or energized after accomplishing a difficult task or closing an important business deal. Some say stress has been the driving force behind many of their achievements, and a few even impose unrealistic deadlines on themselves to improve their job performance.*
>
> (KIEV & KOHN, 1979, p. 5)

Kiev and Kohn's apparently enthusiastic acceptance of pressure, competition, tension, and risk is in striking contrast to the alarm expressed by research scientists and organizational psychologists over findings that implicate these same factors as precipitators of stress-related illnesses, particularly coronary heart disease. Members of the manager's family generally share the researcher's alarm.

The same AMA survey indicates that managers perceive undesirable stress as emanating from several sources. Both middle and top management identified as most stressful and as likely to occur often:

- heavy workload/time pressures/unrealistic deadlines.
- disparity between what I have to do on the job and what I would like to accomplish.

Other leading interpersonal causes of stress on the job are discussed in Chapter 7. These causes are:

- the general "political" climate of the organization.
- lack of feedback on job performance.

It is my impression that acceptance of intense work pressure is more apparent that real. Experienced managers try to live with, rather than change these managerial stressors, not because of a conviction that such pressures are benign, but because they are seen as characteristic aspects of the United States management process and beyond their control. An organizational emphasis on striving is regarded as unchangeable except through intervention at the highest levels.

### External pressures

Managers and executives at all levels tend to implicate stressors external to the management process as the source of "extraordinary pressures" while work pressures are perceived as presenting little or no problem. A quote from the AMA survey about causes of stress away from the job illustrates this point:

> *Years of experience on the job normally condition a healthy, balanced individual to cope with job-related stress. My associates and I have more problems coping with stress off the job and unusual problems such as problems with the contractor on building a house, the automobile dealer—the picky outside problems of staying alive.*

(KIEV & KOHN, 1979, p. 36)

At first glance this statement appears to be a declaration of confidence by a "healthy, balanced individual." But a closer look reveals its true function as a rationalization of intense preoccupation with work and career at the expense of other areas of life. If years of experience on the job normally condition a healthy, balanced individual to cope with job-related stress, then do not years of experience with life normally condition a healthy, balanced individual to cope with the picky outside problems of staying alive? And why do managers and their associates complain about problems with a contractor or an automobile dealer when they take in stride the much more difficult negotiations that undoubtedly arise in their everyday work?

The answer to these questions is clear. Job and career-related pressures are assigned a higher priority and are endowed with greater importance than are outside problems. Managers and executives seek to find, and are encouraged by their organizations to find, greater satisfaction and rewards from their work efforts than from external activities. But coping with work demands as the first order of priority exacts a cost. *Striving monopolizes the manager's adaptive capacity and renders the individual more vulnerable to the harmful effects of threat from other external pressures.*

Stressors from all sources have a cumulative impact. If the manager's capacity to bind and neutralize pressure (adaptability) is taken up with the need to deal with the ordinary pressures of every day work (heavy workload, time pressure, unrealistic deadlines; anxieties over accomplishment, getting ahead, and job security) then any stressful life event, external to work, may overload the adaptive coping capacity and adverse stress responses may appear (see Chapter 13).

Managers and management tend to view such adverse responses as consequences of an overload of external pressures even when work stressors consume the greater proportion of the individual's coping capacity. Thus, financial worries, problems with children, physical injury, illness, or marital problems appear as the *real* stressors (the "picky" problems of living). The pressures of striving at work are perceived as presenting *"no special problem."*

Managers certainly *do* learn to cope with their job pressures in a professional, proficient way. The relative contributions of work and nonwork stressors as depicted in the AMA quote may, in fact, be appropriate in many instances. But the competence of the experienced manager to cope with job-related stressors is used as a rationalization for *not* questioning the impact of the institutionalized stressors of the United States management process on the adaptability of managers.

## MANAGEMENT ATTITUDES TOWARD STRIVING

Only top management has the power to change organizational policy and practices and thereby reduce the coronary proneness of the work setting, or increase job satisfaction. But there are several reasons why those in control are not likely to become sufficiently concerned about the intensity of striving among their managers to take action:

1  Work pressure and striving are perceived as *constructive forces.*

2  Responsibility for the undesirable consequences of striving is laid to the *coronary-prone manager* rather than to the management process.

3  Strategies to cope with the adverse effects of striving may involve complex changes in conventional *career progression* and job design.

4  Management is reluctant to interfere in the individual's efforts to achieve *personal goals,* even when these goals are overly ambitious or when there are indications that the struggle to achieve personal ambitions may be damaging to the manager's health.

These generalizations about top management attitudes toward striving are discussed in detail below.

### Constructive forces

Upper echelon managers tend to visualize work pressure and striving as constructive forces. Their attitudes are based on the consequences of fulfilled career ambitions. Having achieved power and control of their own work situation, job pressures become less threatening. The stressfulness of striving is modified by the satisfactions of accomplishment, success, status, and financial reward. Senior managers then assume their experience should be applied throughout the organization.

In the United States, management tends to regard individualism and competitiveness as constructive forces because these are cultural values, and their effects on health go unquestioned. But individualism and competitiveness, characteristics of the life style in the United States, which are encouraged and rewarded by the interpersonal dynamics of most of its organizations, have been linked to relatively high levels of coronary heart disease.

Different cultures produce very different statistics, however. The rate of CHD in the United States (350 per 100,000 population), is among the highest for industrialized nations, seven times that of Japan (50 per 100,000 population), for example, which is the lowest.

Research indicates that this difference is related primarily to differences in life styles. Japanese-Americans who adopt the United States life style of individualism and competitiveness are five times more likely to have CHD than their Japanese-American counterparts who retain their traditional cultural norms and who live quiet noncompetitive lives as members of a tightly knit social network. In the United States management culture 45 percent of the executives surveyed work all day, in the evenings, and during weekends. An additional 37 percent of the executives surveyed keep weekends free but work extra hours in the evenings. In many United States companies this type of behavior is a norm to which all feel they must adhere (Uris, 1972). Imagine the problems of fit when a Norwegian executive, whose custom it is to leave work weekday afternoons during the winter to ski, joins an American organization, or when an American with the work ethic just described, manages Norwegians whose work habits (based on a national law which limits work to 1733 hours per year) they misperceive as laziness.

### The coronary-prone manager

Instead of looking toward leadership style and organizational stressors as exerting a harmful effect on vulnerable managers, top management emphasizes factors in the managers personality and life style as critical variables.

Scientists themselves are partly to blame for this shift of focus from the organization to the individual. Cardiologists Meyer Friedman and Ray Rosenman (1974) explored the relationship between life style and the prevalence of CHD. They identified a *coronary-prone behavior pattern* (the Type A personality). The style of living of this group is characterized by extremes of competitiveness, striving for achievement, aggressiveness, impatience, restlessness, explosiveness of speech, and feelings of being under pressure of time and under the challenge of responsibility. People with this behavior pattern are often so deeply involved and committed to their work that they neglect other aspects of their lives such as family, social pursuits, leisure, and recreational interests.

By contrast, the Type B personality—significantly less prone to CHD—is more easy going, patient, takes time to appreciate leisure and beauty, is not preoccupied with social achievement, does not feel driven by the clock, and is less competitive.

Rosenman, Friedman and Strauss (1966) studied a national sample of 3400 men free of CHD. They were rated for behavioral patterns following in-depth interviews with psychiatrists who had no biological data about them. After two and one half years Type A men, ages thirty-nine to forty-nine, had 6.5 times the CHD found in Type B men of the same age. Type A men in the fifty to fifty-nine age group had 1.9 times the CHD found in Type B men of that age. The same relationship between behavioral patterns and incidence of CHD was found four and one half years later.

It is not known whether genetic traits, early childhood experiences, or "general emotional upsettedness" are responsible for the Type A behavior, nor is it known how work environment demands activate predisposition. It is known, however, that *reducing pressured striving helps recovery from CHD*. It can, therefore, be assumed that an appropriate balance of striving and satisfaction can be as helpful in avoiding the onset of CHD or its recurrence as it is in promoting recovery once the coronary event has taken place.

### Career progression

Behavioral scientists note that the management process in the United States exposes ambitious young managers to the trauma of defeat as well as to the satisfaction of victory. For the striving young manager, stress intensifies with either achievement or frustrated ambition. Achievement and recognition lead to promotions and new assignments, which in turn involve new uncertainties and challenges. By the time adaptation to a new situation has taken place, the somewhat older, ambitious manager is striving for further recognition and achievement, and once again faces the alternatives of achievement or frustrated aspirations.

This cycle is repeated. Striving continues until two major problems are encountered: (1) demands of a job exceed an individual's capabilities, or (2) the opportunities for achievement diminish as the organizational pyramid narrows toward the top. The process ends in defeat for the by now, middle aged manager; or in victory—with the executive's achieving a level of control over organizational conditions—the power to make relevant decisions, the ability to carry out self-initiated objectives. The victorious executive ultimately creates a psychological environment of greater tolerance for uncertainty and ambiguity, of relative invulnerability from evaluation and control from above. The senior executives who have achieved control over their circumstances may be less prone to an "executive disease" than those still striving to achieve control, or those who live with the consequences of defeat.

Crises and transitions that result from the interaction between organizational pressures toward striving and conventional career progression pathways seem to produce several populations at risk with relation to "executive disease:"

1   Young, competitive managers who are thwarted in their original ambition to reach the top of the organizational pyramid, but have not thought through career alternatives more suited to personal needs and capacities.

2   Young, ambitious, competitive managers who fail to make the transition from driving performers, oriented toward personal achievement, to competent leaders and coordinators of the efforts of others.

3   Somewhat older managers whose skills, drive, capacities, and interests have matured and changed so that their personal needs, motivations, and sources of satisfaction are no longer compatible with a pressured job emphasizing vigorous, competitive striving.

4   Long service middle managers with dim prospects for advancement and limited career options who feel defeated and boxed into their present situation, who are waiting for retirement, and for whom no concerted effort is made to provide sources of satisfaction more compatible with their circumstances, that is, new responsibilities, flexible use of their time, and more creative use of their experience and capabilities.

Some of the problems linked to organizational emphasis on striving develop because career progression pathways generally do not have the flexibility necessary to maintain individual–organization compatibility throughout the various stages of the manager's growth and development. Top management is often to blame for maladaptive managers through the encouragement of power seeking among young high-potential performers (H. Levinson, 1965).

As a reward for valuable performance management promotes the bright, promising individual performer to a position of leadership. This leadership requires the ability to mold individuals into a cohesive, cooperative group of subordinates, as well as sensitivity to their personal concerns. The manager will now be evaluated on leadership ability rather than drive and will be open to the criticism, "He is a great individual performer but can't manage people."

The promising young star was trained in driving and power seeking but not for what was to come next: the transition from energetic individual performer to effective leader and coordinator of the efforts of others. Both management and the manager may be so dazzled by individual accomplishments that they fail to provide training in the leadership of people early enough in the star's career for this training to be effective in broadening the self-image and talents of the younger person focused on individualism and competitiveness.

The mature manager faces still different transitions. Ambition is usually the driving force early in an individual's career. Later, with experience and maturity, a new definition of personal capacities and interests is achieved. Personal goals become less conventional and more individual. Aspirations change from those that are strongly influenced by organizational pressures toward striving, to goals more suited to newly realized personal needs and interests. The shifts described here take place within each of us as we grow and develop throughout the life cycle. The phase under discussion is often referred to as the mid life transition by Daniel Levinson (1978) and others who have written on the crises and transitions that characterize adult life. The implication of these insights into life cycle changes is that natural forces tend to bring about a shift in what will be perceived as sources of satisfaction in the manager's usual work and roles.

Career progression pathways that fail to take these natural forces into account may create individual–organization incompatibility. The individual manager or executive may be forced to adjust to a mismatch between individual characteristics and organizational career patterns. With maturity there may be a shift in sources of satisfaction to the pursuit of more personally gratifying accomplishments such as the training and development of others. Accomplishments in this area are certainly valuable to the organization (subordinates promoted to responsible and important positions, a cohesive, productive work group). However, accomplishments in the area of personal development receive less enthusiastic acknowledgement and reward from top management than do the results of successful striving that have bottom line implications.

Because of this hierachy of values that rewards bottom line results more than achievements with people, top management often fails to establish career pathways that provide mature managers with the opportunity to use their wisdom and experience in the care and nurturing of young executives, as internal consultants on special projects and plans, or as consultants to outside groups in the community or elsewhere.

Mature managers derive their satisfaction and self-esteem from the use of competence and experience in the application of skills. But to derive satisfaction from their work, their workload must be appropriate to their capabilities. There must be balance of responsibility and authority. They must feel a sense of involvement in work and roles they consider to be worthwhile, and they must be permitted a sense of accomplishment and importance.

To summarize, for mature managers, an emphasis on individualism and competitiveness in a group setting can be particularly stressful. They must either be buffered by opportunities for personal satisfaction from accomplishment deemed worthwhile by them or modified by social support systems that value and preserve group affiliation, cohesiveness, and morale or a sense of common purpose.

### Personal goals

*Management is reluctant to interfere in the individual's efforts to achieve personal goals, even when these goals are overly ambitious, or when there are indications that the struggle to achieve personal goals may be damaging to the manager's health.* Management is often caught in a dilemma: "If we move Jim out of the job he has been looking forward to ever since he joined the company, it might make his heart condition worse. Even though there is a lot of pressure in that job, having to give it up might kill him."

But management *is* inevitably involved in the health of that manager. Keeping Jim on the job or moving him to a less stressful one involves a decision that affects the manager's health. "Doing nothing" is as much "interference" as initiating a change of job.

Clinical observations of the context in which managers develop CHD point to interpersonal conflict and dissatisfaction or frustration at work as contributing factors. This conclusion is based on empirical observation rather than systematically collected data. However, one study of 100 young coronary patients indicates that CHD onset was preceded by work overload in 70 percent of the cases, *but emotional distress preceded the onset of CHD in 90 percent of all cases.* Similar stress was observed in only 20 percent of the controls (Russek and Zohman, 1958).

To the executive's family, CHD represents the inevitable outcome of years of striving to get ahead, long working hours under intense work pressure, little free time to relax, vacations not taken, family relationships neglected, and personal interests ignored. The coronary event is often anticipated by family members as the culmination of recently increasing complaints about being unappreciated and misunderstood by the boss, or unsupported by an inadequate staff, or overburdened by the need to learn a new work system considered to be unnecessary in the first place, or any other combination of frustrations, interpersonal conflicts, dissatisfactions, and psychic pain.

Retrospective clinical research indicates that among coronary-prone individuals the illness event is often preceded by premonitory signs of accelerating job dissatisfaction or various complaints about social relationships at work (Kasl, 1978). From my experience, complaints can be considered as premonitory signs if these complaints mount in intensity; are unrelieved by reassurance or time away from work; or if the manager's reactions appear to be extreme in the face of mildly disturbing events, indicating a loss of ability to cope with additional (even mild) stressors.

These clinical observations, if verified by subsequent research, raise an important issue –to what extent is it a management (or personnel or medical department) responsibility to intervene in anticipation of a manager's ill health as a preventive measure? If management had been more responsive to the coronary-prone individual's complaints could the triggering of the illness event have been modified?

Generally, management's practice is to be unresponsive to such complaints (being hurt or unappreciated by coworkers or superiors, for example). These are viewed as weaknesses, personality conflicts, or personal problems rather than as signals that health maintenance intervention may be necessary. The issue seems to be under what circumstances, and in what way is responsibility for the health of the coronary-prone individual (or an individual predisposed to any executive disease) shared by the organization? This issue is illustrated in the following interview:

## INTERVIEW 3 – Combat Fatigue

Robert Lepson, age fifty-three, has had a long and successful career managing the construction of complex technical systems throughout the world. One of Bob's talents is his ability to manage local personnel. His usual personality style is forceful but benevolent. Although authoritarian, he is fair. He takes great pride in past accomplishments as a teacher, bringing local workers up to higher standards. He tirelessly drives himself and those he manages to get the job done as planned, giving special attention to meeting time requirements. His present assignment abroad is an important venture involving a significant commitment of organizational resources. Time is a critical factor. Profit margins that figure significantly in the planning of such a commitment have been based on a projected completion date.

Bob was selected to be in the vanguard of his organization's build-up of local facilities. His personal goal has always been to complete construction with the time period projected by management. When I met Bob the project was already taking longer than planned, costing more than expected, and facing unanticipated sociopolitical obstacles. For a variety of reasons, all of which were beyond Bob's control, the job would require more time for it to come on stream.

The interview was a lengthy one, starting well before lunch and extending far into the afternoon. It can be summarized in a few paragraphs as his complaints and dissatisfactions were repeated over and over again. Problems were described in a tone of unrelieved agitation as if he were trying to master frustrations that were clearly getting the better of him. Any frustration, no matter how small (a delay in being served lunch, temporarily misplacing his wallet) were triggers for explosiveness and impatience. Bob seemed brittle, without any emotional margin for error. The smallest thing that went wrong precipitated a reaction far out of proportion to the insult suffered.

The incidents cited to substantiate his complaints came out in increasingly strident tones. "I can't understand these people. Are they lazy? Here we have all this work to do and they seem quite content to leave the work unfinished in the middle of the afternoon (4:30 P.M.) and go home just because that is the scheduled office closing time. And you can't tell them what to do. They think they know better. It's so frustrating. I try to teach them. They just listen in silence or occasionally nod their heads, then do it the way they were going to do it in the first place. You can't teach them anything!

"With all this time pressure to get things done wouldn't you think they would show some concern? Some loyalty? Wouldn't you!? Every day's delay in completing this project means tens of thousands of dollars. Profitability is the name of the game. They don't seem to care if the company makes a profit. They just want to leave their desks on time to go home and sail or ski or do whatever they do in their leisure time. That's such an important thing here! I have time to play tennis but I also finish the job when I have to, no matter how long it takes!

"They want me to follow their rules, do it their way! They don't come right out and say that, but if you don't do things their way around here they go over your head to some government authority and complain. Then we're tied up with new regulations, or a request to make a new study on which to base new regulations. We're doing things in this country the way we've been doing them at other locations where we have been very successful. The job will never get done at this rate.

"These young engineers don't seem to want to get ahead! The fellows working closest to me just don't give a damn. That's because everything is provided for them in this welfare state! They don't have to compete to advance themselves as we did!"

Bob went on to describe his original ambition—to see the venture through to completion within two to three years of his coming on the new assignment. This goal was doomed to failure. Realistic estimates of completion dates were impossible because of unknown and uncertain factors requiring resolution. Bob ended our interview with a very emotional statement about how disappointed he would be, how much a sense of *personal failure* he would feel, if this vast project, of which his unit was but a very small component, were not completed on schedule.

### Comment

It was my impression that Bob was suffering from a form of combat fatigue, a prolonged exposure to a combination of culture shock and interpersonal conflict. The fatigue grew out of personality characteristics that had served him well in the past, but were too inflexible and authoritarian for the present situation. The culture shock was evident from: (1) his hostility toward local practices and values (different attitudes about use of authority, use of leisure time, quality of work life, priority assigned to profitability), (2) his constant reference to the "we–they" theme, and (3) his taking as a personal affront his subordinates' cultural attitudes that were unfamiliar or causing complications in his usual management style.

Bob was aware of these cultural differences. They were also experienced and discussed widely by almost all Americans and locals. Although he understood them intellectually, he was emotionally unable to accommodate these differences, although he had done so on many occasions during his long career of working abroad.

Bob was also suffering from thwarted personal ambition. His self-imposed goal to see construction completed within the time frame originally planned by management was obviously doomed to failure, and could in no way be attributed to him. Yet Bob perceived it as a personal failure and felt a loss of pride. He redoubled his own efforts, pressured those around him, and finally when failure appeared to be inevitable, he attributed it to the work culture of the host country.

The role of pressures from above can not be defined in this case but they must have contributed to Bob's drive to complete the construction as originally planned. Management, too, was disappointed with the delays and frustrated by previously unanticipated complications stemming from differences in the work culture of two developed countries (the United States and the host country) in which the construction was taking place.

Pressure flows downward. Bob is a typical "Type A Personality." In this instance management demands activated individual predispositions toward striving. However, the relative contributions of individual and organizational stimulation of striving to achieve unrealistic goals cannot be determined.

I remember thinking at the time of the interview that Bob should be sent home for rest and rehabilitation before something more drastic took place. His inability to cope was evident in that he could no longer tolerate even the ordinary pressures and stimuli of everyday life. Others in management were also aware of Bob's growing irritability but were reluctant to pull him off the job knowing how much it meant to him to see the work through to completion.

Several months after this interview I learned that Bob took a very active role in labor negotiations dealing with work rules. At stake was the issue of how things were to be done—in the local mode following local regulations, or in the company mode using standard operating procedures applied successfully at various other worldwide worksites.

Bob distinguished himself during the labor dispute and the difficult negotiations that followed. A short time after these negotiations, he suffered a major illness (presumably a coronary event) and was completely disabled for several months. Happily, he recovered gradually with a greatly reduced work load.

## WORK UNDERLOAD

The manager's self-esteem and job satisfaction seem to be based on expectations that are somewhat different from those in other occupations at other levels. Work overload is related to job dissatisfaction in almost all occupations. But *work underload* is a source of increased job dissatisfaction for managers, but not for others surveyed such as assembly line workers and policemen (Caplan, Cobb, French, Harrison, and Pinneau, 1978).

Managers and executives look for a high level of intrinsic gratification in their jobs, gratification based on the use of competence and experience or the application of skills. Work underload provides insufficient challenge, too little opportunity to use their talents, and consequently reduces available job satisfaction.

If an assembly line shuts down for equipment repair the blue collar worker may greet the event as an extra vacation day. It is intolerable, however, for the executive to have nothing to do. Not being assigned projects of major importance to the organization is often taken as an indication, rightly or wrongly, that the manager is no longer desirable or respected, and should look elsewhere for another job.

Work underload raises a variety of career-related anxieties and defensive reactions about one's competence, value to the organization, future career prospects. Those so predisposed will review personality conflicts, the state of office politics, and troubled relationships with superiors searching for reasons why the work stopped flowing in their direction. As the anxiety builds and the underload continues, reasons for the slack in workload may be misattributed. "They want me out." "He has it in for me." "My boss never delegates authority." "He sees me as too much of a threat and keeps work from me so I won't outshine him."

If underworked executives lose confidence then the tendency might be to become defensive, dependent on the job, to hold on for survival. At this point they may try to control whatever work there is more rigidly than before, to delegate less, to obstruct the actions of others more to seek reassurance of value, competence, or respect in the eyes of others. In short—a manager rarely enjoys a vacation day at work. Some level of challenge and satisfaction from accomplishment in day-to-day work is necessary for managers' and executives' occupational mental health.

This issue brings to mind one of the most unhappy executives I interviewed during the executive stress study—a man unhappy in his work, but not dissatisfied with his personal life.

### INTERVIEW 4 – Unoccupied

Peter Faulkner is the manager of a specialized department in the comptroller's office. "I've been in this position for almost ten years, and I'll be here 15 years from now when I am old enough to retire. Management tells me I am irreplaceable and they will not consider my leaving to do something else.

"I have become so highly specialized, and I am so familiar with what I have to do, that my job occupies only 10 percent of my time and attention. The rest of my time is spent on the telephone looking after my community responsibilities. In the evening I rush home on the 5:03 P.M. train, have a drink and early dinner with my family, then go to my *real* job as Village Trustee. How many more years of this life style can I take? I watch the clock all day. During the summer when there is less action as Village Trustee all I think of is playing tennis in the evening when I get home.

"I've been around a long time, twenty-seven years to be exact. I know the ropes. I could be an adviser to some of the younger managers—on an informal basis, of course. They could benefit from a relationship with an experienced manager who does not evaluate their performance or have authority over their compensation or promotion. I remember how much I wanted such a relationship when I was making my way up the organizational ladder.

"But I am reluctant to bring up the idea. First of all, it has never been done. Everything new seems to challenge someone. Secondly, there is a formal career development program to give high potential young executives wide exposure to company operations. And finally, I suppose the power structure would think of an informal relationship outside the regular chain of command as under-cutting the authority of those who supervise the younger people who have a Big Brother relationship with someone else. So I haven't mentioned the idea. I do the same thing, however, in my commu-nity. Before I became a Trustee I coached the High School hockey team and worked as a counselor at a Teen Center. I like to be in-volved with young people, and help them develop.

"There are several young people in the company right now who might appreciate a mentor or godfather. I would have at their age. Perhaps I could have avoided getting myself into the unde-sirable position in which I am so good at my job that I have become indispensible—and unpromotable.

"The inactivity is starting to get to me now. The real crunch will come when my term as Trustee expires next year and I won't have a job to look forward to when I get home. I'll have to find something else to do at night. During the day I am essentially unoccupied."

### Comment

Following this interview I asked a senior executive why some ex-perienced managers are allowed to function at only a fraction of their capacity. He replied, "We can't all be chiefs in this organiza-tion. We need some indians too. Those jobs must be done and the managers who are in those positions perform very well. We are satisfied with the situation as it is."

Evidently the manager was filling 100 percent of the organiza-tion's needs by working 10 percent of the time. But, the organi-zation was depriving the indispensible manager of an opportunity for continuing job satisfaction through involvement in challenging work.

Peter Faulkner adapted to the "misfit" between personal and organizational needs by looking elsewhere for his satisfactions (community work, counselor to teenagers, Village Trustee). His re-sourcefulness and initiative will probably result in a series of new and challenging jobs outside the organization, each providing a source of satisfaction and self-esteem. His outside involvements serve as an external social support system that buffers against the managerial stressors of a boring job and work underload.

Similar external supports can be valuable for mature managers struggling with midcareer and late-career problems of insufficient challenge and work underload. Personnel practices and policies might do well to encourage external involvements where appropriate, even to the extent of lending managers to other organizations, where their wisdom and experience could be a source of help to the borrowing organization, a source of satisfaction to the consulting manager, and a means of retaining redundant managers until separation through retirement.

## REFERENCES

*Business Week* (1976). The corporate woman: Stress has no gender. (November 15, 1976) 73–76.

*Business Week* (1979). Executive stress may not be all bad. April 30, 1979, 79–103.

Caplan, R. D., S. Cobb, J. R. P. French, Jr., R. V. Harrison, and S. R. Pinneau, Jr. (1975). *Job Demands and Worker Health*. Washington, D.C.: HEW (NIOSH) Publication No. 75–160.

Cooper, C. L., and J. Crump (1978). Prevention and coping with occupational stress. *Journal of Occupational Medicine* 20 (6):420–426.

Friedman, M. D., and R. H. Rosenman (1974). *Type A Behavior and Your Heart*. New York: Knopf.

Kasl, S. V. (1978). Epidemiological contributions to the study of work stress. In C. L. Cooper and R. Payne (eds.) *Stress at Work*. Chichester, England: Wiley.

Kiev, A. and V. Kohn (1979). *Executive Stress*. An AMA Survey Report. New York: American Management Associations.

Levinson, D. J., C. D. Darrow, E. B. Klein, M. H. Levinson, and B. McKee (1978). *The Seasons of Man's Life*. New York: Knopf.

Levinson, H. (1965). Who is to blame for maladaptive managers? *Harvard Business Review* (65607):143–158.

Rosenman, R. H., M. Friedman, and R. Strauss (1966). CHD in the western collaborative group study. *Journal of the American Medical Association* 195:86–92.

Russek, H. I., and B. L. Zohman (1958). Relative significance of heredity, diet, and occupational stress in coronary heart disease of young adults. *American Journal of Medical Science* 235:266–275.

Uris, A. (1972). How managers ease job pressures. *International Management* 27:45–46.

# 6

# EXECUTIVE COPING STYLE

Messages from senior executives shape the approved and characteristic ways managers are expected to behave when faced with crises, transitions, and stressful conditions at work. This *executive coping style* sets the pattern for dealing with a wide variety of stressors, from interpersonal pressures within the organization, to career decisions, to the more personal issues of how to manage one's personal life so that it interferes as little as possible with work performance and organizational goals.

Executive coping style is an informal and implied code of behavior. It is related more to how the organizational climate is perceived than to explicit rules or requirements. Nevertheless, coping style has a powerful influence on the outcome of the stress process. Several characteristics of style that are common to most organizations tend to impede rather than facilitate successful coping with managerial stressors. For one, any indication of distress is viewed as a weakness to be eliminated quickly, rather than as a signal marker pointing to adjustments that must be made before competent managers can achieve mastery over challenging conditions. For another, career-related personal crises are viewed as the manager's private and exclusive concern despite the fact that both manager and management share in the benefits of successful coping. This view prevails even when successful coping requires a change in organizational policy rather than individual adjustment to organizational demands.

This chapter:

- describes how senior executives provide an example of coping style for their subordinates.

- contrasts how the manager is expected to behave (usual coping style) with the psychosocial realities of the coping process (stressor + coping process = stress process).

- presents principles to harmonize style and reality, thereby increasing the benefits of effective coping.

- reviews the dilemmas facing senior executives who must make decisions and establish policies related to stress management. It emphasizes how a realistic coping style can contribute to the resolution of these dilemmas.


### MESSAGES FROM ABOVE

Senior executives set an example for the behavior of subordinates, often without realizing it or without intending to do so. Their reputations, their past exploits, as well as the myths surrounding these exploits, combine with their attitudes about aggressiveness, striving, work style, loyalty, and individual priorities to provide messages from above about how managers should behave. Often, attitudes imposed on subordinates about proper business behavior, personal behavior, and ethics or what they must do to get ahead, stem from senior managers' own experiences rather than from objective reviews of the needs of the organization.

The impact of key executives on organizational personality and coping style can be seen most clearly by outside observers. Personnel practitioners familiarize newcomers with "how we do things here" by quoting the founding fathers' or the present chief executive officer's attitudes about issues ranging from drinking to divorce, from loyalty to the organization to family priorities—or how one is expected to manage almost any aspect of personal and family as well as working life. From such messages managers develop impressions about which actions and attitudes are condoned and which are not, about how far they can go in opposing personal and organizational interests, and how opposing interests can be resolved.

To illustrate, take the case of the manager who has just been told he is very highly regarded and is offered a promotion. The promotion requires that he relocate abroad, a contingency he has not anticipated. The highly-thought-of manager wonders what the consequences may be if he turns down the proffered promotion for personal reasons. His teenaged children require two more years to finish high school. His wife needs just six more credits for her master's degree in social work. He will undoubtedly ask himself many of the questions listed below and will look for "messages" from top management to help resolve the dilemma of whether he should risk damaging his career and turn down the promotion to remain behind so that his family can develop their interests. Questions every manager asks silently but rarely dares verbalize to management include:

- If I turn down the assignment will it be held against me? Is it up or out, take it or leave it?

- Does "take a few weeks to think it over" really mean "say yes tomorrow?"

- Will my resistance be seen as an act of disloyalty? Do they expect me to put organizational interests before family interests?

- What are the approved reasons for opposing what management wants? If I tell them my wife will be so unhappy we may not make it abroad, will they respect that?

- Will they let my wife travel to the new location to see where we will live before I must give them an answer? Will they help find her a job there?

- Is there room to negotiate? Will they place me elsewhere, put me on the shelf, postpone my promotion until my teenagers are out of high school and my wife and I are free to travel?

Problems are likely to develop when messages transmitted downward lead undecided managers to assume the answers to these questions, assess career risks accordingly, and then make decisions about whether or not to go abroad without ever discussing these questions with superiors. Unless there is an explicitly stated policy, or organizational practices are otherwise clearly defined, these questions will be answered by undecided managers on the basis of what they expect (fear, hope) the attitude of top management to be. Their perceptions, however, may not coincide with the realities.

The struggles experienced by managers when they perceive an incompatibility between personal inclinations and behavior approved by the organization are clear from confidential interviews. Such struggles are heightened by ambiguous organizational practices and procedures, and by not knowing where they stand because of insufficient feedback about performance or career prospects. Managers often make hasty and ill-considered decisions just to avoid open conflict between personal inclinations and behavior approved by the organization. I have seen experienced and competent managers resign abruptly without another job to go to, or make precipitate commitments without consulting family members, or simply become ill when nothing else succeeds. These are all means of reducing the discomfort of perceived conflict with established executive coping style.

## CONVENTIONAL COPING STYLE

Maturation is not an automatic process of personal growth—of acquiring wisdom and useful experience with age. According to behavioral scientists studying human development throughout the life cycle, maturation is the result of periodic new understanding of the self and the environment. These insights are gained through the resolution of crises and the working through of transitions from one behavioral plateau to the next.

Middle-aged managers who have acquired the wisdom of experience and the perspective of maturity have "made it" by successfully coping with the challenging and extraordinary conditions of organizational life rather than by dealing with its ordinary day-to-day pressures. Their activity and productivity are in full flower: their successes are models for emulation.

Managers or executives who avoid challenge fail to develop new techniques for mastery. They remain dependent on old techniques that may eventually become obsolete as conditions change and threaten individual–organizational compatibility. Crisis can be distressing and transition tumultuous, but these eventually lead to new competence, security, and inner peace once the necessary career, personal, and social readjustments are achieved.

If the advantages of successful resolution of career-related crises are so apparent, it seems logical for management and managers to join forces and plan ways to assure that the mutual benefits of successful coping will be achieved. It is something of a paradox, therefore, that features of conventional executive coping style threaten rather than promote satisfactory resolution of career challenges and crises. The attitudes that make coping more, rather than less, difficult are listed here and later discussed in detail:

1   Indications of distress are signs of weakness.
2   The goal of coping is the rapid relief of distress.
3   Coping is the manager's private and exclusive concern.
4   Coping is a do-it-yourself process.
5   Using help to cope makes the manager dependent.

1   *The conventional executive coping style, reinforced by organizational mores, encourages the view that any outward indication of distress associated with crisis and transition is evidence of weakness or failure.* The executive is expected to project the image of an aggressive, rugged individualist, always in control, capable of functioning at top form at all times. As a result executives tend to deny or hide an awareness of crisis and distress. They are rarely guided by their own distress into effective problem-solving pathways.

2   Further difficulty stems from the *common misconception that coping is complete when signs of distress abate, rather than after the much longer and more difficult process of defining, then practicing, and ultimately mastering new solutions to challenging conditions.*

This distress-oriented, rather than mastery-oriented view of the goals of coping, places unrealistic time limits on the coping process. It becomes a matter of pride to cope in as short a time as possible. Many managers thus become concerned about approaching their level of incompetence, and many superiors come to regard the performance of their subordinates as unsatisfactory, just because the manager takes longer than expected to cope with challenging conditions, when, in fact, the coping process is progressing at a realistic and appropriate pace.

A much more serious consequence of the distress-oriented view of coping is that learning from experience is suppressed. Distress is often an important signal that the coping process has hit a snag. It may be a marker to indicate that additional knowledge or training, or alterations in organizational support systems, or new personal decisions and accommodations must be made before competent managers can achieve mastery over challenging conditions.

Without this distress signal, midcourse corrections in the coping process may not be made. A mastery-oriented concept of coping helps individuals to seek the missing factors that can facilitate the resolutions of crises, transitions, and challenging conditions. A distress-oriented view of coping that results in a race against the clock to eliminate all signs of distress (that is, "weakness") may produce temporary tranquility, but avoids dealing with stressors and ultimately impedes learning from experience.

3  *The myth that personal crises are executives' private and exclusive concern threatens successful coping.* There seems to be an unwritten agreement between management and managers that all career-related personal crises are intimate family matters or questions of personal life style, but not the appropriate concern of management. Any intervention by the organization is seen as an intrusion into an executive's personal space. In return for this privacy executives are expected to manage their private lives so that they are a source of sustenance from which to emerge refreshed each morning to do battle for the organization.

In fact, almost every management decision invades and shapes the executive's private life. Organizational policies and practices determine to a large extent the framework or parameters wtihin which the executive must live that private life.

Successful resolution of career-related personal crises, therefore, may require a change in organizational policy rather than an adaptation of personal life style to meet organizational demands.

4  *Coping style influences the way managers use practical and emotional assistance in times of need (social support).* Generally, coping is viewed as a do-it-yourself experience. A high value is placed on appearing to deal with stressors without depending on outside help. It is ironic that formal support systems tend to be regarded unfavorably as paternalistic (hand holding, encouraging dependence), and seeking professional counseling is viewed as an indication of weakness or even mental illness. But the informal gossip-rumor-speculation communications systems present in every organization is eagerly pursued in times of crisis.

A coping style that places a negative value on formal and explicit support systems encourages managers under stress to use informal (secret, private, confidential, carefully guarded) channels of assistance instead. Thus, conventional coping style emphasizes reliance on office politics or recourse to informal power structures as sources of practical and emotional assistance in times of need.

5   *There seems to be a general misconception that helping key managers through crises and transitions will create dependent and less effective managers. They should not need outside help to cope with management stressors.* But it is neither dependence nor weakness to make good use of available help from any and all sources while coping with stress. Dependence is related to how this help is used, not to how much help is available.

Providing the distressed manager with appropriate and timely help will enable the organization to benefit from the employee's best judgment and informed self-assessment, in short, that individual's best coping and adaptive efforts.

In fact, by *not* providing managers with as much help as possible in these circumstances, management encourages their dependence on the organization. A manager cannot make independent choices, follow career pathways, or cope with stressful conditions without being informed about how management regards present performance or about future prospects and available options.

It is not considered dependence when business decisions are made with the help of a computer, or the feedback from an attitude survey or a market research report, or the advice of an experienced colleague or mentor. By the same token, it should not be considered a sign of weakness or dependence to cope with personal adjustments by using the practical and emotional assistance available from the organization's social support system.

## THE COPING PROCESS

To understand the differences between conventional coping style and what actually takes place when managers or executives deal freely and successfully with a problem, it is necessary to examine the coping process in detail. Coping with managerial stressors has much in common with reacting to other stressful life events such as the loss of a loved one, or relocating to a foreign environment. The process of coping is similar, whether the stressor is wanted or unwanted, catastrophic or only slightly threatening. It is a process that begins with the threat impact of changing life patterns. It requires psychological working through, takes time, proceeds in a characteristic sequence, and ultimately ends in mastery over threatening conditions or in adjustment or maladjustment to these conditions.

Coping is a universal, biological process that can be defined in four phases: impact, crisis, adjustment, and reconstruction. These phases are discussed here in an effort to compare their psychosocial realities with those features of conventional executive coping style, previously identified as impediments to successful coping.

### Impact phase

*The impact phase is characterized by a paralysis of effective action of relatively short duration.* "I can't cope!" "I'm helpless." "I don't know what to do" are common initial responses to challenging conditions. Almost everyone reacts to the impact of stressful events with at least a short period (hours to a few days) of shock, disorientation, and confusion.

Stunned helplessness can be precipitated by a wide variety of events perceived as stressful because of the meaning they have for the individual involved, as when personal hopes and illusions are shattered.

Observers may not be able to empathize with this latter sense of loss but it is nevertheless real for the person going through it. For example:

> *All is lost! I know I'm not going to get that promotion because the top brass had a career development meeting yesterday and my boss did not greet me as warmly as usual this morning.*

This reaction may appear to be extreme and perhaps illogical. In fact it may reflect an early awareness of themes such as ambition doomed to disappointment, or the waning compatibility between the individual and the organization. What has been lost is the hope that ambition will be fulfilled, or that harmony between the person and the job can be preserved.

The psychological working through to be accomplished during the following phases of the coping process must define what has realistically been lost and then formulate new personal or career strategies to replace lost goals and illusions with more attainable satisfactions.

The ability of individuals to respond to their own sense of loss and panic and thereby start the psychological process of coping is of great practical importance. It is a sign of strength rather than weakness. If the psychological impact of threatening stressors is denied, constructive problem solving will not progress.

### The turmoil or crisis phase

*This phase represents the peak of subjective and objective distress.* As shock and paralysis wear off individuals are confronted with the uncertain and the unknown. They realize that changed conditions can never be restored to their former state of familiarity, comfort, and security. This realization is followed by a full awareness of the emergency, threat, challenge, or frustration. The peak of distress (crisis) or turmoil is fortunately short in duration— usually several days to several weeks. But at its height, this state seems as though it will last forever.

The overt expression of strain and emotion helps restore the ability to think constructively and to solve problems. Emotions concealed behind denial, overcontrol, or detachment perpetuate the loss of constructive energy that began during the impact phase.

It is useful while in crisis to hear from others that it helps to "let things out," or that they have had similar experiences, from which they were able to recover and go on to a successful crisis resolution.

### Adjustment phase

*During this phase the damage to ongoing life patterns is assessed and new ways of adjusting are explored.* "I can't cope!" gives way to, "All is not lost" or "Life must go on" as the individual regains vitality and takes the time to define what has *really* happened. The individual then synthesizes a solution or plan; gets an idea that promises to resolve the crisis; conceives of a new solution that may work. Adjustment is an internal process of fitting needs to new environmental conditions. External help in the form of advice, suggestions, instruction, or emotional support is useful as input to this internal decision-making process. Ultimately, the one who is adjusting must take the credit and the responsibility for the "independent" action of synthesizing input from all sources (even input offered in the form of being told what to do) and formulating a new plan of action that fits individual needs.

It is not dependence but an act of assertiveness to seek advice and counsel at that point. The ability to learn from social interaction with others if this interaction instructs, orients, or clarifies the individual's thinking and provides helpful ideas to resolve challenging conditions demonstrates independence and strength. Sometimes instead of coping, individuals merely adopt the advice of others without altering this advice to fit personal needs. In such instances of dependent behavior the coping process will not proceed to a satisfactory conclusion. Future difficulties can be anticipated.

### Reconstruction phase

*Confidence and productivity return as effective solutions are practiced and consolidated.* In some cases the environment is altered to suit personal needs (coping). In others, the person's life style and behavior are altered to suit a changed environment (adapting). In most cases successful problem solving involves a combination of the two aspects of adjustment—coping and adapting.

Six months after the original stress impact, the individual may feel the beneficial effects of having coped successfully. An internal peace is achieved. A new confidence develops from mastery of any of the major career and personal transitions, crises, or challenges that life inevitably has in store. Surmounting one major challenge teaches us to anticipate and be better prepared for the next one.

A comparison of the usual executive coping style and characteristics of the coping process suggests that:

1   Indications of distress can be used constructively as a guide to effective coping.

2   Management can develop support systems in the work place that will help managers cope with both organizational and personal pressures.

## A CONSTRUCTIVE VIEW OF DISTRESS

Distress, as used here, refers to the uncomfortable feelings and reactions that result when individuals cope with threatening or challenging conditions. Indicators of distress likely to appear during the impact phase include:

• feeling tense, anxious, depressed, or irritable.

• acting troubled, indecisive, or distracted.

• thinking of themselves as helpless, unable to take action, or in need of assistance.

The appearance, frequency, intensity, and duration of signs of distress in a group of managers adjusting to the same set of challenging conditions can serve as a guide to timely intervention.

A realistic coping style encourages managers to view distress constructively, as a stimulus to problem solving. Usual style that views distress as evidence of failure or weakness, to be denied or suppressed, can have a destructive effect.

The distressed manager who is concerned about appearing weak is likely to become inflexible, impatient, or angry—to appear "strong." Conventional social mores tend to equate displays of anger or impatience as forcefulness or strength. Ultimately, outward displays of irritability that defend against distress, tend to erode the individual's capacity to deal with stressors. "Defensive" managers also reduce the capacity of the organization as a whole to respond effectively to challenging or changing circumstances.

### Management offers assistance

The use of advice, support, and assistance when coping with management stressors should not be equated with dependence or incompetence. A more realistic coping style should emphasize management's role in providing social supports in the workplace, and in encouraging the manager under stress to use supports as necessary. Such supports include:

- opportunities to share experiences with colleagues.
- group discussions of current or anticipated stressful career or life events.
- preparation and orientation programs to plan for known or anticipated crises and transitions.
- briefing of managers who have just been through stressful experiences related to work.
- professional counseling in personal stress management.

### DILEMMAS FACING TOP MANAGEMENT

Senior executives face a number of dilemmas when deciding on programs to cope with management stress. These dilemmas are described in relation to their roles as superiors, decision makers, and resource allocators.

### Superiors

Messages from above determine the organizational personality, behavioral mores, and coping style. Stress management programs designed to influence interpersonal behavior and attitudes often require the direct involvement of senior managers. Programs to detect and rehabilitate employees with drinking problems, for example, flourish under the explicit commitment and direct involvement of superiors. Similarly structured programs flounder without support from the top. Experience with alcohol and drug abuse programs, or employee assistance programs, can be generalized to any stress management program that bears on the manager's relationships and attitudes. To be effective, the program requires the commitment and direct involvement of the managers' superiors.

This type of involvement, however, differs from the usual behavior of superiors. Superiors make policy, assign tasks, and indicate expected results. Managers at lower levels interpret these requirements and translate often vague requests into specific programs and procedures. Top management is involved more in deciding *what* should be done than *how* it should be done. They are rarely involved in actually carrying out the program.

Top executives must be convinced of the need for such programs if they are to send appropriate messages to their managers. The more realistic coping style described here will help top executives send such messages.

### Decision makers

Top executives are most likely to act on matters relating to human behavior under stress only when there is a clear indication for such action. Their attention is attracted by problems—(1) high turnover, (2) troublesome resistance of personnel to transfers, and (3) morale problems that impair organization effectiveness, for example.

The appearance of such consequences of management stress indicates that stressors are already having an adverse effect, and support systems designed to cope with these stressors are ineffective. Establishment of stress reduction policies only after undesirable stress consequences have become so widespread that the problem is forcibly brought to management's attention is often too little, too late.

In many instances problems arise in response to major organizational change in the works for some time (reorganization, relocation, reduction of personnel). Usually, there is ample opportunity to anticipate what might happen, and to plan a coping response. But to plan, prepare, or anticipate may be difficult before problems become evident, as there may be no reason to expect that the usual social support systems will not be adequate to the new stress load imposed by organizational change. The need for intervention is usually more clearly perceived by top management than is the need for prevention.

The problem of prevention is that it cannot be carried out without a cost, which is measured in terms of such valuable organizational resources as time, interest, and involvement. Successful prevention requires assigning the task a high priority on the list of necessary programs so that it will not be postponed or delayed until prevention is too late to be effective.

The dilemma for top managers in their roles as decision makers and resource allocators is that they rarely have appropriate and relevant data (a needs analysis by objective professionals, for example) to justify giving a stress prevention program high priority in the absence of known stress consequences. Top management requires accurate feedback to make decisions on stress prevention programs with confidence and conviction.

### Resource allocators

Decisions to risk resources on one venture may involve withdrawing resources from another and permitting the latter venture to fail. Top management must make these difficult decisions, must balance the advantages and disadvantages.

When human relations decisions are balanced against other decisions involving the allocation of organizational resources, preventive stress management programs, which have difficult-to-document cost effectiveness, may be decided against, regardless of the humanitarian value of these programs. To illustrate, consider a common stress management decision organizations must make with increasing frequency: how carefully, and at what cost should employees and their dependents be screened and prepared for working abroad?

*The setting.* An organization needs a rapid and extensive build-up of personnel in a key area abroad to fulfill recently negotiated agreements to construct and operate a large manufacturing installation. The start-up of work is to take place in the very near future. The area is one in which living conditions are extraordinarily difficult. Work pressure is expected to be intense. The labor pool from which the organization must draw has no experience living and working under these conditions.

*The potential cost.* Repatriation is, of course, costly. Statistics indicate that one organization, with a carefully prepared group of professionals and managers experienced in working abroad, reports a 3 percent repatriation rate. Another organization with casual selection and preparation procedures has a 15 percent repatriation rate; a third organization, new to the area, has a 70 percent per year turnover rate.

*The problem.* Management is faced with a choice. Should they invest time, effort, and money in establishing recruiting, selection, preparation, and on-site support procedures? Or should they dispense with such precautions and take a chance, if employees and their dependents will take the chance, that a maladjustment to living and working abroad might require repatriation? Is it more important to take a risk and fill the slot immediately, or is it less expensive in the long run to select and prepare the right family for the right location?

*Professional advice.* Advice is available in a study of the problems of adjusting to working abroad by a committee of experienced mental health professionals (Working Abroad, 1958). Their in-depth evaluation of the United States Foreign Service experience as well as that of other profit and nonprofit organizations can be summarized as follows:

> *Recent experience suggests that sending the right kind of person is so vitally important that it is worthwhile to lower the technical requirements on occasion, even better at times not to fill the job at all than to send someone well-trained who is likely to fail on a personal basis or who may cause embarrassment in his public relations. (pp. 510–511)*

Physicians examining candidates for Foreign Service have been instructed to reject persons who do not enjoy "more than average" physical and mental health. Studies of the health of United States citizens working abroad indicate:

- adjustment to new conditions usually entails physical strain.
- worry over health matters can assume greater proportions overseas.
- chronic ill health, even though minor, has been known to give rise to increased psychological strains abroad.
- persons with histories of psychosomatic illness have been repeatedly found to do poorly in difficult foreign climates.

It has been the experience of a number of agencies and industries that persons given medical waivers and allowed to proceed overseas to work have:

- shown poor efficiency in their work.
- returned to the United States for nonmedical reasons prior to completion of service more often than other employees.

Professional opinion of the likelihood of adjustment problems among United States citizens working abroad under various circumstances, when added to the relocation rates experienced by other organizations under comparable circumstances, provide management with an estimate of the "human stress cost" factor. This cost factor must be weighed against other costs when making business decisions about staffing new ventures.

*The dilemma.* Weighing all the costs and risks and making the difficult decision is the work of top executives. Risking the mental and physical health of any employee or dependent poses a serious dilemma for top management. Is it cruel, nonhumanitarian policy to expose an inexperienced and relatively unprepared manager to a position associated with a 15 percent to 70 percent risk of serious maladjustment? The human stress cost must be evaluated against the cost of delayed start-up, when there is inadequate staffing or an important position is not filled. Ultimately, top management will make the business decision that best fulfils broad organizational strategies and objectives. A delay in one venture may adversely affect other ventures.

Accurate assessment of the anticipated human stress cost of organizational change will enable top managers to make considered business judgments with the result that the human cost factor will not be ignored altogether because "the cost-effectiveness of personnel actions is so difficult to define."

Human stress costs can be thought of as those costs associated with the near-term and long-range consequences of stressors on the health, effectiveness, and turnover of personnel. Thus, the cost of recruiting, preparing, transporting, repatriating, and replacing an employee unable to adjust to working abroad can be considered a human stress cost. Similar costs can be assigned to the consequences of any extraordinary organizational change event such as a new aggressive marketing policy that demands much greater competitiveness from sales personnel, or the stress impact of organizational restructuring, or of a change in the management team.

### Help for top management

If a human stress cost factor is to be included among the planning assumptions underlying policy decisions, then useful estimates of human costs must be made available to the decision makers. Unfortunately, systems to evaluate human costs have long been neglected in favor of systems that estimate other costs associated with organizational change such as the cost of relocating a plant or an office building. An excellent source of relevant data about the human stress cost factor is the systematically collected experience of competent managers as they cope with similar stressful experiences. Candor about the process of coping with the natural experiments of a manager's career will yield the most useful data for planning purposes. A realistic executive coping style encourages such candor.

### REFERENCE

Working Abroad: A Discussion of Psychological Attitudes and Adaptation in New Situations (1958). Formulated by the Committee on International Relations, Report No. 41. New York: The Group for the Advancement of Psychiatry.

# 7

# PRESSURES
# FROM WITHIN

Surveys of what experienced and competent managers find stressful in their customary work and roles show remarkable consistency. The following constellation of factors appears on every list of managerial stressors:

- work pressure (heavy workload, time pressure, unrealistic deadlines, long hours).

- the discrepancy between what individuals would like to do and what they are required to do.

- the "political" climate of the organization.

- ambiguity or lack of feedback about how performance is regarded by superiors.

- the gap between responsibilities and the authority delegated to carry out those responsibilities.

- unsatisfactory relationships with superiors.

This chapter and the one that follows explore the manager's interpersonal environment at work through an evaluation of this constellation of factors in an effort to identify the pressures and crises that may originate within that environment.

## MANAGEMENT STRESS SURVEYS

Robert Kahn and his colleagues at the University of Michigan's Institute for Social Research (Kahn, Wolfe, Quinn, Snoek, and Rosenthal, 1964) are well known for their studies of role stress, one of the earliest frameworks proposed for management stress. Role stress includes as components role ambiguity, role conflict, and work overload. Kahn found evidence of widespread role stress in modern organizations. Of all employees 35 percent had complaints about *job ambiguity;* 48 percent reported frequent *conflicts* between what was expected of them on the job; 45 percent suffered from *work overload*—having more work than could be finished by the end of the day and more than could be done well enough to preserve self-esteem.

Ambiguity, or lack of feedback about how performance is regarded by others, appears prominently as a stressor in all surveys. Uncertainty is an outgrowth of ambiguity and has a deleterious effect on competent performance and self-confidence. Most people tend to be overly self-critical in the absence of information to the contrary from superiors. No news is always bad news even to individuals who know their performance is competent by objective standards. The uncertainty–doubt–self-criticism sequence lowers self-esteem and leads to forms of defensive behavior that are frequently counter productive and self-defeating.

Especially damaging to competent performance is the lack of evaluation during procedures (performance appraisals) that are specifically intended to provide such feedback. The superior may feel reluctant to criticize, guilty about giving bad news, embarrassed about giving praise or good news; or the superior may simply not respect the need for a candid appraisal process. The subordinate inevitably reacts to the uncertainty created by the lack of feedback with frustration, dissatisfaction, and self-doubt. "If he didn't tell me how I'm doing when he was supposed to, things must be really bad."

Even more stressful is a performance evaluation that is evasive, lacking in candor, or incomplete. The question "What am I *not* being told?" is always answered by the uncertain manager in a way that turns the superior–subordinate relationship into one with a negative rather than a positive "support quality." The feeling of being unsupported lies dormant only to be reactivated under situations of pressure, emergency, or conflict. These are the very conditions under which positive social support reduces stress while negative support intensifies it.

A further source of role stress is the manager's interpersonal communications network. The more extensive and diverse the communications network, the greater the stress, particularly for those who function at the boundaries of their organizations where they interface with outside organizations. The role that is at a boundary between departments or between the company and the outside world is one of extensive communications networks and of high role conflicts. It is therefore potentially highly stressful.

The American Management Associations survey (Kiev and Kohn, 1979) of stress factors among middle and top management divides stress-producing factors into personal, interpersonal, and organizational categories. The general "political" climate of the organization was considered as most stressful by almost half of the respondents. Other factors considered stress producing included:

- lack of feedback on job performance.
- lack of authority to make decisions that match responsibilities (emphasized by middle management).
- uncertainty about the organization's or industry's future (emphasized by top management).
- unsatisfactory relationships with superiors.

### Comment

Approximately half the participants indicated they were currently experiencing more stress than they had three years before, while approximately 20 percent reported stress had decreased. The net increase in stress was attributed almost entirely to managers age thirty-five or under who had been in their present positions only a short while. Older managers in their positions for some time did not report the same increase in stress.

There is a strong emphasis on the stressfulness of relationships with superiors in the anecdotal material also collected in the survey. Only excerpts were reported so that the focus of superior–subordinate difficulties is not apparent. But these findings support those of almost all observers of organizational behavior in the conclusion that the hierarchical structure imposes a severe strain on interpersonal relationships.

It is my opinion that career progression anxieties and problems in the quality of interpersonal behavior within the superior–subordinate relationship are the significant sources of stressfulness indicated in these surveys. The young executive occupies a special position of risk within this hierarchical structure.

## THE YOUNG EXECUTIVE

Problems confronting striving young executives who are in their present position for a short time and report feeling increasing stress over the past three years can be illustrated by the following interview with a rising young executive of obvious high potential.

## INTERVIEW 5 — The Top of a Pyramid

The subject is Jim McFee, in his late thirties. Following a brilliant record of achievement as a salesman he was chosen in the previous year to head up a large regional sales force.

"Let me show you what stress really means! This is the organization chart for my department. These twenty-five people at the bottom want to be promoted into the five positions at the next higher level. The five at that level want the two jobs at the level above that. The name at the top is mine and nobody is going to get my job!

"Everyone wants to get ahead. If they don't they become dissatisfied. I don't want to lose anyone because experienced salesmen are hard to find. How do I fit twenty-five people into five positions?!"

I suggested lateral moves to give them all a sense of challenge and career momentum. The suggestion evoked a cry of frustration. "I can't! Hugh won't move because his wife has asthma and must remain in that climate. Curt refuses to relocate without a promotion because even with a promotion the costs of moving just about eat up any salary increment he's likely to get. And Bill can't move at this time because he still has kids in high school and doesn't want to disturb their adjustment by exposing them to a new social group.

"Bob is older than the rest. His children are on their own, but his wife is tired of moving. She has her roots in the community where they're living now. She warned Bob that if he were to be transferred again, he would move alone. He thinks she was just kidding but doesn't want to risk finding out for sure.

"And finally there's Harry. He's barely making it in that job. It's a small territory and not very profitable. He's been in the area a long time so people know him and remain his customers out of friendship. He couldn't survive anywhere else. My boss mentioned merging that territory with the one adjacent to it. He knows we're carrying Harry. What would happen to poor Harry under those circumstances? I hope he leaves before we have to do that to him. I hope he retires early.

"And the rest," he said pointing to the remaining twenty names, "they are after me all the time to promote them." He put the organization chart away and said sadly: "We are facing stiff competition. At the annual sales meeting next week we will announce a new system of sales quotas with compensation based on results. The older guys haven't had to go out and beat the bushes in years. I don't know if they are up to it. My boss hasn't come right out and told me, but I think not too far down the line we will reduce headcount by about 20 percent.

"Think of what I'm going to look like to those guys. I was just promoted. To them my job seems secure. At that meeting I'm going to have to tell them that there is a freeze on promotions, that they will have to work harder, and that compensation is no longer guaranteed but will depend on sales.

"We all used to be buddies. I have the feeling they don't talk to me any more except to complain or tell me what they want from me. It's lonely in this job. At times I wish I were a salesman again. I haven't been able to concentrate on my job thinking of what's facing me at that meeting."

### Comment

Making the transition from solo performer to leader of the organizational unit is the major challenge facing Jim McFee. As a salesman his aggressiveness was admired and rewarded. No one else was hurt as a consequence of his drive to make a track record that would impress superiors and enable him to get ahead. He could be totally self-interested in the sense that his performance, or perhaps the performance of his sales group, was his major interest. He was not called upon to be concerned about the future of others. Neither was he dependent upon the performance or cooperation of others in establishing his record.

But, as leader of an organizational unit, Jim McFee has had to shift focus. Aggressiveness and drive alone no longer assure success and may create interpersonal problems as they affect the careers of those over whom he now has the authority to evaluate performance and determine compensation.

New leaders become an important reference point for the members of the group they lead. They become the group's source of information about organizational policy. Leaders interpret management's expectations, demands, and plans for the future. They must be concerned about how management's plans affect the careers and personal lives of those for whom they are now responsible.

An important shift in focus is the growing dependence of leaders on the input, backup, and performance of others. As solo performers they could get the job done alone. As superiors, they have the nagging problem of how much responsibility to delegate and to whom, of how much to rely upon the product of their subordinates. For new leaders, the issue of delegation of authority and responsibility is critical. Their performance will be evaluated by their superiors on different criteria: the productivity of the organizational unit they lead and the management and development of other people.

The interpersonal aspects of leadership have greater prominence for such executives than they have previously experienced. They are the source of guidance, support, and reassurance, but also the object of wrath, envy, and complaints. Those for whom they are responsible may or may not be reasonable, objective, or temperate in their demands. An important requirement of the new leadership job is that the leaders be concerned about the future of their people, in terms of career development, the fit between their skills and competence, and the requirements of the jobs available to them.

In summary, leadership requires a much more balanced reaction along many more personality dimensions than is required of an individual performer. The absence of such balance can bring about morale and performance problems, lack of cooperation, even rebellion in the ranks—dissatisfactions that significantly influence the effectiveness of the organizational unit as a whole.

Superiors will judge a leader's performance only by the "bottom line," and whether the unit achieves the results expected of it that year. The process whereby these results are achieved, including expertise in manipulating and handling the many superior-subordinate relationships that determine the effectiveness of the unit, is usually left entirely to the leader to cope with. Good, happy relationships without results is not acceptable to management.

No wonder Jim McFee thinks of going back to being a salesman again before the moment when he must face his people as a leader and interpret to them management's new policies, which are clearly unfavorable to their advancement prospects. Of course, the outcome of that meeting will be determined neither by Jim McFee's personality characteristics alone, nor his level of experience as a leader.

Many systems within an organization guide such interactions so that the complications of leadership that is too aggressive, too passive, too concerned, or too indifferent will be avoided. Management training and development programs, the process of choosing, placing, and educating superiors at every level, the organizational personality with its prescribed modes of behavior and executive coping style are all systems that determine the guidelines within which a leader at Jim McFee's level must function. These systems in turn will shape and educate his performance as a leader and help determine the ease or difficulty with which he adapts to his new role.

## THE SUPERIOR–SUBORDINATE RELATIONSHIP

In hierarchical organizations the relationship between superior and subordinate is complex. There is, of course, the natural desire to relate to one another as concerned human beings showing consideration, support, even affection, or as teammates harmonizing efforts toward a common goal, and sharing the benefits (or frustrations) of the outcome of mutual effort.

But, both superior and subordinate are involved in a struggle for survival within the same organizational system. Career progression anxieties dominate the consideration–support–teamwork–job satisfaction (that is, social support) system in most organizations. Office politics, power struggles, fulfilled or disappointed ambitions shape the superior–subordinate relationship more profoundly than do the human welfare or supportive elements.

The dominance of career progression anxieties over mutual support considerations is fostered by a hierarchical organization modeled after the military chain of command. There roles are rigidly defined, responsibilities and authority formally allocated, and distances between levels carefully maintained. Rigidities of the superior–subordinate relationship within such an organizational structure tend to suppress certain important aspects of affection, support, approval, consideration, and the communication of mutual concerns. Organizational norms do not encourage, and may actually discourage, the expression of affection, support, and approval even when such expressions are clearly called for. "I'm not going to hold anybody's hand," is a frequent comment by persons in authority.

Perhaps even more destructive to the supportive qualities of the superior–subordinate relationship are the power aspects of that relationship imposed upon it because both parties are involved in a struggle for survival within the same system. Each has a power to use against the other. The superior has direct power over the fate of the subordinate through appraisal of performance and the ability to influence compensation and advancement. The subordinate's power is more indirect: the power to cooperate or obstruct; the power to make the superior look good or bad; and the power to produce or fail to produce the backup, input, or implementation on which each superior must depend.

## TO PRAISE OR NOT TO PRAISE

Suppression of expressions of approval is not confined to American organizations. A colleague who consults with a large Scandinavian conglomerate on issues of organizational behavior reports the following experience.

*At the annual budget review meeting all Divisional Vice Presidents present results achieved in the previous year. One Vice President rose to deliver his report and quite matter-of-factly described how he had saved millions of dollars in expenditures while at the same time he increased sales significantly beyond projections. The brilliance of his strategy was obvious to all. His accomplishments were outstanding.*

*After completing the report the Vice President sat down, never betraying his eagerness for an acknowledgment of his accomplishments. The Chief Executive Officer listened attentively throughout. When the presentation concluded he called for the next item on the agenda without reacting in any way to the Vice President's outstanding performance.*

*The Vice President, greatly disappointed, screwed up his courage and confronted the CEO. "You never say anything favorable or compliment competent performance," he complained.*

*"We expect competent performance," replied the CEO. "But maybe you are right, I'll have to think about it."*

*Think about it he did, and two weeks later circulated a memo saying, "We do not express approval often enough in our organization. Of course, we expect people to meet their objectives and that should be reward enough for them. But when someone clearly exceeds objectives* by a wide margin *he or she may be congratulated for doing so."*

*The Chief Executive Officer thought of his memo as a radical departure from usual organization practice.*

## Comment

Despite all the objective criteria for performance, even the most competent individuals need approval and confirmation of their competence from their superiors. Yet in most organizations such approval is not forthcoming. People seem to know where they stand only when they are threatened or criticized.

Superiors who are unwilling or unable to provide adequate support and approval tend to provoke anger in their subordinates. The consequences of this anger depend upon whether it is vented against others or kept inside and directed against the self. Anger directed at others leads to absenteeism, accidents, sabotage, resistance, scapegoating, internal strife, even sadistic behavior—all common incidents in most organizations. Anger directed against the self is expressed by demoralization, apathetic performance, lack of drive, loss of interest or motivation, loss of self-esteem, and tension, anxiety, insomnia and depression. All too frequently, anger is "passed on" to the executive's family.

## GUILT AND AWE

Guilt about the exercise of power over others, or fear of its anticipated destructive consequences is a common problem for superiors. Awe of the person in power is a common problem for subordinates. Together these themes can suppress candor to an extreme degree. The results are bizarre distortions of the otherwise natural tendency for two individuals to communicate in an effort to solve a problem in which each has an important interest.

Failure in communication growing out of the power aspects of the superior–subordinate relationship are illustrated in the following pair of interviews:

## INTERVIEWS 6 AND 7 – Next Door Neighbors

John Williams, age sixty, offered his own situation as a prime example of management stress. "The last two years have been very difficult ones for me. My doctor tells me the tensions of my job are not good for my heart condition but I can see no way out of my predicament.

"I'm a special assistant to an officer of the corporation. I got along very well with my former boss. I had his respect and confidence and he was not reluctant to tell me so.

"His successor is not pleased with me; our styles are not compatible. I would leave the job immediately if I didn't have just two years to go before I can elect early retirement and assure my pension.

"The worst of it is that I think I'm about to be fired. My boss hardly speaks to me, never takes me into his confidence. He is almost certainly looking for someone to replace me. He does not confront me directly and I am reluctant to raise the issue for fear I'll open Pandora's box and find myself on the outside without a job."

At this point I interrupted to ask if he could suggest a solution to the problem. "Yes. After I retire I plan to teach at the business school where I have been giving courses through the years. We have an understanding that I will join the full-time faculty when I leave the company. It would be ideal if I could join the faculty now and still be listed as an active employee until I have enough service to elect early retirement. Occasionally this arrangement is offered to executives who have become redundant or so highly specialized that they cannot be placed within the company. I would accept this arrangement tomorrow if offered the opportunity to do so."

"Then why don't you suggest this to personnel?," I asked.

"I don't think my boss will take kindly to my solution. He is exasperated with the situation as it is and so am I. I'm afraid our negotiations will end in an unpleasant confrontation, even with personnel acting as an intermediary. I'll just have to hold on as long as I can and hope my health holds out."

A few days later I interviewed Paul Stone, a senior personnel officer whose portfolio includes high level executives. He described the problems facing him following a change of leadership. "Any change in top management brings about a shifting of personnel. Sometimes the new management does not work well with supporting staff inherited from their predecessors. They usually prefer their own team. Old supporting staff become redundant and often difficult to place in other positions.

"There are several executives who present problems in placement. One officer is very unhappy with the assistant he inherited
and is putting pressure on me to either place him elsewhere or let
him go. Of course we prefer to find something inside the company
until he retires, but there really is nothing else for him. We'll have
to place him outside, if possible.

"We place a number of our executives in outside situations if
there is nothing for them internally and they need only a few more
years until retirement. I've contacted a number of nonprofit organizations that might need an experienced executive but so far I
haven't found anything that I would even suggest to this executive
as suitable.

"In this case I have to work fast because his boss has his own
candidate in mind for the job. I'd feel very guilty if I couldn't place
that man and we had to let him go so near retirement."

Paul Stone was obviously referring to the same person I had
interviewed just a few days before. I asked "Have you spoken to
this person to see whether he has plans for retirement or ideas
about what he might be interested to do outside the organization?"

"No," said Paul Stone. "That would be opening Pandora's
box. Until I have a position lined up for him I cannot raise the issue
without appearing to be promising something I might not be able
to deliver."

I reinforced my point. "Executives often have very good ideas
about how to resolve their own career problems but may be reluctant to express them because they do not expect a favorable
reception. I wonder what would happen if you spoke directly to the
person involved."

I later learned that Paul Stone and John Williams, who frequently met to discuss routine matters, finally came around to a
discussion of their mutual dilemma—and that it was resolved. John
Williams was given a leave of absence to teach at the business
school and his retirement was not jeopardized.

### Comment

All too often management attempts to resolve difficult placement
problems by moving people around on the company chessboard
without meaningful discussion or consultation with the persons
involved. Such a process does not take advantage of the self-

assessment of experienced and competent managers or their often creative solutions to knotty career problems.

The lack of candor and communication about issues known to be of mutual interest that this pair of interviews demonstrates is more the rule than the exception among managers, particularly at higher levels. Even those who come in contact with one another frequently in their customary work tend to avoid communicating on important issues for fear of confronting potentially unpleasant controversy in which the superior feels guilty about exercising power over the subordinate, and the subordinate is in awe of the superior's power to control. Consequently open discussion leading to a creative solution that would be mutually satisfactory does not take place.

### FRUSTRATION FLOWS DOWNWARD

It is not uncommon for one person to vent frustration and disappointments on another. Such interaction between superior and subordinate is more likely to take place when an organization is facing hard times and ambitions, job security and job satisfaction are threatened. The following interview illustrates one type of superior–subordinate interaction during a period of high organizational stress.

### INTERVIEW 8 – Cut Off

The interview took place in a large corner office. Ralph Hudson was only fifty but his troubled expression and obvious agitation made him appear much older. As we began it was apparent that he was trying to decide whether it was safe to reveal what was on his mind.

After a while he broke the flow of superficial conversation. "We are in the process of reorganizing the department and moving our offices to another floor. Last week my boss sent me this without a word of explanation. We haven't spoken since."

With obvious rage and indignation he handed me the floor plan of the new department with the name of each manager written in the office he was to occupy. The corner office was missing. What was the equivalent of Ralph's present office on the new floor had been cut off the blueprint entirely. His name was nowhere to be seen.

"What do you make of this?" I asked, "Where do you stand?" He said that at first he took this as a signal that he had no place in the new setup. He went through the anxiety of suddenly being confronted with the need to think of employment outside the company. Like almost every manager of his age he expressed extreme concern about duplicating his present position in the job market. The reflections provoked by the incomplete floor plan obviously caused him great emotional distress.

The subject soon turned to his relationship with his superior. For quite some time now the department has been struggling with severe profitability problems. Some people in the unit even thought of themselves as the laughing stock of the company, a humiliating organizational self-image. His boss had been charged with the responsibility for turning the situation around. When the situation did not improve his boss became more demanding and critical of his staff.

Ralph connected his boss's failure to improve profitability with his behavior toward subordinates. Finally Ralph verbalized what was really troubling him. He was convinced that his boss achieved satisfaction by creating insecurity in his subordinates and watching them cringe and suffer. After he expressed these suspicions of his boss's character Ralph was noticeably more relaxed. On further reflection, he realized that there was no one else who could occupy his position at the time, and concluded that the office cut off the blueprint must be his after all.

The interview ended here. He was still somewhat agitated and uncertain about his future but much less so than when we began to talk. To this day it is unclear why the office had been cut off the blueprint and by whom; whether this action was motivated by the boss's desire to exercise power and to be held in awe, or for some benign and perhaps entirely coincidental reason. When the department moved to new quarters Ralph Hudson occupied the corner office removed from the blueprint. His boss left shortly thereafter for a similar position with another company. Within the year Ralph was out of work for some time with a stress-related illness.

### Comment

Ralph Hudson's boss was charged with the challenging assignment of turning around an unprofitable organizational unit. When faced with difficulties in accomplishing this objective he pressured and drove those under him in a manner subordinates considered to be both unreasonable and intentionally hostile. The overall morale of the unit suffered significantly when intimidated subordinates could not react overtly.

Social constraints in an organizational setting are such that frustrations are expressed more indirectly through criticism of others, unreasonable demands, scapegoating, and simply foregoing the usual interpersonal considerations in favor of exercising the power and privileges of position, or "pulling rank."

It is characteristic of reactions to disturbing uncertainty that fears, concerns, and morbid thoughts are aroused in an effort to explain and clarify what is uncertain and unknown. Ralph Hudson might have found it less stressful if his boss had said he wanted to get rid of him than it was for Ralph to speculate about that possibility. Coping behavior is guided by reality and knowledge but is paralyzed by uncertainty. Distress aroused by this conflict may have contributed to the triggering of Ralph's stress-related illness.

## ORGANIZATIONAL BURNOUT

In times of stress, social interactions within an organization can set in motion a destructive process that adversely affects individuals who under normal conditions would not be so affected. The outcome of this destructive process on a group level is referred to as the "organizational burnout" syndrome (Hall et al., 1979).

Indications of organizational burnout are lowered morale and dissatisfaction expressed through group interaction such as:

- high personnel turnover.
- increasing absenteeism.
- frequent scapegoating.
- antagonism within pairs and groups of individuals working together.
- dependent individuals who manifest their dependence through anger at superiors and expressions of helplessness and hopelessness.
- maintenance of critical attitudes toward coworkers.
- lack of cooperation among personnel.
- progressive lack of initiative.
- increasing expression of job dissatisfaction.

- expressions of negativism concerning the role or function of the unit.

Dr. Richard Hall and associates encountered organizational burnout with significant frequency in various units in their hospital. It was particularly evident in high-stress units such as medical or surgical intensive care, where performance demands on personnel are excessive and where the conditions treated preclude a favorable outcome, and thus produce a low yield in terms of work satisfaction. Hall et al. believe their observations can be extended to executives and other professional groups whose work serves as the primary source of self-esteem and demands intense commitment of time, energy, and interest. Business and industrial units going through crises (reduced profitability, loss of important markets, contraction, layoffs) can be thought of as high-stress units comparable to the intensive care units of a hospital.

In general, burnout has occurred in units where:

- there are excessive performance demands on personnel.
- there is a heightened sense of personal responsibility or involvement.
- the nature of the unit frequently precludes a successful outcome (a terminal oncology service where in spite of the best medical efforts the majority of patients die; a declining or highly competitive market where in spite of the best managerial efforts profitability cannot be maintained).
- work priorities have low yield in terms of personal satisfaction (the need to reduce staff or cut back production) take preference over those producing job satisfaction (expansion into new markets).
- there are ambiguous lines of authority; actual authority to make and implement decisions is different from that defined by the organization.
- members are assigned responsibility for decision making without having appropriate authority.

Coping strategies to manage organizational burnout focus on improving social forces at work through planned group interaction while at the same time improving sources of personal satisfaction and support external to the work environment. The following steps are recommended to manage organizational burnout:

- meetings with administrative personnel to define the nature of the problem as organizational rather than as unique to the individuals involved.

- a series of carefully planned unit meetings to ventilate distress; to identify problem areas as organizational rather than personal.

- reorganization of work priorities and staff interactions, based upon information provided in the unit meetings.

- focus on allocation of authority and responsibility; distribution of frustrating tasks; and the concept of a team approach.

- encourage group discussion of the social effects of burnout such as the elimination of outside interests, development of physical symptoms, and disruption of family functioning.

- a clear-cut message that encourages referral for private, confidential counseling for individuals interested in discussing personal issues.

The symptoms of organizational burnout and the pressures that produce these symptoms are summarized here. If previously adequately performing managers seem to just wear out and gradually show a decline in efficiency, initiative, interest in work, or a change in their ability to maintain performance in times of stress, then the problem may arise from within organizational social forces rather than from within the individuals affected. All too often such declining performance is attributed only to factors in the individual manager. Morale problems, the symptoms of burnout, point to seriously destructive forces within the social atmosphere that require a remedy of organizational rather than individual coping strategies. The appearance of more than an occasional burned-out manager should make superiors look for causative social factors and appropriate remedies on an organizational level.

### CONCLUSION

In the beginning of the chapter a constellation* of personal, job-related, interpersonal, and organizational factors that competent

---

* (Work pressure; discrepancy between what individuals would like to do and are required to do; the "political" climate; lack of feedback about performance; uncertainty about their future; a gap between responsibility and authority; unsatisfactory relationships with superiors).

and experienced managers regularly designate as stressful on surveys of management stress were identified. Upon evaluation, this constellation seems to reflect the ordinary pressures of the manager's day-to-day work and roles, the pressure inherent in the management process that can be made more or less severe by variations in internal organizational structure and practices.

Periodic crises and peaks of extraordinary stressfulness emerge from this background of ordinary pressures from time to time through the dynamic interaction of career progression forces, organizational viability and change factors, and the effectiveness of social support systems to deal with the stressfulness of change.

Pressures from within the manager's social interactions become more severe around the time of specific events such as career transitions (from star performer to leader); changes in management (working for a new boss); or problems and changes in the fortunes of the organization itself (as when new management fails to improve the profitability of a problem unit).

Surveys of management stress do not reflect the dynamic character of the forces inherent in the manager's work over time. Only through questions formulated to capture the stressfulness of transitions, challenging conditions, and change can we fully appreciate the periodic crises and peaks of extraordinary pressure that arise from time to time, and from these data identify subgroups of managers at risk and plan coping strategies accordingly.

The following chapter on organizational dynamics discusses the forces acting on managers as they establish a fit with the organization and then struggle to maintain this fit over the full course of a career with that same organization.

## REFERENCES

Hall, R. C. W., E. R. Gardner, M. Perl, S. K. Stickney, and B. Pfefferbaum (1979). The professional burnout syndrome. *Psychiatric Opinion* (April):12–17.

Kahn, R. L., D. M. Wolfe, R. P. Quinn, J. D. Snoek, and R. A. Rosenthal (1964). *Organizational Stress: Studies in Role Conflict and Ambiguity.* New York: Wiley.

Kiev, A. and V. Kohn (1979). *Executive Stress.* An AMA Survey Report. New York: American Management Associations.

# 8

# ORGANIZATIONAL DYNAMICS

The manager must secure a place in the narrowing hierarchical structure of an evolving organization if the momentum of career advancement is to be maintained. But that place, established under one set of conditions, is soon challenged by changing organizational forces. At the same time, what the manager wants from the job also changes.

The coping problem confronting the manager is one of maintaining compatibility with the job environment in the face of changing organizational, career, and personal goals and functions. Compatibility is a dynamic equilibrium of many interacting forces.

This chapter discusses how managers' compatibility with the job environment is affected by:

- changes in career goals that accompany personal growth.
- the gradually diminishing opportunities for advancement available in a hierarchical organization.
- changing roles and responsibilities at progressively higher levels of management.
- the problems of late career.

### CHANGING CAREER GOALS

Bursts of energy, spontaneous inspiration, and creativity are characteristic of *managers in their twenties and early thirties*. Young managers seek opportunities for training and development, a forum in which to exercise initiative and test their creative ideas. In return they expect recognition of their efforts as evidenced by advancement, and compensation commensurate with their potential. Salaries are designed to attract young talent. Starting salaries are going up at a significantly higher rate than increases given to managers already on the payroll. Salary increases for managers are highest in early career stages.

What young managers want from their personal life during the period of family formation is undergoing redefinition. Starting a family is being deferred until career directions are well established. Young couples in their twenties and thirties are reluctant to go through the complex tensions of developing a career and a family at the same time. They prefer to remain mobile to take advantage of evolving career opportunities. Having a family is perceived as limiting options and mobility. This focus on work at the expense of the satisfactions available from family life causes young managers to seek and expect more career satisfaction than was required by their more family-conscious counterparts of a decade ago who derived satisfaction from both work and family.

Around age 35, however, a change in emphasis as to what the manager wants from the job becomes perceptible. By age 40 that change emerges clearly, brought about by a new set of personal priorities. The old ambition and intense concern with success is relinquished in favor of a new form of individuation or self-realization. Managers no longer aspire to be Chief Executive Officer but seek instead to apply what they have found through experience to be their abilities and interests. They seek to use those capacities that are identified as particular characteristics of themselves, those abilities and talents that are proof they have "made it." At this point managers are advancing toward "marker events" of special significance—events or changes (such as a key promotion) that define what they have become as individuals.

Those managers who see no such opportunity for successful advancement to a new level of work and social functioning will be looking around for a better job in a new company or a new function. They will seek a new way to "make it" (consultant or entrepreneur), to define their special place and settle into it. Some managers will spend several years exploring various possibilities before they make this transition to a new career. But many managers resist this transition. They remain rutted for years in a painful work situation without a future, doing work that has lost importance for them, feeling a private sense of humiliation, but unable to take the initiative to look for a change. In the end they may be forced to face the incompatibility with a job that has no desirable future. Some combination of inner readiness and external pressure will force them to leave. Although the struggle of finding a new fit may be painful, it is preferable to remaining in an unsuitable job that offers no opportunity for advancement or self-realization.

Breaking away from the influence of those who have been guides or monitors is another aspect of the process by which managers and executives find themselves. During the formative stages of their careers many managers have mentors who help, encourage, and support them as they "learn the ropes." But just as young adults leave home, seek independence, and defy the parents they admired and emulated, *managers, at about age forty,* leave their mentors, often in defiant disagreement over key issues, and go off to become distinct individuals with personalized management and life styles.

*Managers in their fifties* want to be respected and esteemed for their unique talents of developing others and for their wise reformulation of experience. They focus on the opportunity to use their accumulated wisdom to solve the fundamental problems facing the organization. Many of these managers will tell how they enjoy acting as mentor, developing new talents, or helping others handle the power structure.

But if managers in their fifties are asked if they would like to change their current work environment, they become irritable, impatient, and change the subject. They see themselves with limited options and no real ability to alter their career direction through their own actions. They seem not to recognize their roles as choosers or their responsibility for choices.

Even among executives, more often than not, change during late career comes about only because of contingencies and external influences. They seek esteem, respect, recognition. They want to feel important, to contribute, to be involved, to have their talents appreciated and used. But they want these rewards in their current environment. They are challenged by the thought of breaking away, of having choices or alternatives, of developing another niche. Suggestions along these lines provoke irritation or are ignored entirely, as if they are impossible. These executives are "locked in."

In late career the need to survive until retirement is the predominant theme. The need to feel important, to contribute, and to be involved is still there. Mood varies with how managers or executives regard their present status. Managers who feel they are needed and will be actively involved in the affairs of the organization until they themselves choose to retire are usually the most effective in their jobs. Managers who are actively making plans for the future (consulting positions, second careers, plans for an active retirement) will remain contributors in their present roles. But managers who are marking time until their careers in an organization come to an end, and who have nothing of interest or value to look forward to will gradually fall into a depressed, demoralized, downward spiral. This spiral points to major maladjustment when the time comes for them to separate from the organization.

## PYRAMIDAL STRUCTURE AND DEFEAT

Reasonably competent managers who remain with an organization because of a perceived fit between their goals and the opportunities provided by the organization expect to achieve a sense of accomplishment, status, and security as the reward for long and loyal service. *But* those managers or executives will also be exposed to factors inherent in organizational structure and practices that predispose to defeat, failure, obsolescence, lowered self-esteem, painful loss experiences, and a sense of being unfairly treated.

Management motivates managers with the promise that competent performance will enable them to climb the organizational pyramid toward power, status, and financial reward. But the pyramid narrows at the top. For each person who is promoted, a number of loyal, experienced, career people who have consistently met the requirements of their job and achieved their objectives are left behind to feel defeated, redundant, forced to hold on until retirement while fighting off the challenge of younger rising stars.

### Position in the hierarchy and health

Some observers believe that man follows the universal biological pattern of defeat. Those who lose the struggle for power with their peers and are forced to take lower positions will have signifi-

cantly poorer mental and physical health than their victorious
rivals who occupy higher positions.

My own studies of the stress repsonses of key executives of
a large corporation following a change in leadership and subsequent internal reorganizations, and of their health profile three to
five years later, confirm that a relationship does exist between
position in the hierarchy and health. However, it is important to
define this relationship, to discover the many meanings of victory
and defeat, and to clarify how health is ultimately affected by these
experiences.

The strongest impression left by these studies is that *any
change* in position within the hierarchy at upper management levels
is stressful for the individual undergoing that change, whether it
involves a promotion, a shift to a different level of reporting relationship, a transfer, relocation, demotion, or retirement. Any new
job involves giving up old, familiar, trusted supports in favor of
new responsibilities, cues, and techniques for getting things done,
and entry into a new and uncertain power structure. For those who
are promoted it means approaching the loneliness and isolation at
the top of the pyramid where they are progressively cut off from
vital informal sources of information and peer support. Thus, a
change of position within the hierarchy involves painful loss as
well as gain.

Remaining in the same position within the hierarchy is also a
painful loss experience. When individuals are passed over for
promotion they take it as an indication that they can no longer
view themselves as valued and contributing members of the organization. Involvement and the feeling that their competence is
valued are both major sources of self-esteem in contemporary organizations of all kinds.

From my studies a spectrum of health-illness responses to
change in the management hierarchy emerged. At one end were
those executives who were promoted to new functions and new challenges. Although they may have initially experienced tension, elevated blood pressure, irritability, insomnia, and the adverse health
consequences associated with these responses to stress, they generally did not go on to develop major and incapacitating health
problems.

At the other end of the spectrum, the health impact of defeat
and demoralization was much more profound. Over a period of

three to five years there was a greater incidence of life-threatening or major incapacitating illness in those who had been passed over, particularly among executives in later career who had remained in the same position for five years or more prior to the change in leadership.

Executives and managers who were disappointed with their position in the new hierarchy fell in the middle of the health–illness spectrum. The effect of disappointment on health was more subtle than the effect of either victory or defeat. Over the long term, a persistent sense of disappointment from the loss of cherished hopes, expectations, and ambitions resulted in heightened susceptibility to stressful or changing conditions and in a predisposition to serious depression or other disabling psychological reactions.

To the outside observer, virtually all executives appeared to cope with their new assignments in a professional, business-like manner. Victory and defeat were accepted as a way of life in an organizational setting. New in-groups and out-groups were regarded as a rational consequence of a shift in leadership. During the first six months most individuals appeared to work through mourning the loss of what was old and familiar to accept changed circumstances and to direct their full attention to new roles and responsibilities. The stimulation provided by new responsibilities and challenges, and by their continuing involvement in matters of importance to the organization helped them to cope with change. Those who experienced their new responsibilities, roles, and relationships as uncertain or ambiguous had the greatest difficulty with near term adjustment. Uncertainty seemed to be even more stressfull than adversity.

Within themselves, hopes and expectations—secret and often unconscious, realistic or impossible, private or shared with others— were tested against how they perceived and evaluated their role in the new hierarchical structure. Disappointment resulted when, after sufficient time to absorb the meaning of changing events, the executives interpreted these events as signifying a serious blow to cherished hopes and ambitions, or as a violation of an implicit agreement that defined the mutual expectations of the individual and the organization.

Over the long term (three to five years) executives who felt strong disappointment, or who saw themselves as having been unfairly treated, did not adjust to the new organization hierarchy without psychological disability. This disability took the form of:

- *chronic apprehension* about approaching obsolescence, the threat of forced early retirement, and concern about not being able to collect an undiscounted pension.
- *a conviction of limited options* (e.g., they felt they could not object to any subsequent assignment, transfer or relocation offered them, no matter how undesirable they or their families considered the move to be, for fear of being forced to leave the organization).
- *feeling locked in* to the organization to protect benefits already accrued.
- *pessimism* about chances for employment in the outside job market even at lower salaries or in jobs of lesser responsibility.
- *despair* at the thought of learning new skills.

There seemed to be an increased psychological brittleness among this disappointed group that left them much more apprehensive when reacting to new, changing, or challenging circumstances; less able to respond flexibly to unexpected contingencies; more prone to acquiescence as a method of survival; and more prone to depression, repressed anger, demoralization, and blaming others when something went wrong.

In other words, the psychological cost of adjusting to disappointment was to become more dependent on the organization for survival and more concerned about obsolescence. As a group, they were remarkably uncreative and unimaginative in considering new alternatives outside the organization. The more angry or dissatisfied they were with their present circumstances the more threatened they were by even the thought of developing alternatives for themselves without help from the organization.

Disappointment was occasionally expressed by questioning their loyalty to the organization. Some managers suppressed these feelings out of shame or guilt. After all, failure to receive a desired promotion was to be "taken like a man." Suppressed anger often took the form of tension, irritability, depression, and demoralization. A few developed an increasing sense of having been unfairly treated by the organization. Occasionally this developed further into a sense of having been betrayed and resulted in bitterness, and thoughts of revenge or restitution. In rare instances an enemy or persecutor was singled out to rationalize the sense of defeat, or these reactions culminated in serious clinical depression.

## MANAGEMENT OF DISAPPOINTMENT

Reactions of disappoinment can be expected following any major organizational shift in which important career changes result from the unilateral decisions of those in power. Three sources of disappointment stemming from the management process can be recognized:

1   a violation of the implicit mutual expectations of manager and management.

2   an organizational value system of "up or out."

3   the frustration of the manager's personal ambitions.

Responses of disappointment are so directly related to effective performance and health that the management of disappointment both from an individual and organizational point of view becomes an important part of any strategy to cope with stress.

### Violation of mutual expectations

Experts in organizational behavior describe an implicit set of mutual expectations between the manager and the organization, an unwritten psychological contract. These expectations define what the organization requires of the individual (often referred to as loyalty), and how the individual expects the organization to react in return (often based on subjective factors rather than on objective appraisal of realistic prospects.)

When these implicit expectations are violated by one party, the other will react with anger, frustration, and disappointment. Work events that challenge a well-established equilibrium between the manager and the organization may be unconsciously perceived by the manager as a violation of mutual expectations by the organization, leading to a response of serious disappointment.

Work events likely to trigger such disappointment include:

• requirements that managers learn new material or take on new responsibilities to meet work objectives, particularly if their background has not prepared them to do this readily.

• arbitrary management decisions such as the unilateral assigning of objectives without the agreement and acceptance of these objectives by the manager—often a consequence of the management by objectives process.

The psychological contract is either entirely unconscious or not clearly realized as such. It surfaces only when managers become disappointed at what has happened to them, that is, after the damage has already been done.

Psychological forces that individuals are not aware of often overshadow objective reasoning or the ability to see the other side of a conflict. Thus, managers will not understand the organization's point of view if they are reacting to disappointed expectations for which they hold the organization responsible.

Awareness of expectations and demands that constitute the psychological contract, will help reduce disappointment and free other psychological forces such as the use of objective reasoning to find alternative nontraumatic responses.

An agreement involves *two* parties. The organization can also become disappointed or displeased with the manager who is perceived as having violated the conventional mores, ethics, and behavioral modes of the organization's personality. In many instances the manager's violation of expected behavioral modes involves resistance to planned job change and relocation.

Managers who disappoint the organization may suffer severely. They may be passed over or develop an undesirable reputation. Their performance, which otherwise meets acceptable standards may be evaluated as unsatisfactory. Once labeled a violator, or disloyal, or poorly motivated, or unwilling, that individual's career progression can suffer substantially.

## Organizational value systems

A value system of up or out, taken for granted in organizations oriented toward productivity and profitability, heightens the sense of defeat and insecurity among those passed over for promotion. Acceptance of the "up or out" ethic ignores the costly effect on performance of angry, demoralized, defeated managers who remain with the organization, as well as the impact of this sense of failure on their families and social relations outside the workplace. It reinforces the popular notion of the "Peter Principle" that claims people inevitably rise to their level of incompetence.

I agree with H. Levinson who emphasizes that many people become incompetent because they are made so by the underlying depression that paralyzes their activities after they had been defined as defeated, as failures. "This phenomenon is made even worse by the intense pressure toward early retirement, which is essentially a castration of mature people who have had little opportunity and less support to adapt to rapidly changing economic circumstances. As a consequence they see themselves as utter failures" (H. Levinson, 1976, p. 56).

### Frustrated personal ambition

No one is immune to encounters with the disappointments in life. As Zaleznik (1967) points out in his article on the management of disappointment, individuals who want power and responsibility or seek creative expression are especially vulnerable to episodes in which reality does not conform to their wishes or intentions.

Circumstances are likely to arise during the course of a manager's career that can trigger a sense of frustrated personal ambition with accompanying bewilderment, disappointment, and painful loss experiences. Most managers and executives will go through such experiences. A reexamination of sources of satisfaction, self-image, and what the manager is internally compelled to achieve can be profitable. Ambition originating in early life is often based on subjective themes that can be altered in the light of objective review during adult life. Managers also pass through a traumatic series of specific age-linked phases.

*The Seasons of Man's Life* by Levinson, Darrow, Klein, and Levinson (1978) and the predictable life stages conceptualized by Erikson deal with the subjective reorientation all people go through during the transitions from one life phase to the next. Each transition has its career-related component anxieties, frustrations, and disappointments followed by restored comfort and newly achieved perspectives when the transition to the next phase is accomplished.*

Far from being a prelude to continued failure in career, these critical episodes may actually be occasions for accelerated growth and even the beginning of truly outstanding performance. However such an outcome requires individuals to face the issues. People seldom need to examine their motives or review their ambitions until they meet an impasse in life.

---

* Jaques (1976) describes how institutions must grow to accommodate changing individual capacities at different life stages by changing complexities of tasks assigned to managers as they grow older, and the implications of task life stage congruity on personnel selection and compensation systems.

Present disappointments may reopen problems arising from past experiences of frustration and disappointment. Resolving present crises may involve getting over the mourning of past losses. Thus, resolution of crises triggered by frustrated personal ambitions requires high quality personal psychological work and depends on the individual's receptivity to and ability for constructive introspection.

Management of career-related disappointments does not necessarily require psychotherapy or some other form of counseling. Constructive introspection and the thinking through of life's crises can be accomplished under a variety of conditions depending upon personality style and the availability of suitable supporting relationships. It is the receptivity to some form of constructive introspection that is the crucial issue here. The managers' and management's coping strategies should be geared to anticipate, encourage, and support the constructive resolution of those painful career-related loss experiences that are so much a part of the life of every manager and executive.

Zaleznik supplies the following optimistic conclusion to the management of disappointment

> *In the course of examining reactions to disappointment, a subtle change may take place in the individual's perspectives and attitudes. While he may come to recognize the impossible quality of certain goals and wishes, and be willing to relinquish their demands on his behavior, he may at the same time discover unchartered possibilities for productive work and pleasure. Those imminent possibilities remain obscure so long as the individual is intent in his quest for restitutive rewards to make up for his felt losses of the past.*
>
> (ZALEZNIK, p. 70)

## MIDDLE MANAGERS IN THE MIDDLE

The next two sections deal with stress arising from changing roles and responsibilities at two levels of management. Emanuel Kay (1974), in a position paper commissioned for *Work in America*, examines the special problems of middle management and their patterns of coping. The middle manager's problems and complaints are used here as the basis for a discussion of the genesis of obsolescence among managers.

### The position

The middle manager is defined as one who manages managers, supervisors, or professional and technical people, but who is *not* a top executive (who sets policy and deals with the total resources of the organization); is *not* a general manager (with profit and loss responsibilities); and is *not* a supervisor (who is often closely related to the employees supervised in terms of background and experience).

As a group, middle managers are responsible for interpretation and implementation of organizational policies and goals established by top executives. They manage a portion of a total function or specialty providing expertise through knowledge, performance, and through the persons they manage. They coordinate with other middle managers to provide the smoothest and most efficient realization of organizational goals. Various complaints of middle manager merit closer scrutiny.

### Threat of job loss

Unemployment among middle management may not presently be as high as during the 1970–71 recession, but the loss of a sense of invulnerability against unemployment is perceived as an ever-present threat.

> The significant thing about the 1970–71 recession with respect to middle managers is that they suddenly went from a traditionally low unemployment rate to a relatively high one. For the first time in many years, they felt threatened with the loss of a job. This experience and its attendant publicity will be a source of continuing concern for many middle managers for years to come. To them it is grim evidence that they are not in a uniquely favored and protected position because they are the echelon immediately below the top executives.
>
> (KAY, 1974, pp. 110–111)

Another example of a perceived environment being more threatening than objective conditions is described by Kay, who, from his extensive personal experience (no specific statistics on the effects of merger on middle manager tenure were available) observes that:

> A significant number of middle managers believe that mergers have a negative effect, and although this may be one of the myths that has crept into the management folklore from the

*perspective of dissatisfaction and job insecurity this perception is a "fact" and must be dealt with as perhaps as important as the actual statistics.* (p. 111)

## Boxed in

The chain of events leading to a boxed-in feeling among middle managers demonstrates a highly significant source of management stress: the extreme specialization and departmentalization of managers that results from career development pathways based on training for promotion, at the expense of developing the manager as a generalist capable of performing more than one function. This process begins when the manager is hired as a college graduate to perform a functional speciality (engineering, manufacturing, finance). Or it may begin after relatively short experience in rotational assignments when the young manager is appointed to a particular function because of demonstrated competence in that area. Subsequent training and assignments are promotional; they are designed to make the specialist a better manager of people within a specific functional area. Training and career development do not rotate the specialist out of one functional area into others to broaden interests or test for new talents. The process is thus fixed by promotions, compensation, and respect for demonstrated competence in the specialized function.

Middle managers who, after a few years, feel the need for a change, may want to move laterally to a less crowded, more satisfying or promising career pathway. But they are now hemmed in either by a lack of experience in other areas, or a salary that is too high for the experience level at which they will enter other functional areas.

Aging middle managers are concerned about diminishing powers (the midlife transition) and feel vulnerable because:

- "Old skills" are being used on an "old job" with limited incentive to develop, except for promotion within a functional hierarchy.

- Defensive attitudes begin to develop of protecting their turf, resisting adaptation to changing conditions, and refusing to learn new skills, thereby promoting obsolescence when top management decides that for reasons of organizational health their positions should be changed, abolished, or downgraded.

• During periods of economic decline or other organizational evolutionary changes their positions are risky for they may be seen and dealt with by top management as narrow functional specialists with little potential outside that speciality, who are now too old and too high salaried to be trained for other positions.

When the threat of organizational change does not evoke a sense of vulnerability in middle managers, middle age does. Managers pass successive milestones. Each milestone emphasizes the perceived vulnerability of the specialist's position. The first intimations of failing powers during the midlife transition years (early forties) often results in the managers' taking some new direction in their personal lives. But if personal reorientation does not really provide new and broader perspectives organizationally or in career approaches, the succeeding milestones of middle age will take their toll. After age forty-five middle managers fear approaching obsolescence. These feelings reach a crescendo at age fifty when middle managers finally realize that they have missed the portal to top management. Then they feel not only boxed-in, but also *locked-in* by pension plans and benefits that are too promising to give up for other, undoubtedly very risky, jobs outside the organization. The benefits may not be realized for five to fifteen years from the point at which they begin to feel locked-in, which can be a long time to "defend" one's position.

Middle managers, boxed-in and locked-in, then proceed to throw away the key by abandoning self-assertive efforts to improve their uncomfortable position out of fear of entering the outside job market in which the same problems that interfered with mobility within the organization are anticipated—too high a salary to be placed elsewhere, too specialized, or too old for career development in new directions.

### Lack of authority

"We have responsibility but no authority," lament middle managers. "We are expected to produce results but have little influence over the policies and events that determine these results. Top management does not ask us for our input when they establish policy or make certain decisions, even those that affect us directly. They do not value our opinions. Decision making is seen as the prerogative of top management. They will relinquish none of their influence or control. Those of us who have been around a long time know the ropes and get things done in our Machiavellian ways. Some of us stick our necks out occasionally and usually get our heads chopped off. Others play it safe and never take any initiative at all. Those who are more self-confident leave for other jobs where they can feel more effective. When something unexpected happens top management takes over and we just wait for them to make a decision or take action. We're ashamed to let our subordinates see how little power we have to do the things we are being held responsible for."

Middle managers in the middle, suffering and dissatisfied, receive no sympathetic understanding from below or above. Subordinates view middle managers as without influence, indecisive, inflexible, burdened with undesirable jobs, or occupying positions to be avoided at all costs. Top managers lament, "Middle managers are unrealistic about their roles; are unrealistic about who makes the decisions around here; are obsolete, unambitious, and resistive to change; complain too much without realizing that top executives have been under pressure too in recent years."

The pattern of power distribution in the management hierarchy can be a stressor of great significance. Obsolescence, apathy, demoralization and defeat—all too common outcomes of the management process—are not necessarily related to the pyramidal organizational structure and defeat. As illustrated in the series of executive stress interviews, experienced managers and executives can accept losing out in a competition for promotion as an inevitable consequence of limited opportunities in an ever-narrowing organizational structure. Far more demoralizing for many managers is the frustration caused by the middle manager's impotence to exercise responsibility without power, a frustration to which many adapt by becoming apathetic, fearing incompetence, and thereby actually becoming obsolete. Some managers leave the situation altogether for greener pastures while those who stay and stagnate become serious personnel problems.

### Comment

Psychologists have observed that for large numbers of individuals, life in the middle years can be a gradual or even rapid stagnation or alienation from the world and from their sense of self. Surely, severe decline and constriction are common enough so that they are seen as part of normal middle age. But according to Daniel Levinson (1978) although a good deal of decline is statistically normal in the sense that it occurs frequently, such *decline is not developmentally normal.* Drastic decline occurs only when development has been impaired by adverse psychological, social, and biological circumstances. *If obsolescence and fear of reaching their level of incompetence is found commonly among managers, but less commonly among equally intelligent and experienced individuals in other professions, then this obsolescence must be viewed as an occupational hazard of management and not as a fact of life or the consequence of the midlife crises.*

## THE GENERAL MANAGER

The greatest challenge of a rising manager's career is the transition from functional specialist to general management. Managers with outstanding achievements as specialists in areas where they know more and more about less and less (finance, marketing, manufacturing, research and development, planning) may be chosen by virtue of this accomplishment to step into the role of middle level general manager who is required to know less and less about more and more.

Hugo Uyterhoeven, (1972) emphasizes the demanding requirements, pitfalls, imperfections, and misunderstandings inherent in the position of middle-level general manager. Uyterhoeven's purpose is to help the manager formulate a job strategy to emerge an effective, successful manager rather than an ultimate victim. My reason for going into detail about the general manager's job is *not* because it is inherently stressful, although it is. My purpose is to use this material as a springboard for a discussion of the importance of the process of realistic self-assessment and job choice.

All the challenges and ambiguities notwithstanding, the middle-level general manager's position provides appealing opportunities for the aspiring executive. The job is under the manager's own control to a great degree, can be creative, offers an opportunity for contributions to be noticed, and leads to further career advancement.

But risk and opportunity go hand in hand. It is not a job for everyone, but only for those who perceive a compatibility with the special demanding requirements of these positions, who are willing to take the risks, and who are prepared to cope with the failures that may be involved.

## The position

General managers are responsible for the profit and loss of a particular business unit at the intermediate level of the corporate hierarchy. Although general managers are the chief executives of their units, they are at the same time subordinates taking orders from executives at a higher level. Even these higher executives may take orders from still higher levels. Only the top-level general managers act primarily as superiors. All other general managers find themselves in the middle, taking orders from a boss, giving orders to subordinates and relating to peers or organizational equals with whom cooperation is essential to fulfill their own profit and other objectives.

According to Uyterhoeven, the middle-level general manager:

• has a boss's responsibility without the boss's authority.

• receives abstract guidance from superiors about what is wanted in the form of goals (expected profits and other objectives for the year) to be accomplished within specified restrictions (budgets and other organizational limitations).

• is not told how to go about accomplishing these goals but must translate abstract guidance into concrete actions (plans and strategies) which ultimately appear as measurable results (profit and loss, markets entered, new products introduced, inventories trimmed).

• must get things done through others using accommodation and compromise. This involves meeting the often conflicting and changing demands of superiors, subordinates, and peers and confronting the inevitable politics of organizational life centering around positions of influence, prestige, and career objectives of others, while still getting the job done.

• must handle the responsibility–authority discrepancy or "imperfection" of the position, a discrepancy generally misunderstood by the top executives who judge the "results" produced by middle managers. Top-level general managers incorrectly understand the scope and characteristics of the lower-level position as having the same opportunities, prerogatives, and power that they do, and therefore expect middle level general managers to shoulder similar responsibility.

General management positions are becoming increasingly common as a direct outgrowth of the shift from the functional form of organization requiring only one general manager at the top to the divisional form with a variety of business units often extending several levels down into the organization (group, division, department). Each unit requires its own general manager.

The divisional form of organization and the shift from specialist to generalist has several advantages for the organization. Only a small segment of the total enterprise is entrusted to an unproved general manager. A large number of general management slots enables a corporation to attract and retain capable managers. The middle manager phenomenon is conducive to management development and training, with challenge increasing as the manager moves up in rank, enhancing confidence, versatility, and individual and organizational competence.

To achieve maximum benefit from this management style, the company must transfer and promote its large reservoir of capable, specially trained general managers as new opportunities arise. This procedure then involves managers and executives in the well-known consequences of frequent relocations, expatriate assignments, and often painful decisions about relocation and career development versus conflicting family priorities.

Some of these assignments require specific personality characteristics. General managers working abroad interface with the host government, the local business community, and the public. In the role of top executive, figurehead, or chief representative of the organization (or of the United States) in the eyes of the local business, political, and social community, general managers must function as diplomats, teachers, and models. Public exposure may be stressful, even dangerous. Implications of their role as liaison with the local community must be considered among the highest priority requirements of that position. Family life must be organized around the general manager's role as figurehead. The adjustment, health, and safety of dependents is a related stressor for expatriate general managers.

### Challenges and risks

For aspiring general managers, each move up the organizational pyramid involves new problems of fit. Rewards and risks must be assessed anew before each job choice or decision to relocate. Assessments of fit must take into consideration the career progression patterns they are committed to as general managers, the mobility requirements of that career, and the intensity of work pressure and interpersonal politics that are an integral part of the role.

*The transition.* The specialist functioning successfully in a specific narrow area risks a misfit when attempting to make the transition to general management, a position that may require drastically different skills and personality characteristics. The general manager must get things done through others as a delegator and a doer, a strategist and an operator, a player and a coach, and a leader who is constantly influenced by the demands, expectations, and abilities of superiors and subordinates. A specialist with indepth knowledge and control of a functional area such as marketing may find the new position of responsibility for specific results to be too challenging.

The previous experience of a functional expert is not transferable to the type of leadership required as general manager. For the specialist with an outstanding record of achievement the transition to generalist may be too risky.

*Risking defeat.* Once having made the transition to general manager the individual is committed to the challenge of advancing up the organizational pyramid and risking defeat. Competition and rivalry for the next highest position can be intense. Those young managers who are designated as high potential performers may be encouraged by some superiors, and resented and regarded as rivals by others. But the action is always exciting.

Once individuals lose the high potential label in the eyes of management, their career progression slows remarkably. Managers are almost never told when their rising star has fallen. Instead, management support is withdrawn and the tarnished general managers are looked upon as obstacles occupying a slot that blocks the flow of career development assignments for others. For the general manager it is usually "up or out."

*Office politics.* The exposure to office politics is essential to getting the job done. But office politics often bring about psychological trauma. Coexistence in an intensively competitive political atmosphere is not always peaceful. As long as general managers must get things done through accommodation and compromise with others on three different levels (superiors, peers, subordinates) and these others have their own personal and organizational objectives in mind, the risk of exposure to the pain of office politics is great with every action, strategy, decision, meeting, or review of results. The general manager's position is not for individuals who wish to be dependent or whose sensitivities are affected by the confrontations and battles of the general manager's everyday work and roles.

*Work pressure.* The intensity of work-related demands must be taken into consideration when a manager assesses a fit between personal, professional, family, and life-style factors and any new job. The role of general manager demands first call on the manager's best efforts. Even if the internal shop is in order, external demands must be responded to—routine and emergency meetings with top management about their special concerns; the needs and requests of peers and subordinates; and external community events, ceremonial roles and public initiatives that require the general manager's top priority attention.

Personal and family requirements often take second place to managers' roles and work. All too frequently managers have little energy and interest left to give to outside interests. Middle-level general managers must assess the impact of the intense involvement of job demands on personal, family, and other interests, and develop a strategy to cope with and resolve these conflicts.

*Mobility.* A commitment to a life style requiring a high degree of mobility means taking the risk that changing family priorities will ultimately conflict with career progression priorities. Even when a manager's career is totally within the United States the mobility of the family unit may become a critical factor in career progression, when personal and family priorities shift to complicate relocation and job choice decisions.

For the woman manager or the childless two-career couple the decision about whether or not to have children is postponed until the mid thirties when the decision to make the transition from functionalist to generalist must also be made. The social adjustment of teenaged children presents a serious problem. Relocation usually disrupts the stability so essential to their socialization. The manager's wife, who was previously preoccupied with the needs of small children, now has time to devote herself to personal interests and community affairs, factors tending to reduce the mobility potential of a manager's family unit.

## Summary

The position of general manager is one of great importance to the organization and of great appeal and interest to an individual interested in advancement. But the pace is intense, the work pressured and absorbing, requiring single-minded concentration on the requirements of the job. These requirements often include figurehead and other important roles within the community and a commitment to a mobile life style.

Each new move is a new challenge, raising problems of fit between the job and personal interests and personality, professional skills, family needs and interests, and overall life style. As career progression continues, mobility problems, family interests, and the narrowing of promotional opportunities combine to raise a new series of risks—those involved in successive job choice and relocation decisions.

## PROBLEMS OF LATE CAREER

Problems that are likely to develop among long-service managers and executives in their late forties and fifties render this group relatively resistant to change and complicate management efforts to reassign personnel. The following interview illustrates the problems of a manager with long service in late career for whom there is no appropriate placement in the standard organizational setup.

### INTERVIEW 9 – Waiting to Retire

I began the interview with George Sorensen, a distinguished looking, gray haired man in his late fifties, with the usual opening remarks about my interest in the sources of management stress. Without his saying a word in response, he got up from behind his desk, and slowly walked across the room. There he pointed to a photograph of a large apartment complex hanging on the wall, and said, "I manage the Division's real estate interests now. I've been doing it for almost two years." He briefly reviewed the real estate in his portfolio. That was all he had to say about his present work. He returned to his desk and slowly recounted the positions he has held during his long service with the company.

He started working at nineteen as an office boy while going to college at night to study engineering. Gradually he worked his way up to become the manager of a large manufacturing plant in the Midwest. There, he was respected and well liked. The plant was the largest employer in that small midwestern town. His position as Manager gave him status in the community.

The only indication that he derived pleasure from his work came when he described the circumstances following a serious explosion at his plant many years before. He conducted an investigation into the cause of the explosion, found the source of the difficulty, installed the appropriate safety devices, then reassured the community that the situation was under control. He smiled as he recalled the grateful response of the community to his effective handling of the situation.

The last decade of his career was described in very few words. He paused frequently and his speech became less audible. When the company acquired another firm with more modern facilities to make the same products, his plant was shut down and he was transferred to New York.

"This really isn't much of a job. It was created for me because I have long service and they didn't know where I fit in. My secretary takes care of most of the details. My young assistant does the traveling to the construction sites. There's nothing left for me to do now but to wait until I am old enough to retire.

"My wife and I don't like living in an apartment in New York. We are far from our roots in the Midwest. We don't have any family left, now that my brother Arne died just a few months ago.

"He worked hard all of his life to maintain his lumber business. Just when he sold the business and acquired enough money to enjoy his leisure time, he had a heart attack. Never fully recovered. Just downhill from there. What is life about, anyway? I wonder if it's worth the struggle."

George Sorensen was obviously depressed. Signs of depression —slowed speech, labored thinking, loss of interest in work and personal matters—were evident from the start of the interview. By recounting the highlight of his career, he communicated the source of his depression, namely, the loss of an image of himself as an important and respected manager to whom others looked for support. By telling about his brother, who worked so long and hard but could not enjoy the fruits of his labor, he indicated how he himself was feeling at this point in his life.

His range of present interests was very narrow. Future planning was restricted to calculations of how much longer he had to work before he could retire on full pension. He lacked confidence that he could sustain himself in the present job for the three years that remained until retirement.

As I left his office I looked at my watch. I was surprised to discover how short the interview had been. George Sorensen had so little to say. To me, the interview seemed a long session of hard work with little enjoyment or reward for all the effort. I then realized that George Sorensen had succeeded in communicating to me how *he* felt about his current life. It was a long session of hard work with little enjoyment or reward for all the effort.

### Comment

George Sorensen is faced with a problem that is all too common among managers and executives in their fifties. He is not obsolete. He has wisdom and experience gained from long service to the organization. There is simply no position available to him in which his value to the organization can be realized. In the opinion of his management, the greater organizational need is to fill available positions with managers of higher potential, or with longer service still ahead of them. The solution was to create a position he can occupy until he retires.

Unfortunately, George Sorensen could not find a place for himself either. No options were developed in anticipation of late-career problems, or of approaching retirement. Life and career planning that he engaged in when younger were not continued into the later phases of his life and career.

In this illustration the executive's career ends on a depressed note. Certainly, only a minority of careers end that way. On balance, careers in management are sources of self-esteem, pride in accomplishments, and a position of respect in the community. The depressed note, however, reflects a problem in the American management process. All too often the older manager or executive ends a productive career with less dignity, with less sense of worth and self-esteem, and with less independence than seems appropriate for the effort invested over many years of loyal and effective service.

Managers most likely to develop problems in late career (Table 8.1) are those who, for a variety of reasons, are dissatisfied with the status quo but see no way of making changes or of developing new options. These problems may be a result of personal inertia, extreme dependence on the organization for career planning, having advanced beyond their competence, inadequate management education and career development programs, or the absence of opportunity in the organization in which they have invested so much time and effort.

The complacency with which American management regards the late-career problems of managers and executives with long service, reflects American cultural values. Career development and management training are directed toward helping younger managers to climb the pyramid toward top management. Late-career and life planning is generally neglected.

By contrast, the Japanese system assures managers a place in

**TABLE 8.1**  *Profile of managers likely to develop problems in late career.*

| | |
|---|---|
| 1. Managers with Long Service | This group seeks to protect its considerable personal investment in a career within the company and benefit plans. |
| 2. Advancement-Discouraged Managers | Manager and/or company consider further advancement unlikely for a variety of reasons such as poor performance or organizational change. |
| 3. Managers Immobilized without Options | Life and career planning engaged in when younger was not effectively continued into the later phases of business life. |
| 4. Managers Vulnerable to Stress | This group tends to resist change and to develop severe morale problems in response to the stress of any organizational change. |
| 5. Managers with Low Job Satisfaction | In this group, waste of experience, talent, and wisdom through poor utilization of resources is a frustration to manager and management alike. |

the organization until retirement through ongoing training and through a series of planned career transitions. At age forty-five the managers are selected to become members of top management, or general managers of smaller organization units. Involvement with the organization is assured until the retirement age of fifty-five when active employees are continued on temporary status as long as there is a use for their wisdom and experience within the organization.

In the United States, late career planning presents a challenge for both manager and management. Each has a role in the resolution of this soft spot in the management process.

## REFERENCES

Jaques, E. (1976). *A General Theory of Bureaucracy*. London: Heinemann.

Kay, E. (1974). Middle management. In J. O'Toole (ed.) *Resource Papers for Work in America*. Cambridge, Mass.: MIT Press.

Levinson, D. J., C. D. Darrow, E. B. Klein, M. H. Levinson, and B. McKee (1978). *The Seasons of Man's Life*. New York: Knopf.

Levinson, H. (1976). *Psychological Man*. Cambridge, Mass.: Levinson Institute.

Uyterhoeven, H. E. R. (1972). General managers in the middle. *Harvard Business Review* (72212):75–85.

Zaleznik, A. (1967). Management of disappointment. *Harvard Business Review* (67612):59–70.

# 9

# THE EVOLVING ORGANIZATION

Changes in the characteristics of organizations adapting to ever-changing internal and external environments may lead to disruption of a previously established harmony between individuals and the organization, or may produce an incongruity between the functions required of those individuals and their capacity to perform those functions. To preserve compatibility individuals and the organization must evolve in parallel ways.

Three examples of how incompatibilities can develop from gradual changes within an organization are presented in this chapter. In each instance changes in operating procedures and practices required to assure the viability and competitiveness of the organization violated long-established, but largely unacknowledged, expectations of employees. Severe career-related personal crises within the groups most directly affected by these changes were the result.

The first example discusses the consequences of a shift from a paternalistic management style to a system of management by objectives. The second example describes the health consequences among a group of telephone operators and supervisors when the company changed from voice switchboard operation to the dial system. The third example demonstrates how factors similar to those affecting the telephone operators subsequently affected a broad spectrum of employees in the same organization. In this last instance lower- and middle-level managers were the population at greatest risk.

Strategies to identify and cope with the effects of organizational evolution on individual–organization compatibility are discussed at the end of the chapter.

## MANAGEMENT BY OBJECTIVES

In the first chapter I referred to the sudden and remarkable increase in employee visits to the Medical Department at a corporate headquarters for stress reactions that followed a major reorganization and changes in management practices. The stress consequences of an important phase in the evolution of the organization are illustrated by the following review.

During the period in question, changes were instituted by management to improve the competitive position and effectiveness of the corporation as a whole. Subsequent events have confirmed the wisdom of that decision. Three companies were merged into one and a paternalistic management style was replaced by a system of management by obectives, which based promotion and employability on defined performance standards. The credibility of the new system was established immediately when, for the first time in the company's history, old employees were let go and new personnel were hired from the outside to fill key positions.

Within months following the reorganization announcement there was a significant increase in employee visits to the headquarters medical clinic for tension and anxiety states, depression, elevated blood pressure, and personal crises. Shortly afterward a similar increase in the incidence of hypertension and peptic ulcer occurred.

Stress reactions remained at a high level over the next several years, declining only slightly after the last of many organizational changes, but continuing into the years of economic recession a decade later. It would seem logical to explain the significant increase in physical and psychological complaints as the response of those employees whose jobs were most threatened and who were ultimately separated from the company. Such was not the case. The clinical observations referred to here were made among those who survived the initial reorganization and remained through a series of subsequent changes.

Information about the sources of stress during that period is available from interviews conducted more than a decade following the original announcement of the reorganization; from anecdotal material offered freely by participants in various management education programs; and from discussions of sources of management stress. The following interview is representative of the opinions of many employees who lived through that critical transition in the life of a large corporation.

## INTERVIEW 10 – The Deafening Silence

Tom Henderson is an executive with long service who came up through the ranks of one of the smaller companies involved in the merger.

"I'll never forget those days. The old company was a great place to work. We were like a close family unit. No one worried about job security. When you wanted time off for personal reasons others would cover without asking for an explanation. We almost hated to see the weekends come.

"In the old company you felt the job was yours for life so it was like hearing a cannon being fired in the office when the first employee was let go as a result of new management practices. After the easy going way we were managed it was shocking to have to meet objectives and to go through an annual performance appraisal.

"What was most stressful, though, was the way in which the changes came about. The merger itself was a total surprise to us. Strangely enough, there wasn't even a grapevine to alert us to what was happening. The secrecy surrounding the planning of this change was exceptionally tight.

"I was in the field when the first notice of the merger came. It was in the form of an announcement that our company was to merge with two others and no one was certain of employment in the new organization until notified by clarifying announcements to follow. Well, we waited for that follow-up announcement, and waited, and waited. No one heard anything at all for the next three months. Some of the rumors were wild.

"Those who were very confident of their abilities took matters into their own hands and found other jobs outside the company. Some just left without another job to go to because they could not tolerate the suspense of the unknown. We had absolutely no way to find out what we should be planning for ourselves and our families.

"After three months an announcement came that changes were being made first at headquarters to be followed later by changes in the field. Six weeks after that I heard about my job, but only because I was the head of the department. Others didn't hear about their situations until some time after that.

"That was over ten years ago. When I don't sleep well I still think about that experience. Something I'm going through must remind me of what happened then. I have a funny habit. I startle at the sound of footsteps behind me in the corridor as if the management consultant who planned that reorganization is creeping up behind me to tap me on the shoulder and give me the bad news. It could happen again at any time. You can't trust a consultant.

"I made out fairly well as far as my career is concerned. I received a rather good promotion and came to work here at headquarters. At first my wife had a little trouble adjusting to living in this area. Customs are different from those in the small town where we both had lived all of our lives. My wife's family is very close and she was not too happy about leaving her mother and sisters. It took time, but everything worked out all right.

"I hope we don't have to go through another experience like that one again. I'd quit first—if I could afford it, that is!"

### Comment

Two issues are raised by this material: (1) the impact of organizational change on established individual–organization compatibility and life patterns, and (2) the impact of the process of organizational change.

Before the reorganization, employees at all levels had clearly established expectations of what was or was not demanded of them in the way of performance and what the company promised implicitly in terms of longevity and job security, according to usual management practices. Employees then based their own life practices on the assumption that these implicit promises would always apply.

Changes, acknowledged as necessary for a more effective organization, were nevertheless perceived by employees as a violation of a long established psychological contract that promised them an organization concerned about individual welfare, an absence of performance demands, and freedom from worry about job security. The new system of management by objectives based job security on performance and confronted the employee regularly through performance appraisals. This system was perceived as a violation of the former psychological contract, and led to a high level of mistrust of the organization, feelings that resurfaced periodically during subsequent periods of extraordinary work stress.

Even many years after the reorganization, lingering evidence of the trauma felt by employees could be found in the often repeated myth that a management consultant was coming to make things worse than they already were. It was quite common when discussing management stress for employees to joke by pointing to an unfamiliar figure at corporate headquarters and saying, "Watch out for him. He's a management consultant." Mistrust of the organization was displaced by employees from management to consultants to make day-to-day living with the suspect organization more comfortable.

Mistrust of management was dissipated through the years as top management led the organization through an economic recession without a reduction in headcount at a time when customarily secure middle- and upper-level managers were being laid off by other companies.

The second important source of stress in the reorganization was the way in which the transition was managed. The long silence between announcements of plans compounded the uncertainty and fear of the unknown that inevitably accompany even gradual organizational changes. In this instance the deafening silence about how employees would be affected raised fearful images of the future. Consequently many who were unable to assess their own situation for lack of adequate and relevant information jumped the gun and left with or without another job, just to reduce the unbearable tension of uncertainty and the fear of the unknown.

Preparing for change by providing employees with relevant information from which they can form a realistic assessment of future prospects, and by providing support for employees to cope with unfavorable as well as favorable eventualities are important organizational coping strategies.

## THE DIAL SYSTEM

The following description tells how a group of telephone operators and their supervisors reacted to a change from the voice system of switchboard operation to the more efficient dial system. The change meant retraining to meet new job requirements and exposure to a different work ethic. It illustrates how evolutionary events in the life of an organization can be a source of stress for long-term employees with firmly established (and often unconscious) expectations about individual–organization compatibility. Similar stressors that came at a much later date had a comparable effect on most employees in the same company, but most particularly on lower- and middle-level managers.

### Epidemic of depression

This was my first opportunity to observe the selective effects of occupational stress on a specific group of employees. It occurred while I was completing my psychiatric residency training and moonlighting on my day off as a physician at the New York Telephone Company. Although I did only psychiatric evaluations, we couldn't use the word psychiatrist in those days.

Young physicians have a tendency to think they know it all when they complete intensive specialty training and start practice —a wishful denial of the challenges and uncertainties that await them during this important transition from student to independent practitioner.

Know-it-all was exactly what I was. Each time the nurse handed me the list of consultations for that day I would show off. Without looking at the list I told them "I know all about these three patients. They are telephone operators or supervisors, women between the ages of forty-five and forty-seven, who have been with the company from twenty-seven to twenty-nine years. One had the flu six months ago and has not been able to return to work. Another has been complaining of fatigue, dizziness, and headaches at the switchboard recently. Clinic physicians cannot find anything physically wrong with them so they have requested a psychiatric consultation. The third woman was sent here by her supervisor, a longtime close personal friend. The supervisor noticed that the operator was crying at the switchboard because of "personal problems" and that she has become alarmingly quiet or frighteningly irritable, very much "unlike her usual self."

Week after week my predictions were borne out. We were witnessing an epidemic of mild and severe depression among a specific subgroup of employees at that particular location. In all, I collected forty-five such patients over the period of about one year, summarized the case histories, and presented the findings at a meeting of personnel managers.

Clinically, this group of women was suffering from one or another form of depression: some mild, some severe, others masked by fatigue, headaches, or severe stress reactions. As is often the case, many were unaware of depressed feelings but preferred to think in terms of physical symptoms of fatigue or headaches or just not feeling well enough to return to work. An epidemic of flu about six months before apparently triggered the onset of depression in some of these women. They were either too slowed down to function well or too discouraged to confront what was facing them should they return to work.

The dynamics of the epidemic of depression became clear as interview data began to accumulate. The similarity of emotional and work-related experiences triggering these symptoms, and the life history context in which the epidemic of depression took place made this a natural experiment.

As a group these women felt bitterly betrayed by the company. They remembered how things used to be. The company could do no wrong. It was the greatest employer to work for. They were proud to be loyal, devoted employees, placing company interests above personal interests. The Telephone Company was worn proudly like a badge of status and belonging.

It was often only at the conclusion of an interview that I realized they rarely referred to husbands, children, a home life, school, family or community interests. There were indeed husbands and children, but through the years these relationships were relatively neglected out of "loyalty to the company." Throughout their working lives they traded loyalty to the company for a type of security that had a very special meaning for them—the prospect of lifetime security; an assurance that the company would stand by them and support them in times of need.

As girls in their late teens, these operators were able to get and hold jobs during the depression years of the early 1930s. Often they were the only ones in their families to be employed, the sole source of income upon whom several generations of adults were dependent. What made this position of special importance and even more satisfying was that the Telephone Company promised job security during those times of struggle for economic survival.

The narrow age range of the group was a result of two factors: having been very young girls when they began to work for the company and having been thrust into positions of financial responsibility in the family at a very early age. As adults, loyalty to the Telephone Company and the paternalistic, organization-centered social involvements and the security this implied, influenced their subsequent marital relationships and attitudes toward their children.

For a long time the compatibility between the security-esteem needs of the operators and the extreme loyalty fostered by the company was unchallenged. But in the few years before the outbreak of depression among older operators, young women coming into the company began to express totally different attitudes toward authority, financial security, and what they wanted as a reward for their work. They worked for the pleasures their earnings could buy. They were defiant of authority and thought only of what the company had to offer them in the way of benefits and days off. It was a buyer's market. They could go elsewhere and get as good a job. One job seemed like the next to this new generation. They talked back to their supervisors, chewed gum at the switchboard, took all the breaks and time off to which they were entitled, and then tried for even more.

Inevitably these young women clashed with the experienced older operators. The older operators sat next to them at the switchboard and were envious of their new freedoms and self-interest and resented their defiance of authority, their lack of respect for the company, and their lack of respect for older, more experienced co-workers. It was in this atmosphere of endemic conflict between these two groups that the triggering event took place.

The company initiated a change in operating procedures, switching from voice to the dial system, a change that required all operators to go through a short, intense training program. The younger operators, more adept at understanding the new technology and less set in a customary way of doing things, picked up the new system easily and moved ahead. The older operators were threatened by the change, offended at being asked to learn something new after many years, and resentful of having lost the opportunity to feel superior. "I'm older and more experienced and can do it better than those young kids." was no longer quite true to the facts. The pride and self-esteem of the older operators were trampled! The unspoken promise of the company to provide security, to guarantee self-esteem, importance, and protection against challenge, seemed to the older operators to have been broken. Their rivals, younger women who were less responsibility-ridden and freer to enjoy pleasures of young adulthood, were now getting ahead faster.

As the company fell from its pedestal in the eyes of the older operators, love, as it will do, turned to hate, bitterness, and a sense of betrayal. Almost as a domino effect, family problems began to emerge as their attitude toward the company changed. Husbands said "I told you so." or began to berate them for years of neglect. Children began to demand their due, tired of taking second place in their mothers' interests. Home for these unhappy women was certainly no source of support. Above all, this group mourned the loss of that special relationship of loyal employee to ideal company.

In most cases the depressions eventually cleared although the generation problems between the two groups at the switchboard remained. Some women decided they had worked long enough and retired to recoup as much as they were able of the pleasures of family life.

### Comment

This illustration of a natural experiment—a study of the effects of a change in switchboard procedures on the health of operators and supervisors—shows that the effects of work pressure experienced at one moment must be understood in relation to the total life context of those undergoing this pressure. It demonstrates that context can include an individual's entire employment history. Mutual expectations are taken for granted over years, and emerge again with violent impact in response to changes and transitions in personal life (middle age), changing social conditions (attitude of younger persons toward authority, responsibility, personal satisfactions), and organizational evolution (change to the more efficient dial system).

The resulting "epidemic of depression" can be understood only in the broader context of the entire past history of person–organization compatibility. Why else would the simple requirement to attend a short training program to learn a new switchboard system set off such an epidemic of depressive illness?

This illustration emphasizes the importance of individuals being aware of what they really want from an organization and why. Such an awareness must be updated and renegotiated as personal needs and the character of the organization change over time. Had the older operators been aware of some of the psychological themes involved in their resistance to the new training program, their sense of betrayal and subsequent bitterness might have been diminished considerably. Their learning new operating procedures might then have progressed more efficiently. Certainly, depression and family conflict might have been reduced.

Employees' dependencies on the organization account for much of the stress impact of changes in the life of that organization.

## A COMPETITIVE ENVIRONMENT

After writing about an epidemic of depression among an older generation of operators at the New York Telephone Company that occurred more than twenty years before, I sat back to relax with a copy of the New York Times. In the business section was a prominent headline, "A.T.&T. Trying to Lift Morale: Worker Stress Linked to Rise in Competition" (April 14, 1979). It was like déjà vu. I had just written about the fortifying effect of employment on the lives of Telephone Company employees, about loyalty fostered in older employees by company practices, about younger employees with different attitudes toward authority, and about morale problems that followed efforts to modernize operating procedures. Now, over two decades later, I was reading about the same issues generalized for all employees.

Published data on how employees rate the Telephone Company as a place to work clearly show that morale is sinking rapidly. Morale used to be higher among managers than nonmanagers, but now the figures are reversed indicating that triggering factors may be having a greater effect on managers at lower and middle levels. The article about Ma Bell, the Biggest Company on Earth, and its impact on United States life and business, attributes dissatisfaction and worsening morale among formerly loyal employees at all levels to internal restructuring and competitive practices designed to meet the challenge of greater external competition. Michael Maccoby, author of *The Gamesman* and a student of A.T.&T. is quoted as saying in the *New York Times* article (April 14, 1979, p. 29):

> *A.T.&T. used to be the most different of the big corporations. A kind of noncorporate atmosphere prevailed. The feeling*

*among employees was that it was more than a business; it was here to do more than just make money.*

*Now, with the competitive environment, it will have to become more interested in making money. The gamesman who takes risks will surge to the top. The new marketing people being brought in create some stress. They think the old people are too stodgy; the old people think they are too pushy.*

What is so striking is the consistency over time of:

- the Ma Bell corporate personality.
- the type of individual–organization compatibility fostered by this personality.
- the new social values attributed to the younger generation of employees that appear to the older generation as a defiance of authority and a lack of interest in their work.
- the dissatisfaction and morale problems triggered by internal changes resulting from the need to remain competitive in the external world.

The comments of managers quoted in the *New York Times* article are used here to explore the effects on managers of an evolutionary change in organizational personality as Ma Bell adapts to external competitive pressures.

### Corporate personality

The company prides itself in a "greenest grass" corporate image, smothering its people with a pleasant employment package, pay and benefits that are generally considered quite good, and most important perhaps, company assurances of virtual lifetime job security ("You have to be very bad, I suppose murder is a firing offense"). In return, "Ma Bell expects a good deal of respect. But loyal employees with lots of drive can steadily move toward the atmosphere of leadership, enjoying comfort and sometimes riches."

### Individual–organization compatibility

Evidence of this compatibility is to be found in the community, in the employee's family, and of course in the employee who remains loyal even in retirement. The article points out the fortifying effect that the company has had on tens of thousands of high school and college students who thought that a phone company worker was one of the best things one could be. Stories of heartfelt devotion among family members were quoted. "My family was like a tree that decided to put down roots in the phone company. It was automatically thought that once you got out of school you sprinted to the personnel office and signed right up."

Devotion continues even after retirement. Most former phone company workers are united in a gigantic fraternity called the Telephone Pioneers of America with 526,000 members. They periodically get together at chapter meetings and talk phones. "When you're a phone worker, you're a phone worker every last day you're on this good earth. I suspect there may be a Pioneer group up above."

### New social values

Older managers are quoted as describing the younger worker with new social values. "The younger employees don't have the loyalty to the system. It's rather frustrating trying to get eight out of eight from them." Another manager states, "There's a new employee. Much less amenable to external discipline. He has the work ethic, but he wants to be talked to. If you transfer him, he wants to know why. I never had to be told why. I was told to move and I moved. The new worker needs more interaction."

### Performance measurements

In an effort to meet the challenge of external competition, and to encourage new aggressive leadership internally, A.T.&T. now places great emphasis on measuring each employee's performance in detail and on encouraging internal competition. A.T.&T. pits one employee against another, office against office, and carefully rates each performance.

Observers hold the new internal competitive environment responsible for the extreme decline in morale among managers. New techniques to cope with the stressfulness of performance evaluation measurements are (1) goals determined by customers and not by other managers, and (2) results reported qualitatively (high, objective, low, unsatisfactory) rather than by actual numerical scores. Nevertheless, the prevalent attitude among those who have been around for some time is that "There's just all this change. The

Company's gotten like a monkey on your back. We're sure not the close-knit Ma Bell family anymore."

## MANAGEMENT OF ORGANIZATIONAL CHANGE

In the three examples cited, changes in organization personality and practices resulted from the need to react to an increasingly competitive business environment, to new technology, and new social values. A number of factors contributed to the stressfulness of these evolutionary changes. Almost any change that challenges long-established working and living patterns can be stressful, but unilateral employer-initiated change is certain to be highly stressful for those most directly affected.

Any change will be resisted to some degree. But where change is brought about entirely at the initiative of the organization and those most directly affected are not included in the planning process and are not informed about how plans are to be implemented, the resistance to change will be intense.

When the stressfulness of change can be anticipated, the techniques for managing change are of critical importance. In the case of the merger referred to previously and the accompanying changes in business practices:

- The long silence between the announcement of the merger and follow-up clarification of how each employee would be affected only served to heighten the uncertainty and fear of the unknown associated with any major organizational change.

- Secrecy and the lack of clarifying information deprived affected employees of the opportunity to assess how career and personal plans might be affected. There was no opportunity to plan a personal strategy to cope with new circumstances, whether favorable or otherwise.

- The prolonged uncertainty not only increased short-term distress, but adverse consequences were evident over the long term when favorable attitudes toward the company were replaced by a mistrust of change that lasted for over a decade.

Remedial measures should include timely, relevant, and realistic information about the reasons for the change and how it will be implemented. The informed employee can be expected to be less resistant to employer-initiated change, particularly if the explanation is accepted by those most affected. Even if the reasons for change are not entirely accepted, managers will eventually cope with the bad news as well as the good if given the materials, time, and support required to do so.

It is my impression from observations of job loss following organization-initiated change that the way job loss is managed significantly influences the ultimate consequences of such undesirable events. The quality of organizational support together with the abruptness of the career change are often more important factors in determining the stressfulness of the experience than is the desirability of that change. Employers who support managers through the experience of job loss and job change help the separated manager to remain healthy, find a better job sooner and retain a positive attitude toward the former employer. Managers who are dismissed abruptly as a consequence of organizational change but without such support are much more prone to illnesses and have less success in finding satisfactory and appropriate career alternatives.

The importance of continuing employer support through the phase of separation from the company is evident even when the manager leaves abruptly under what can be considered favorable circumstances. These can be early retirement or a mutually satisfactory separation agreement following such organizational events as a merger that results in a redundancy of managers and executives.

Latent dependencies are likely to surface after long established and often unacknowledged individual organization compatibilities are disrupted by evolutionary changes in organizational personality and practices. The past history of what the individual expects from the organization and the way in which the organization encourages such expectations is often a critical factor in determining resistance to change.

Generally, dependencies are personal and private psychological constellations with roots that go back to the early life history of the individual. As such, they are the responsibility of the individual to deal with in a personal way. The most common problem results when individuals wait until the change that has already taken place disrupts established compatibilities; only then do they realize that personal action is required to resolve personal dissatisfactions.

- In the case of the telephone operators who neglected personal relationships out of loyalty to the company, it was not until they became seriously depressed and bitterly disillusioned with the company that they realized the necessity to recoup the lost pleasures of family life.

- Managers who left their job without securing another one because they could not tolerate the suspense of the unknown might have reacted less precipitately under the same circumstances if they had well-defined career alternatives.

Remedial measures for the individual manager include periodic self-assessment of career plans, expectations, goals and alternatives, and a continuing awareness of the necessity for realistic career alternatives and options in anticipation of unexpected contingencies. All too often clear signs of the impending obsolescence of personal skills or changing organizational personnel needs are ignored by managers, who prefer to believe that the comfortable present will continue forever.

An obstacle to realistic self-assessment is that it often requires personal change in anticipation of challenges to individual organization compatibility. Rather than learn new skills or develop new options, the individual often becomes apprehensive and leaves personal career development to the initiative of the organization. The organization, in turn, may be perfectly satisfied with the way the manager is performing at the moment and does not require, and certainly does not encourage, training for jobs or functions for which the organization can see no immediate and practical use.

Thus, the personal predisposition to dependency on the organization combined with organizational practices that encourage dependency, create an implicit agreement that the manager's career needs will automatically be taken care of, and that job security is assured. When evolutionary forces change the organization's personality and practices, the dependent manager without immediate options resents the changes and various stress reactions are likely to develop over the longer term.

The perception of stressfulness comes not only from challenges to long-established patterns in the working and personal lives of employees, but also from their need to adapt to radically new aspects of an altered work environment.

- According to the *New York Times* article quoted, within A.T.&T., women now hold 36 percent of management jobs compared with 32.2 percent in 1972; women's employment in outside craft jobs has increased from 0.2 percent in 1972 to 4.7 percent at present; the number of men in operator jobs has surged from 1.4 percent in 1972 to 7.9 percent at present.

- Representation of minorities in management has risen from 4.6 percent in 1972 to 10.1 percent at present.

Oldtimers in Ma Bell who are disturbed by new management practices that stimulate internal competition are also disturbed by concurrent changes in sex roles at work, minority participation in management, and new attitudes toward authority. These new social changes heighten the oldtimers' perception of the workplace as different and consequently uncomfortable, less satisfying, and ultimately, more stressful.

Newcomers entering the workplace with these new values and new attitudes, but without the background awareness of established practices within the organization, have expectations that are different from those of older employees and therefore, feel less challenged by change. But they also feel less supported by established organizational social support systems.

In times of accelerating change at work, the new and the old employees are likely to view each other with suspicion as was the case with the telephone switchboard operators, and as is apparently the case over two decades later with newer and older employees at all levels. Differences in values between new and old employees are probably not as apparent when internal conditions are stable, but emerge as stressors under circumstances of organizational change.

### REFERENCE

*New York Times* (1979). A.T.&T. trying to lift morale: worker stress linked to rise in competition. April 14, 1979: p. 29.

# 10

# EXTERNAL SOURCES OF STRESS

Stressors from outside the organization shape the manager's work and roles and influence the interaction between career and personal life. Among the sources of external stress are:

- a rapidly changing business life.
- new social values and political developments that affect established organizational practices.
- shifting personal and family values that affect the context in which career-related personal crises arise.

Most often it is the cumulative effect of stressors from more than one source that triggers the adverse consequences of stress, consequences that are usually misattributed to only one area of the manager's life such as work pressure alone or personal problems alone. In fact, stress from only one source may not have the same adverse effect without the simultaneous impact of stress from other sources as well.

This interactive quality of stressors leads to "peaks of extraordinary stress," which implies a cumulative effect from several sources. "Career-related personal crises," refer to how managers perceive and react personally to the totality of interacting pressures, threats, challenges, and frustrations they may be experiencing at the time.

Since different stressors require different actions, a clear definition of stressors acting on the manager singly or in combination is important to the planning of coping strategies. This chapter:

- describes stressors originating from sources outside the organization that influence the manager's work and personal life.

- discusses recent research into stressful life events and the implications of research findings for strategies to cope with managerial stressors.

## CHANGING BUSINESS LIFE

Managers and executives today must cope with a rapidly accelerating pace of change in business life. They must plan and make strategic decisions in the face of mounting uncertainties introduced by external conditions over which they have no control: economic uncertainty, monetary instability, and new public and government initiatives. Business planning and strategy is falling victim to the tyranny of circumstance.

The energy crisis in 1975 is an example of such uncertainty. Companies affected by this crisis are well aware of the impact of external pressures on organizational practices. I had the opportunity to study the effect of exposure to prolonged periods of high work intensity under severe time pressure on a top management team. The company studied is known for its highly centralized management style, which I explored several years before by means of confidential interviews with approximately 100 managers and executives.

At that time (*pre-energy crisis*) there appeared to be a favorable balance of stress-producing and stress-modifying factors. The chief source of stress for staff members responding to initiatives from above was the uncertainty of whether or not support materials developed under time pressure were responsive to leadership needs.

Second in intensity, although no less important, was the concern expressed by many staff members that by responding to top priority leadership initiatives they would be left with insufficient time to meet their own previously assigned objectives. "With all these special projects initiated from above I'm afraid some of my own work will fall between the cracks and be overlooked."

Positive factors seemed to outweigh or modify the perceptions of stress. For one, involvement at the decision-making level, although pressured, generated a high degree of job satisfaction among supporting staff members. For another, all persons interviewed had great confidence in the judgment and competence of top management and in their ability to get the company through times that were challenging to all of business and industry.

From the *postenergy crisis interview data* it was clear that top management had felt the same pressures in responding to external government and public initiatives that staff members felt responding to top management initiatives. External demands were likely to be vaguely formulated and often contradictory. Top management was no longer able to control the use of their own time and consequently became concerned that their own company objectives would not be met. "With so much of our effort consumed in responding to external initiatives, often from unpredictable directions and without precedent, we're afraid some of our own work will fall between the cracks and be overlooked."

During the energy crisis all members of top management went through peaks of extraordinary stress. High work intensity under severe time pressure generally was not as stressful as the need to learn new functions or to perform in unaccustomed roles, or the need to do more than one type of work at the same time. Internal organizational pressures were generally less stressful than pressure from the outside. Frustrations encountered in trying to get the company's point of view across to friends and acquaintances was often mentioned as a source of intense stress.

The informal support systems that developed spontaneously among the management team to meet the challenges of the energy crisis proved to be particularly effective in modifying perceived stresses. As a team they drew closer together, met more often, and communicated more freely. The usual rivalries among units found in any large organization were missing.

Perhaps the most impressive development was a new personal support system—a short informal rap session before the start of the daily formal meeting. The rap session began as an opportunity for members to bring each other up to date on their most recent activities, and they began to use this opportunity to express personal frustrations and "blow off steam." All concerned found this informal departure from the usual formal meeting helpful.

Managers at all levels felt the impact of the energy crisis in their usual work. The farther removed managers were from the source of information about what was going on, the more prone they became to listen to rumor and hearsay, and the more uncertain about what and how much initiative or authority they should exercise. A broad, comprehensive communication system from top management to all employees was initiated to reduce the stress of uncertainty and of the unknown.

## NEW SOCIAL VALUES

New social values are challenging well-established conceptions of business practices and organizational behavior. The full impact of these challenges to accustomed management values, roles, and job demands has not yet been felt. With increasing frequency today's managers and executives are being confronted with the task of resolving differences between their own values and job demands and those evolving from such new social developments as:

- a growing emphasis on humanism and quality of work life at the expense of profitability and productivity.

- greater demands for involvement in the decision-making process by younger and better educated managers who are unwilling to accept close control and authoritarian practices.

- shifting social mores at work due to a greater representation of minority groups in management ranks, as well as an increasing number of assertive women managers who are challenging roles and behaving in ways heretofore reserved only for men.

- a trend toward corporate social responsiveness and accountability initiated through the efforts of business critics, environmentalists, consumer advocates, and public interest groups.

Companies are discovering that it makes bottom line sense to treat all employees supportively, to create a work environment of respect, dignity, and trust. In Sweden and Norway meaningful work, involvement in the decision-making process and factors related to the quality of work life for all employees are required by legislation. Cultural changes throughout society, such as the trend toward greater individual freedom in homes, schools, and communities, and the turning away from authoritarian values are reflected in new humanistic values in work organizations. Social changes are creating new expectations among employees as to how they are to be treated by their managers. In short, evolving ethics and values related to the quality of life (including the quality of work life) are redefining what the organization can require of the individual and what the individual can expect from the organization. In addition, business is now held responsible for the social consequences of its management of human resources.

Student (1978) considers the growing dissonance between the values held by managers and the demands of their jobs, to be a new, subtle and highly significant source of management stress.

*Today's managers are noticeably more humanistic in their values and in their approach to the management processes than were their predecessors, while business realities and business-role demands have changed very little. Emotional strain and feelings of tension, anxiety and a sense of futility can result from the inner conflict between a manager's needs for efficiency, profit, productivity and so forth and a heightened concern about the welfare and self-worth of the individuals who work for him or her.*

(STUDENT, p. 20)

Role conflict and situations that arouse contradictory values are known to evoke tensions, feelings of apathy or futility, and other stress responses. The potential for such stress responses develops when "new" managers have to perform in "old" business roles, or "old" managers have to establish and/or implement "new" decisions that are contrary to their values.

Generally, managers do what they are supposed to do unless the conflict is extreme, in which case various forms of resistance including sabotage are likely to develop. Conflicts usually surface under emergency conditions or in response to unexpected contingencies. Managers then tend to revert to their "true selves," and the internal dissonance between new and old values is felt more keenly. Conflict between the new and the old way also becomes personalized, resulting in lack of support, confidence, or trust among managers who hold different values.

### New political developments

Evolving socioeconomic conditions or new public and government initiatives may have the effect of changing the character and goals of the organization itself and thereby threaten the adequacy of fit between the job and the individual. For example, nationalistic trends and other initiatives of foreign governments have had a remarkable effect on Americans working in foreign assignments for multinational corporations with affiliates throughout the world.

Until the late 1960s United States managers and executives staffed the offices of these companies' foreign affiliates using work practices more or less like those at home. At that time most American Foreign Residents (AFRs) planned on an entire career of working and living abroad and looked forward to the financial benefits and ease of living associated with such work. They expected to shift continuously from one foreign post to another until retirement when they planned to build a home at their favorite vacation spot and live comfortably on the nest egg they had accumulated over the years.

AFRs were comfortable with their life style. "I've been with the company twenty-five years and I've moved nineteen times," said with great pride, was a frequent boast by expatriate families. Reentry into the United States would have put them at a competitive disadvantage with managers at the same level at headquarters, and positions with other divisions in the company were not easy to find. But reentry was regarded as a remote possibility of little concern.

During the 1970s, however, local social, political, and economic values have changed. The wave of intense nationalism that has swept the world has resulted in the nationalization of the local offices of United States companies, which involves replacing foreign employees with local personnel whenever possible. If appropriately trained personnel were not available to replace AFRs then the United States company was required to train local workers to do the job.

Relationships with host governments became sensitive and the political and social situations in these countries were often unstable and even explosive. With such changing conditions the personality requirements for AFRs changed rapidly. They now had to be diplomats, of greater than average physical health and emotional stability, willing to perform as skilled teachers, and able to tolerate the process of training their replacements, thereby rendering themselves obsolete.

Perhaps the most stressful development for AFRs was the radical shrinking in the number of positions available to them. No longer could they expect to move from one post to another until retirement when they could take their accumulated wealth and enjoy their leisure time. Reentry into the United States was now a virtual certainty at some point during a career of working abroad. The greatest problem for these career expatriates, so skilled in moving almost on a moment's notice from one post to another, was that they had no home base to go back to, no point of security and support to use in times of crisis. Reentry into the United States was extremely stressful as it meant the loss of a life style to which the expatriate and his family had become accustomed.

The stress impact of reentry into the United States was also increased precisely because it was not another totally unfamiliar foreign location in which the expatriate family expected to endure social isolation for a while until they became familiar with the language and local customs. They were experienced in handling those conditions. In their own country, but without a home base, surrounded by people like themselves, they somehow felt more isolated than ever before.

The shift in job structure and career expectations was extreme, sudden, unanticipated, and unprepared for because of the speed with which changing social, political, and economic values swept the world.

To be sure, a great deal of organizational restructuring has subsequently taken place to cope with and/or adapt to the changing conditions of living, working, and doing business abroad. Programs for selecting and preparing expatriate families for going abroad, providing support while on location, and again during the process of reentry into the home country are receiving serious attention. But the career expatriate without a home base, whose life style involves moving 29 times during 40 years of foreign service until retirement is a casualty of changing times.

## MANAGER'S PERSONAL LIFE

The peaks of stress and personal crises that managers go through are rarely related to the pressures and dynamics of the work environment alone. Most often stress and crises result from the interaction of organizational factors and other important influences in the manager's total life sphere, such as:

- competing personal, family, or social interests, goals, and responsibilities.

- changes in capacity, perspective, and self-image that accompany growth and development during adult life.

Stress that may result when organization pressures compete or conflict with the demands and responsibilities of the manager's personal life can be illustrated by considering the various problems that emerge around the issue of relocation.

Problems involving the relocation of employees and their families have become a serious management concern. For some time organizations have been finding it difficult to convince qualified managers to take highly desirable positions if the promotion requires transfer to another location. Quite often the positions are given to far less competent candidates whose primary qualification for the job is a willingness to move. Reluctance of families to change from one location to another, whether within the United States or abroad, has been increasing steadily over the past decade or more. Some companies are now willing to move to new communities in the hope of attracting qualified managers by offering more desirable living, as well as working conditions. Companies are also taking the serious risk of losing a significant number of their managers who choose to remain in the old familiar location rather than give up established supports to move to a supposedly more desirable community. To move or not to move has become a modern dilemma for management. To move or not to move is a dilemma for today's executive family as well.

Several recent developments have changed the priorities around which such family decisions are made:

**1**   The husband's career progression is no longer the family's primary concern. The wife's need to have roots within the community, her social adjustment, her career, or other personal interests are now given greater weight than they were ten or fifteen years ago.

**2**   The educational and social adjustment of teenaged children has become a serious concern since the upsurge in drug abuse and the challenge to establishment, sexual, and family values of a decade or two earlier. Stability of adjustment within the community over a period of several years during the high school experience has proved important to the avoidance of teenaged behavior problems. Family decisions today take this fact into account.

**3**   Younger employees often present a complicated relocation problem because the career of both husband and wife must be taken into consideration when changes are contemplated. Subtle adjustment complications that are beginning to surface in the two-career family will be discussed.

**4** The monetary rewards of promotion are often negated by the rising expenses of relocation, the costs of sending children to appropriate schools, and inflation.

## The decision to relocate

The following clinical interview illustrates a family problem that began to emerge with greater frequency during the 1960s and beyond, in which the decision to relocate was complicated by conflicting interests among family members.

Conventionally the manager (husband at that time) assumed the family would automatically go along with his career decisions and did not consult with them when offered a promotion that required relocation. The organization, making the same assumption, rarely gave the manager much time for self-assessment or family discussion to reach a consensus about relocation and job choice. Superiors at that time (some still think this way today) regarded a manager's reluctance to relocate as requested by the organization as an indication of poor motivation and lack of interest in getting ahead. It was shocking when managers began to say "No" to promotions if the position called for relocation. It became frustrating to management when their most desirable high-potential performers (the ones with the self-confidence to say "No") were reluctant to move as called for in the organization's career development plans.

In the 1960s it was not clear to the manager whether turning down a position for personal reasons would jeopardize career prospects. The manager assumed it would. Conflicted and uncertain, the manager might engage in decision-making discussions with the family feeling damned if he did move (against the wishes of some family members) or damned if he did not move (against the wishes of superiors).

More than likely the manager avoided such conflicts, by assuming family acquiescence to the move. Motivated by long-standing ambition to get ahead, he automatically made the commitment to accept the new working and living situation, then came home and instructed everyone to pack up within a few days and look for a new home and new schools in the new community.

*Today*, family consensus will probably be reached through a different route. Changing priorities around which family decisions are made place greater weight on factors already mentioned such as the interests of the spouse, the needs of teenaged children, and the relative lifestyle and economic advantages of the new location versus the old. And now the more complicated problems of the two-career couple raise an added requirement of the move, that is, appropriate and satisfactory employment for not one but two persons, each of whom may have career requirements that are difficult or even impossible to satisfy at some locations.

In any case, the process of reaching a family consensus prior to relocation, a process that includes self-assessment, discussion of trade-offs among family members, the meaning of giving up old supports, and the prospects for developing new supports at the new location is now respected as an important step in the job decision process. Factors to be considered in the family decision-making process may be new and changing with the changes in the personal and social values of society. But the consequences of *not* reaching a consensus, or of violating the consensus once one has been reached, remain the same over time in terms of subsequent work and personal maladjustment and stress-related health problems. These factors are demonstrated by the illustration that follows.

## INTERVIEW 11 – All Is Lost

Carl Hoffman, a large athletically built engineer in his late forties was so agitated at the start of his consultation in my private office that he was unable to sit in the patient's chair. Instead, he paced the floor smoking one cigarette after another, all the while trying hard to control a coarse tremor that was clearly evident, much to his embarrassment, whenever he put his hand to his mouth.

Following a performance appraisal by his boss the afternoon before, he had been tense and agitated exactly as he was in my office. He had not slept at all that night. By early morning he felt so desperate that he made up his his mind to speak to someone about it as soon as possible.

That morning he and his company physician talked for quite a while. It was clear that Carl was going through an acute personal crisis triggered by the performance appraisal, which he considered to be unfair and overly critical. In the opinion of his physician, Carl was overreacting to that experience because of a combination of personal and work-related concerns that required sorting out. He was referred to me for emergency "crisis intervention."

I was surprised when he entered the office unaccompanied by a wife, friend, coworker or boss. Usually anyone that agitated appeals to someone close for support and assistance under trying and unusual circumstances. Emotional distress is difficult to bear in any case, but desperation, self-doubt, humiliation, and the feeling of failure tend to escalate rapidly when not kept under control by positive feedback from others.

Carl was eager to tell his story. As an engineer working in a small field unit in the southwest his greatest ambition had been to be promoted to the New York office. His opportunity had come a little over two years before when he was offered a promotion from the regional office to Division Headquarters in New York. He seized the opportunity, and had been working for the same boss ever since.

Once in New York he never really got into the job. Concentration seemed to be very difficult and he found it hard to sleep in his new living quarters. Confidence was replaced by self-doubt. He wondered if he had what it takes. Maybe he was promoted beyond the level of his competence. He must have been a fool to think he could make it in the big time. Maybe he shouldn't have transferred at all. Things were so much more expensive in New York. It was hardly worth it financially even though his rent wasn't very much because he lived alone in one hotel room and ate his big meal in the company cafeteria at noon. A picture of depression was unfolding—self-depreciation, sleep disturbance, poor concentration, and pessimism. And why was he living alone?

Carl went on. His concentration was so disturbed at times that meeting deadlines became difficult. He told his boss he couldn't make the deadline for one project but his boss wanted the job done on time anyway. At a department meeting Carl presented the material he had developed and his boss criticized him publicly. Carl felt humiliated.

At the performance review his boss mentioned that particular assignment as an example of why Carl was not up to the job. Although the word was not mentioned, his boss seemed to be implying that he should be demoted to a lower level more in keeping with his capacities.

At this point in the interview Carl burst into tears. "I sacrificed everything to take the promotion and come to New York. Now they are thinking of demoting me after I burned my bridges behind me." Then Carl described how the decision to relocate was made and the consequences of that decision.

He and his wife hadn't been getting along too well even before the relocation problem came up. She complained about his being so involved with his work that he neglected his personal life. His wife had just taken a job to keep herself busy now that their three children were old enough to take care of themselves.

When the promotion was offered he accepted, then went home and told his family about it. His wife expressed dissatisfaction because she was tired of moving, had roots in the community, and had a job to keep her busy. She protested a great deal but he insisted. Then she told him to go on to New York by himself and she would follow.

He took a room in a residence hotel and started the new job. Within a few weeks his wife consulted a lawyer and initiated divorce proceedings, proclaiming that she would get as much as she could from him because he had ruined her life. To his surprise the children seemed to side with their mother. Because he felt guilty he gave his wife as much as she wanted of their possessions, the house, and their savings. He kept little or nothing for himself.

The week before the meeting when he gave the presentation that was criticized by his boss, he had been involved in the last step of a bitter court battle during which he sued to recover some of what he had given to his wife in the divorce settlement. On the day of the meeting he learned he had lost the case.

When it appeared that his boss was considering demoting Carl, the futility and irony of the situation struck him. He was enraged. He had nothing left of his personal life. Now he was losing what little he had left of his career and his pride in his work. By this point in the consultation, agitation had given way to depression. I was concerned about what appeared to be his total isolation in life. Isolation plus bitterness about having lost everything he had ever cherished—a home, the respect of his children, a successful career—point to a potentially dangerous, self-destructive frame of mind.

Just as we were about to conclude the session he mentioned his girlfriend for the first time. "I hope she won't think I'm too much of a failure. I was hoping we could get married." A ray of hope! All was not lost!

We discussed how his depression had dampened his work performance. What he thought to be incompetence was actually the consequence of depressed thinking and retarded initiative resulting from his reaction to his personal situation. Living in isolation made everything seem worse; he was cut off from any source of support. He was granted a short medical disability leave from work to give him time to recover from his depression and to put his personal life in order before facing the demands of his work in terms of concentration and initiative.

### Comment

With a few more sessions Carl Hoffman's depression lifted. He did marry his girlfriend and they have remained together. Yes, he was demoted, only to be reinstated to his former position once the depression had lifted and he was capable of performing up to his potential. So far as I know, he was forever pursued by his first wife in her bitterness over his having abandoned her when he accepted the promotion and relocation to Headquarters.

Carl Hoffman was clearly a candidate for professional counseling. His psychic pain was severe and disabling. He had lost perspective and could neither plan for nor visualize the future. He had lost all hope that he could work his way out of the acute career-related personal crisis in which he found himself.

It is doubtful that the favorable outcome ultimately achieved in this case could have been accomplished without skilled professional crisis intervention. But individuals do not have to be in extremis, with intense unbearable or disabling psychic pain before seeking professional help.

An opportunity to ventilate concerns in a professional, confidential, and appropriately supportive atmosphere is usually sufficient to bring about the necessary relief in cases of personal crisis originating in an organizational setting in which individuals have been functioning well until then.

### The two-career couple

Changing social values are influencing conventional business practices and the manager's accustomed working roles. New social forces are also having a profound effect on the manager's personal life. Nowhere are these changes more evident than in the case of the young, two-career couple involved in a contemporary triangle, the complicated interrelationships of the working life–personal life–partner's working life triangle. A new sense of woman's entitlement, the desire of young women to take advantage of developing opportunities, and economic necessity are forces behind the rising incidence of two-career couples.

This section does not discuss the older wife and mother who turns her attention to a career to cope with the emptiness of not feeling needed after children grow up and leave home. Her original ego ideal (the type of person she wished to become) included the image of herself as being first and foremost a wifely, motherly, supportive figure. Rather, this section discusses younger women, who today are more ambitious and self-assertive in terms of career. Their attitudes about family formation reflect this difference. Having a family is being postponed or discarded entirely in favor of pursuing available career prospects. Where there are children their care must often be left to others during working hours.

Flexible work schedules, part-time and consulting relationships, and professional work performed at home are all contemporary accommodations to the problems of maintaining a career and at the same time discharging child care responsibilities. Flexibility involves a trade-off. Women (and now men also) are willing to forego the fringe benefits of regular employee status for the greater freedom and control of their time provided by these different types of relationships with the employer organization.

Another accommodation to the rising demand among women for even broader career choice is the sharing of domestic responsibilities (including postnatal child care) between partners. Younger couples find domestic job sharing easier than older generations who are more involved in the self-esteem, strength–weakness, masculinity–femininity connotations of social and interpersonal roles.

If new social values do not drive more women into careers, contemporary economic conditions will. It is now necessary for both partners to work if a couple is to maintain a desired life style, or pay the mortgage, or simply keep up with inflation.

Self-assessment, job choice, and the decision to relocate are based on a rather complicated set of conditions for the young two-career couple. Examined from the point of view of dollars earned per hour of work, the job of the partner who earns more will be preferred over the job that pays less. This choice may be made even when the lower paying job has greater prospects for future advancement, but involves moving to an area where the partner with the better paying job may not be able to find as advantageous a position.

Complications caused by two-career couples are just beginning to surface. For the manager it means choosing a job based on more varied and complex priorities than those motivating managers just a decade ago. For the organization it means changing policies about hiring both partners, and new uncertainties about career development programs. The work of the personnel director has become more complicated. "If you want one member of a couple you have to worry about finding a job for the other. We train managers knowing that somewhere down the line they will have to relocate if they want to get ahead. Now we have to take the risk that after managers are trained they may not go along with the relocation because of the partner's conflicting career plans."

If the two-career couple now complicates job choice and manager–organization fit, what is likely to happen when the careers of both manager and partner progress, become important sources of satisfaction, fulfillment and self-esteem for each, but also lead in different directions? Such two-career-related personal crises are appearing in the offices of psychotherapists in ever increasing numbers. What will happen when they both go through the midlife transition (around age forty) at the same time, and seek new and possibly conflicting sources of self-definition and self-realization?

How these problems will be resolved remains to be seen. But with the present emphasis on alternative life styles, and the absence of barriers to separation, probably more and more managers and executives in midcareer will be living alone or as single parents. The literature on the health and adjustment of separated, divorced, or otherwise unattached adults living alone (with low social support) leads me to speculate that unattached managers or executives in their early forties are members of a population at risk in terms of the adverse consequences of stressful life events (including work events).

One other complication has already emerged. The popular phrase "stress has no gender" refers to the fact that women managers in alarming numbers are falling victim to the same kinds of stress-related health problems that used to be seen almost exclusively among aspiring and achieving male managers and executives. In short, new social values, new sources of stress and new

organizational practices are all converging to create an atmosphere of changing conditions, uncertainty, and above all disruption of the more conventional, well-established support systems
both internal and external to organization life.

Undoubtedly the characteristic career-related personal crises
of the future will be different from the ones now known. The
traditional sources of stress acting on managers and executives
today will be described here. By the time we become thoroughly
familiar with these sources and have practiced strategies to cope
with them, modern trends in a fast moving world will have changed
conditions just enough to force us to take a fresh approach to each
new crisis as it arises.

Present and anticipated complications in career pathways, job
design, and personnel practices that result from the increasing number of young two-career couples confirm what is already known
about management stress from previous chapters: that we must
look beyond stressors in the workplace to the accumulated effects
of all stressful life events if we are to understand and cope with
the origins and consequences of career-related crises in the lives of
managers and executives.

## STRESSFUL LIFE EVENTS

Stressful life events are those that require adaptive responses from
the individual involved. Any change in the individual's personal or
work life will be perceived as stressful if ongoing life patterns are
threatened.

Formal characteristics of stressors (intensity, magnitude, duration, predictability and novelty, timing and context) influence the
individual's perception of them as threatening. An awareness of
the effects of stressor characteristics is important to the understanding of the stressfulness of organizational change or how work
pressure and stressful life events interact to produce career-related
personal crises.

### Intensity (rate of change)

There is a positive correlation between perceived rate of change
and the experience of anxiety and stress, particularly when that
change is regarded as undesirable (Lauer, 1974). While both societal
and personal changes are significantly related to stress level, the

contribution of societal change is greater ("The world we live in is changing so fast that it leaves me breathless at times."). Thus organizational change during intense societal change (economic recession, energy crises, new social values, new governmental initiatives) will be perceived as more stressful than similar changes initiated when external conditions are more stable.

### Magnitude and duration

The magnitude of the stressful event (degree of departure from average conditions) directly corresponds to its impact on the individual and the extent of consequent disability. Individual characteristics or predisposition or social support systems can overcome the effect of stressors of lower magnitude. However, the more extreme the stressful situation, the more variance in outcome is accounted for by the stressor rather than by other factors such as individual difference or support systems. Sufficient stress (exposure to concentration camp conditions, for example) will induce an acute stress reaction in all so exposed, irrespective of variation in predisposition or coping capacity.

Thus, it is totally unreasonable to expect managers or executives to be invulnerable to *all* stressors, or to consider stress reactions signs of weakness. Duration of stress is important, but variable in its consequences. Some individuals, predisposed to stress reactions, will manifest their vulnerability soon after exposure to threatening events. Prolonged exposure to stressors of sufficient magnitude (job insecurity, job loss, uncertainty, job complexity, or ambiguity) is likely to induce severe or pervasive illness consequences in a large segment of the population so exposed.

### Predictability and novelty

Unpredictable events have a more adverse effect than those that are anticipated or for which individuals are prepared on the basis of prior experience. (Rabkin and Struening, 1977). Unanticipated or unpredictable events evoke a sense of helplessness or uncertainty (a state of hesitation or doubt about the appropriate response), which magnify the stress reaction. The inability to control or even anticipate the occurrence of stressors enhances their negative effect on behavior. This impact is seen in the individuals' lowered frustration tolerance, less efficient performance, impaired ability to solve problems or resolve conflicts, and panic reactions to the unknown. Realistic anticipation of and preparation for stressful events seem to modify their adverse impact. Learning what to expect and when to expect it enables individuals to differentiate between what is dangerous and what is safe, and to develop coping mechanisms that reduce the actual danger, panic, or fear response, and the eventual stress consequences. Thus, if managers are trained to anticipate the stressfulness of characteristic career transitions then they will be able to cope more effectively in a transition. Learning what to expect can result from observation of others; instruction by others, including a godfather or mentor; organizational training programs with a managerial stress component; group cohesiveness, and peer group or personal support systems within as well as outside the organization. Novelty enhances the impact of stressful events. Training that simulates exposure to new situations generally increases tolerance for the threatening aspects of stressful conditions and helps produce appropriate responses to them.

### Timing and context

Numerous stressors operating simultaneously or in sequence have greater impact than stressors that occur singly. Stressful life events or a poor state of health are potential contributors to overload when these occur simultaneously or in sequence with stressors at work.

Brown (1974) found that the biographical circumstances surrounding an important stressful life event predicted such consequences as depression as well or better than the individual's self-reported measure of threat. Thus a scientific rationale exists for delaying relocation or job change, (including promotion and favorable change) until the manager's life situation and/or health improve sufficiently to prevent stress overload by the addition of managerial stress. From Brown's work on the relationship between life changes and depression, it would seem that both the manager and the organization are in a position to make such judgments. Organizations regard these judgments as a prerogative of management. All too often the manager is reluctant to ask for a delay or alteration in management's plans for fear of being considered disloyal or poorly motivated, thereby jeopardizing future career opportunities.

Scientific evidence would seem to indicate that a judicious postponement of change until such time as the manager's total life situation can withstand the new stress load may preserve the manager's effectiveness.

### Vulnerability to illness

Changes, transitions and sudden events heighten vulnerability to illness by dissolving former social support systems, leaving people unprotected and unprepared for the new experiences to which they are exposed. Individual vulnerability to illness is enhanced once the social buffer against stressors has been weakened or removed.

Research indicates a temporal relationship between an increase in the number of recent life changes which require adaptive responses from the person involved (stressful life events) and the onset of various stress-related psychological and physical disorders (Rabkin and Struening, 1976).

Environmentally induced stressful life events do not actually cause disease but serve as precipitating factors, influencing the timing but not the type of disorder. Thus, stressors:

- act as precipitating factors in chronic diseases.
- affect susceptibility to infectious diseases.
- can be a component of any disease.

Where there is the presence of a disease agent (tubercle bacillus) or a predisposition to disease (high serum cholesterol, depressive tendency) illness onset results from the interaction of:

- stressful environmental conditions and recent life changes.
- individual perceptions of these events as stressful.
- available social support systems.
- individual adaptive coping behavior.

Many researchers have scaled life events in terms of their intensity and the length of time necessary to accommodate or adapt. Their hope is to create rating scales for use in identifying stress levels and predicting susceptibility to disease or vulnerability to stress-related disorders. Positive relationships have been found between the number and intensity of recent life events and:

- sudden cardiac deaths, myocardial infarctions.
- accidents, injuries.

- tuberculosis, leukemia, multiple sclerosis, diabetes.
- the gamut of minor medical complaints.
- poor work performance.
- indices of general levels of mental health.
- mild depression.
- suicide and other mental symptoms and disorders.

In addition, life events have been related to the course of illness and recovery.

The use of a schedule of stressful life events (both work and personal) most characteristic of the lives of managers and executives might be valuable as a measure of recent stress levels and vulnerability within a specific management group or as a predictor of the onset of stress-related disability should this group become subject to additional organization-initiated changes (stressful life events, by definition).

It is encouraging to note that recent research structured along these lines shows great promise. The introduction of new lists of life events chosen in accordance with the goals of a given study and the characteristics of the populations studied has greatly increased the correlation between stressful life events sampled and episodes of illness (Rahe, 1974).

As a matter of fact, it would be a valuable learning experience if a management education program were to include a module on management stress in which the group is required to construct and evaluate a schedule of stressful events in the life of a manager. From a review of the various sources of management stress mentioned in previous chapters, the schedule adapted to the life of the manager or executive working in an organizational setting might include ordinary and extraordinary work pressures, organizational change events, career progression events, and events in the manager's personal life most likely to interact with work pressures to trigger career-related personal crises.

### REFERENCES

Brown, G. W. (1974). Meaning, measurement, and stress of life events. In B. S. Dohrenwend and B. P. Dohrenwend (eds.) *Stressful Life Events.* New York: Wiley.

Lauer, R. (1974). Rate of change and stress: a test of the "Future Shock" hypothesis. *Social Forces* **52**:510–516.

Rabkin, J. G., and E. L. Struening (1976). Social change, stress, and illness: a selective literature review. *Psychoanalysis and Contemporary Science* **5**:573–624.

Rahe, R. H. (1974). The pathway between subjects' recent life changes and their near-future illness reports: representative results and methodological issues. In B. S. Dohrenwend and B. P. Dohrenwend (eds.) *Stressful Life Events.* New York: Wiley.

Student, K. R. (1978). Personnel's newest challenge: helping to cope with greater stress. *The Personnel Administrator* (November):20–24.

# 11

# COPING WITH STRESS: ORGANIZATIONAL STRATEGIES

The recent surge of management interest in reducing executive stress reflects an awareness that the functioning of key individuals responsible for planning strategies, making critical decisions, and establishing personnel policies has a significant impact on the health and productivity of all employees. The quality of leadership determines both the personality of that organization and its chances of survival. Generally, companies are discovering that treating *all* employees supportively and helping them help themselves makes sense. This view has set in motion a wide variety of employer-initiated programs to maintain employee health and well-being, to prevent manifestations of strain from progressing to actual illness, and to provide employees with the opportunity to gain personal insights, which will help them cope with stress both on and off the job.

## PROGRAMS TO MAINTAIN HEALTH

Programs to maintain health are standard practice for large organizations today. These include periodic health examinations for selected (particularly older and long service) employees; physical fitness and exercise programs, and educational programs that focus on improving habits that threaten health (smoking, improper diet, excessive drinking).

### Tension reducing and relaxation techniques

Tension reducing and relaxation techniques are gaining in popularity as ways of neutralizing manifestations of strain that predispose to illness. Specific techniques range from biofeedback, meditation, and behavior modification, to changing the pace of an overloaded business day or advice about the use of leisure time. These programs are more likely to be used by upper levels of management. They are appealing because they are easy to teach, depend upon the initiative of the individual, and do not involve intrusion of the organization into the personal life of the employee. However, they do not affect the sources of stress or improve the individual's psychological adaptive coping strategies.

### Employee assistance programs

Employee assistance programs have become standard practice for large organizations. Originally, these programs were initiated by employers to deal with employees whose decline in job performance was health related, usually due to some form of alcoholism. As these programs demonstrated their usefulness, rehabilitating up to 80 percent of affected individuals, self-referred employees became motivated to seek assistance for other types of personal problems as well. Presently, over 2000 companies in the United States provide some form of in-house or outside confidential counseling service on a voluntary basis for a broad variety of problems including acute personal crises, advice about financial and legal matters, and preparation for the anticipated changes in life style following retirement. Generally, employee assistance programs are more commonly used by lower levels of management.

Group process experiences are designed to facilitate a better understanding of human relationships, techniques of communicating and responding, a greater awareness of what goes on among people in groups, how it goes on, and what kind of impact the participant has on others. However, confrontation groups, T-groups, and communications activities are becoming less popular with management. On balance, attendees claim such programs help them feel more comfortable with themselves and relate better to others. Management does not see evidence that this sense of personal well-being is reflected in increased effectiveness on the job. Generally, the do-it-yourself ethic, and the forces that inhibit the expression of affection, support, and approval in an organizational setting still prevail.

It is rare to find an employer-initiated program designed to provide specific insights into how to anticipate or resolve career-related *personal* crises. Even less frequent are programs that provide for the active participation of managers at all levels in a critical review of organizational structure, practices, and dynamics with a view toward finding creative solutions to standard management stressors. Active involvement of managers in planning, problem solving, and policy making is potentially the most valuable stress management technique. Yet these activities are the very ones that are reserved for planning groups or high level policy-making bodies such as an executive committee. Such issues are rarely referred to lower levels of management for their input and suggested solutions.

No matter how valuable employer-initiated stress management programs may be, responsibility for formulating and maintaining a successful coping strategy ultimately rests with the individual manager. There are many compelling reasons why the individual should not depend upon the organization alone to provide the stimulus for personal stress management.

The problem of assigning responsibility for interventive actions and preventive programs is difficult. Ideally, it should be a partnership effort to protect an established individual–organization compatibility from the challenging forces of organizational evolution, individual life cycle changes, and external threats to the survival of the enterprise.

In practical terms, however, individual and organizational interests in the outcome of the coping process may differ widely. Coping by leaving a stressful job for a more compatible environment elsewhere may be a desirable solution for the individual, but an unacceptable one for the organization where it is considered an act of disloyalty because it represents a loss of an investment in the training and expertise of an experienced manager. Many organizations discourage looking outside while things are going well inside. Very few organizations teach out-placement techniques as part of standard management education. The unwritten ethics of organizations serve to discourage awareness of approaching job–person misfits or dead-end career pathways until it is too late.

Mounting stress within the individual may be an early warning signal of such an impending danger. All too often the threat of exposing anxiety about performance, or ill health, or fears of incompetence, or any signal that there is something wrong forces managers to suppress or deny problems until it is too late.

Actually, the most satisfied, therefore devoted, employee is the one who remains not out of dependency or lack of alternatives but out of choice because that career pathway is the most desirable of all possible alternatives explored. Yet few managers as a matter of strategy seek to develop viable alternatives to their present positions, or to keep options open as protection against unexpected contingencies.

### RESISTANCE TO CHANGE

All interventive actions involve change. And any change is stressful. Thus the paradox that action designed to reduce old stress is very likely to produce new stress. Change accomplished gradually through established channels and standard practices is always less stressful than more sudden or radical change associated with special improvement programs.

Actions that increase the supportive context within an organization are ideally suited to accomplish gradual change through the usual events in the manager's ordinary work. For example:

• A strong effort can be made to give managers a clear understanding of how their performance is regarded by superiors during *performance appraisals,* or during the process of establishing mutually agreed-upon annual objectives. Removing ambiguity about how performance is regarded by superiors will give the manager feedback necessary for informed self-assessment, job choice, and career planning.

• The use of *usual communication channels* to define how much leeway individuals have in turning down the offer of a new assignment, and under what circumstances this can be done, will help the manager make better choices and cope more effectively once choices have been made.

• Training that increases the manager's awareness of the process of coping, when combined with the establishment of *organization-supported channels to confidential counseling and advice,* can be a remarkably effective means of reducing the stigma usually associated with seeking support.

Abrupt or sudden change through improvement programs that influence job design, allocation of authority and responsibility, or other accustomed practices will create new stress. New stress results from the challenging of established power structures, communications networks, interpersonal relationships, and the informal systems that get things done. Even when there is general agreement that a particular improvement program is desirable, and after considerable effort has been dedicated to its planning and development, characteristic resistances to change are provoked for a wide variety of reasons once the program is initiated.

Resistance can be anticipated from individuals whose power base, authority, or status might appear to be affected. Or they may resist improvements just because such improvements challenge accustomed practices that have been taken for granted for so long they have become unquestioned modes of doing the ordinary day-to-day work.

During the period of most rapid change the environment may appear more rather than less challenging, leading sceptics and those who are unconvinced of the need for change to claim "we were better off the way it was before."

Change, even change for the better, requires agreement that it is necessary, useful, or inevitable so that all individuals involved will go along with a minimum of resistance and discomfort. Preventive programs to cope with a problem *before* undesirable stress consequences appear are particularly difficult to initiate without widespread conviction that change is necessary. As described by Drucker (1971) the Japanese system of management involves personnel at all levels in the process of thinking through the need for change, which postpones action until consensus is achieved. Once change is initiated, however, there is little or no resistance since familiarity and acceptance has been accomplished in advance.

The process of thinking through the question, "Do we have a problem?" may be the most effective stress-reducing strategy of all. "What actions should be taken?" can be decided only after the problem has been defined. Thinking through a problem promotes an awareness of the issues and prepares individuals for the changes to come. Change, once initiated, is then perceived as anticipated and familiar, and is more readily accepted. When individuals have been involved in the process of planning change, by the time that change actually comes about it is likely to appear as gradual and therefore less stressful.

Generally, management's attitudes toward accommodation to the human aspects of management stress and organizational change is thought to range from disinterested to resistant. In my opinion indifference and resistance are based on an incomplete awareness of the psychosocial or relationship components of management stress, compounded by uncertainty about how to integrate available information about individual reactions to stress into organizational policies and practices.

It has been my experience from stress surveys and other in-depth interviews, that for the manager, conviction and creative problem solving follow comprehension of basic issues. Comprehension is accomplished after thoughtful, open-minded consideration of the question, "Do we have a problem?" It is the behavioral scientist's role through training, consultation, and feedback, to increase the manager's or executive's awareness of the nature of managerial stressors and the various means of coping with them. The choice of what to do once the problem is defined is up to the individual manager or management.


### INTERVENTION POINTS

Organizational strategies to cope with stress can be described according to where in the stress process the constructive action is applied. From a review of the Stress Process Model (Fig. 1.1, page 5) it is apparent that strategies can be categorized as interventive actions that:

1  have a direct effect on the stressor.

2  strengthen support systems to reduce the threat impact of stressors.

3  increase the harmony between the characteristics of the individual and the environment.

4  encourage personal support to buffer against the adverse consequences of stress.

5  reduce undesirable stress reactions.

6  treat the illness and maladjustment consequences of stress.

Table 11.1 lists organizational strategies to cope with stress in categories and serves as a summary of principles for coping and interventive actions proposed in earlier chapters.

TABLE 11.1    *Coping with management stress: organizational strategies.*

1. Act directly on the stressor

|  | Stressor | Action |
|---|---|---|
| • Factors intrinsic to the job | Gap between responsibilities and authority delegated to carry out these responsibilities | Delegate sufficient influence or authority to carry out assigned responsibilities |
|  | Insufficient control of work initiatives | Involve managers in the planning of work objectives; obtain managers' agreement to assigned objectives |
|  | Job complexity | Reduce job complexity by limiting the number of boundary and reporting relationships; by reducing the variety of managers' roles; by providing managers with sufficient time and opportunity to learn new tasks |
|  | Intense work pressure | Reduce work pressures (heavy work load, unrealistic time pressure, responsibility for managing people, job complexity, intense striving); avoid simultaneous pressures |
|  | Intense job demands for striving | Reduce job demands (for striving competitiveness, productivity, advancement); balance demands for striving with sources of satisfaction (accomplishment, promotion, financial or status rewards) |
|  | Unclear job requirements | Clarify job requirements, reporting relationships, objectives, priorities |
| • Organizational structure | Hierarchial structure that limits managers' involvement and control | Encourage planning and decision making by consensus; participative management |

TABLE 11.1 (cont'd)

| Stressor | | Action |
|---|---|---|
| | Reduced opportunities at the top of the organizational structure | Eliminate levels of authority, where possible; provide for second career and out-placement training; late career planning; portable pension system |
| • Organizational change | Threat to established harmony between managers and their position in the organization | Institute programs to manage organizational change that provide managers with a clear understanding of why the change is necessary, and modes of action whereby managers can participate in the change |

2. Reinforce support systems

| | | |
|---|---|---|
| • Performance appraisal process | Ambiguity or lack of feedback about how performance is regarded by superiors | Institute performance appraisal system that gives credit for accomplishments; provides information about how current performance is regarded by superiors, about opportunities for advancement, and about managements' appraisal of managers' potential for advancement |
| • Career development program | Uncertainty about future job prospects (fears of redundancy, obsolescence, forced early retirement), frustration at having reached a career ceiling, fears of entering external job market | Institute a career development program for every manager that includes continuing training in new skills, second career and out-placement training, flexible late career job structure |
| • Management education | Peaks of extraordinary stress and career-related personal crises that are related to transitions and changes in work and personal life | Institute training programs to prepare managers for the stressfulness of career transitions and changing personal goals that accompany personal maturity |
| | External pressures from government and public | Train managers to become aware of and to anticipate |

TABLE 11.1 (cont'd)

|  | Stressor | Action |
|---|---|---|
|  | initiatives and changing social values that threaten established organizational practices | the impact of external pressures and to plan accordingly |
| • Organizational behavioral norms | Conventional executive coping style that regards indications of distress as weakness and discourages managers from seeking help while coping with stress | Recognize a more realistic coping style that provides support for managers under stress through shared experiences with colleagues and awareness of anticipated crises and transitions |

3. Maintain harmony between the manager and the work environment

| • Programs to maintain good health | Poor health is a stressor as well as a consequence of stress | Institute organizational programs to help managers maintain good health, including a periodic comprehensive health assessment and specific programs to maintain fitness and control excessive eating, drinking, smoking, and high blood pressure |
|---|---|---|
| • Individual growth and development | Managers' goals and characteristics may change as they go through the various phases of life, thereby creating incompatibilities between the characteristics of the individual and the requirements of the job | Design jobs, benefits and compensation systems, and assign tasks to accommodate the changes that result from individual growth and development |
| • Self-assessment and job choice | Each job choice or decision to relocate raises the possibility of a misfit between the new environment and managers' personal interests, personalities, professional skills, family needs and interests, and overall life style | Provide opportunities for managers to realistically assess the fit between individual needs and characteristics and the new environment through realistic job previews, opportunities for periodic stress review and individual counseling |

TABLE 11.1 (cont'd)

---

4. Enhance personal support

- Use senior managers as advisors to young managers
- Organize self-help groups of individuals sharing the stressful experiences of organizational life
- Add a stress review component to the periodic comprehensive health examination provided for managers
- Provide a personal stress counseling service (see Chapter 14)

5. Reduce adverse effects of stress reactions

- Provide an in-house or outside comprehensive health maintenance program to encourage physical fitness at all times, and to provide programs to control weight, smoking, blood pressure
- Use relaxation techniques, as necessary, to control anxiety and tension
- Use outside counseling resources to relieve distress associated with peaks of stress and personal crises
- Provide advice and counsel to those who are depressed or without energy (experiencing burnout) or who are prone to excessive striving (coronary-prone personality)

6. Treat the illness and maladjustment consequences of stress

- Provide medical benefits for employees and their dependents that include a mental wellness component
- Institute employee assistance programs that include a treatment referral service for troubled employees
- Design programs to deal with such maladjustment consequences of stress as: individual and organizational burnout; coronary-prone managers and their work environment; the problem of discouraged or redundant managers in late career
- Provide a personal stress counseling program

---

The following chapter discusses the role of the organization's social support system (support systems and personal support) as a component of a broad range of strategies to cope with management stress.

Several strategies listed in Table 11.1 may be included in a comprehensive program to cope with an important area of management stress. The next section illustrates how strategies can be combined into a program to deal with the characteristic problems of managers in late career.

### Coping with the stress of late career

Stressors require action. But all too often the action taken is the nonaction of waiting for the stressor to pass. For example, the manager in late career with an unsatisfying and often non-essential job, often waits for the stressor (role stress) to disappear through the passage of time. The organization may also wait for the problem to disappear when the manager reaches retirement age or becomes distressed enough to take early retirement and leave without full benefits.

There are many alternatives to nonaction depending on the reasons why late career problems develop.

Characteristic problems of late career and the principal reasons for the development of such problems can be categorized as follows:

**1** *Approaching Fifty and Obsolescence*—Advancement-discouraged managers will cling to the status quo because of the stigma that exists in the outside job market against hiring and training older, higher salaried persons.

**2** *Waiting to Retire*—Advancement-discouraged managers in their early fifties tend to abandon efforts at career planning because of "being locked into company benefit plans."

**3** *Early Retirement Conflict*—Managers who wish to opt out by taking early retirement rather than making the effort to job hunt, retrain, or relocate also fear the financial problems of reduced income.

**4** *I'll Work Until Seventy*—Economically secure managers who require the recognition, respect, status, and self-fulfillment provided by their present position tend to shun early retirement or further career-life planning.

**5** *Dependence on the Organization*—Many managers who have been in the same position for a long time would like to change career directions but do not know how. They tend to become dependent upon the organization, expect to be provided with satisfactory employment as a reward for long and loyal service, and feel betrayed when these expectations are not met.

**6** *Declining Performance*—Managers who have advanced beyond their competence or seem to burn out with age and can no longer perform as before become frustrating disposition problems.

Management prefers not to retain older managers who fail to meet requirements and block career pathways for others.

7   *Up or Out*—Older managers often accept assignments that are inappropriate to their competence or interests in order to survive within the organization. They expect an up-or-out, take-it-or-leave-it management attitude and are themselves unprepared to switch to more appropriate alternative careers because of lack of planning.

### Age discrimination

Traditional practices and policies may eventually be declared to be age discriminatory. Management education programs and career development practices favor younger managers. Organizational change places older persons at a disadvantage.

1   Considerable management attention is devoted to the establishment of career pathways for younger managers. Little consideration is given to end-of-career planning and placement for long-service employees.

2   Management education programs emphasize the training and development of younger persons for a career within the company. They fail, however, to anticipate the need among older, longer-service employees for a continuous process of learning, redefining goals, reappraising skills, job satisfaction, and growth. Younger employees receive help with their first career. Older employees also require help to remain valuable to the company or to develop second careers. Such help might include out-placement or preparation for retirement.

3   Organizational change places older employees at a disadvantage. Younger, more trainable managers with greater potential are preferred over less flexible longer-service managers. In the process, older managers who are equally qualified for the same job are often selected against in favor of younger persons for whom the position is a step up in the development program.

4   Benefit plans lock older managers into a struggle to survive the late-career years. Retirement without discount is usually possible only at a much later age than the average age at which careers of long-service managers and executives are terminated.

5   With the present focus on Equal Employment Opportunities, the question of age discrimination will undoubtedly be in the thoughts of personnel undergoing the stress of organizational change. Accusations of age discrimination can be expected from those who tend to project blame onto others (including the organization) for disappointment, misfortunes, loss of status, lowered self-esteem or betrayed expectations suffered as a consequence of change.

### Principles for change

Problems that develop in late career are a liability to both management and the manager. Successful resolution should result in mutual satisfaction. It should be possible to salvage the considerable experience, talent, and wisdom that is currently being wasted as a consequence of these problems.

The organization and the individual share responsibility for the resolution of career problems. The organization's responsibilities are:

- through education, to alert individuals to the factors that cause these problems.

- to provide creative planning of flexible end-of-career patterns, benefit plans, alternative kinds of employment and separation procedures, in order to increase the options available to relatively immobilized longer-service employees, managers, and executives.

Ultimately it is the individual's responsibility to take advantage of the opportunities provided by the organization or to develop satisfactory personal alternatives. Adjustment of personnel is important to the success of organizational change. This adjustment involves time for individuals to reconsider personal, family, and career priorities, to mourn what has been lost, and to learn to master new circumstances. In this process latent personal conflicts are exposed and potential fragilities placed under strain.

The organization becomes involved in the personal aspects of a manager's adjustment to changing circumstances at work because it is in the interest of the organization to do so. This involvement takes the form of communication, initiation of education, and counseling on personal adjustment and personal stress management.

Treatment, when necessary, should be referred to outside resources at the individual's expense.

### Recommendations for change

1 Provide a Career Development Program for managers with problems of late career to:

- encourage resolution of late-career problems through participation in a workshop for "Planning for the Fifties and Beyond."

- reduce vulnerability to stress and resistance to change usually found in this group.

- correct the differential that presently exists between employer-initiated career development programs for younger and older managers.

- evaluate alternatives and learn new ways to cope with the stress of adjusting to change.

2 Provide a Retirement Preparation Program as a health maintenance service that will:

- initiate a Preparation for Retirement Program for those between the ages of fifty-three and fifty-five.

- increase awareness of the personal, family, and career issues involved in retirement planning through periodic distribution of information, educational events, group discussions, and group discussions that include the employee's spouse.

- make available to employees on a confidential and voluntary basis retirement planning information tapes for personal and family use.

- refer employees to counseling services for initial consideration of personal problems on a confidential and voluntary basis.

- make available help with legal, financial, and benefit planning.

3 Develop more varied and flexible end-of-career practices and procedures to improve the mobility of long-service managers within the organization and to help resolve the career problems

of those close to retirement who face redeployment or relocation. Suggestions for consideration include:

- liberalize early retirement when precipitated by organizational change.

- create alternative end-of-career positions (at no reduction in salary so pensions will not be adversely affected) such as lateral moves to positions of different areas of responsibility, group level, status. The opportunity to prolong a career within the company during the crucial prepension years and the prospect of using wisdom, talent, and experience in a new way should help minimize concern about lower status and reduced responsibility among employees who choose this route.

- provide for a "sabbatical" within the company, that is, time away from regular responsibilities to be used in consultation, task force participation, planning, and special assignment.

- offer part-time, part-of-year, or periodic work assignments that provide the employee with the opportunity to develop an alternative career while still earning service toward a more favorable benefit package.

## REFERENCE

Drucker, P. F. (1971). What we can learn from Japanese management. *Harvard Business Review* (71202):110–122.

# 12

# SOCIAL SUPPORT SYSTEMS

It should come as no surprise that the support individuals receive from their social environment sustains them through challenging and difficult times and helps them to cope with the unfamiliar, the uncertain, and the unknown. The family, of course, and group affiliations organized around common goals and shared interests are sources of security, satisfaction, self-esteem, and comfort in times of distress.

Yet some people are surprised to learn that good social support is also good for the health of managers. There is clear evidence that the health of managers and executives is affected by the quality of perceived relationships with those at work with whom they are in regular contact, have ongoing relationships, share mutual obligations, and to whom they expect to turn for practical and/or emotional assistance in times of need.

The time has therefore come to study the effect of social support systems on management stress in a systematic way. To do this we must first define concepts to be used, formulate models to help organize our observations, and find methods to collect relevant information.

The following general discussion of social support systems and the application of this concept to the manager's work and roles is at best a preliminary approach to this problem, but one that I find useful in organizing the material presented here. The concept of increasing the "supportive context" within an organization through careful attention to personnel practices that influence social relationships is valuable as a guide to the formulation of coping strategies.

It is also useful to conceive of social support systems in the broadest possible sense. Included here are not only the usual personal relationships at work with superiors, peers, subordinates, and friends, but also all the other interactions in the manager's social network:

- organizational mores, organizational personality, and usual executive coping style.
- personnel policies and practices.
- regularly occurring social interactions such as performance appraisals, departmental meetings, and other regular group interactions.
- management orientation, training, and education programs.
- opportunities for mentorlike relationships and other personal guidance experiences.
- in-house and outside consulting and counseling by professionals on career-related health and personal matters.

This chapter presents basic definitions of social support, briefly reviews some of the evidence that gives rise to the interest in social support as a technique to cope with occupational stress, and then discusses the implications of these findings for strategies to cope with management stress on a personal as well as an organizational level.


### DEFINITIONS

People are said to have *social support* if they have a relationship with one or more persons that is characterized by relatively frequent interactions, by strong and positive feelings, and by an ability and a willingness to give and take emotional and/or practical assistance in times of need. In the stress process model, social support systems are divided into two interrelated components.

*Support systems* include the formal and informal systems that define what is expected of the individual and how the individual can best cope with the environment. Support may be provided by means of education, training, orientation, group affiliation and cohesiveness, sharing of common experiences, or interpersonal communication. Systems may be formal, such as training programs, or informal such as a close group of coworkers. Systems may be located in the organization, work group, peer group, family, or community. These systems help to reduce uncertainty and fear of the unknown by teaching appropriate responses to anticipated stressors, and emergency responses to unexpected contingencies. As implied by their position in the stress model (p. 5), these systems modify the threat impact of stressors and are therefore important to the learning from experience feedback loop. Positive effects are enhanced when available support systems function together.

*Personal support* refers to close, positive personal relationships with specific individuals or small groups that provide care, protection, comfort, and emotional or other assistance in times of need. The critical aspect of effective personal support is the individual's perception of the ability and willingness of others to empathize and help, especially in an emotional sense. It is most important to have strong support from at least one source, be it spouse, supervisor, coworker, mentor, physician, or friend. It is probably not necessary that strong personal support come from several or all possible available sources.

Since 1970, NIOSH * has been conducting research aimed at identifying and evaluating the impact of psychological job stress on physical and mental health and fostering practices that will either reduce job stress or improve the individual's adjustment to it.

The NIOSH study, *Job Demands and Worker Health* (Caplan, Cobb, French, Harrison, and Pinneau, 1975) illustrates how social support is perceived and measured in a work environment. Workers in 23 diverse jobs, including managers and professionals, were asked to rate support expected from "your immediate supervisor or boss," "other people at work," and "your spouse, friends, and relatives" on a four-point scale from "very much" to "not at all" in response to the following questions:

- How much does each of these people go out of his or her way to do things to *make your work life easier* for you?
- How *easy is it to talk with* each of these people?
- How much can each of these people be *relied on* when things get tough at work?

---

* The Stress Research Section, Behavioral and Motivational Factors Branch, National Institute for Occupational Safety and Health.

- How much is each of these people *willing to listen* to your personal problems?

The report anticipates an additional volume on the role of social support in mitigating the strain effects of job stress (House, 1981).

### RESEARCH FINDINGS

In a social environment, factors in the individual's life sphere that form a social support network include:

- support from close persons or groups.
- amount of family support.
- prevailing work, peer, and social cohesiveness, affiliation, and morale.
- ease of access to helping resources.
- community attitudes.
- subcultural processes.
- social position, influence, and status.

This social support network supplies its members with:

- consistent feedback and communication of what is expected of them.
- supports and assistance with tasks.
- instruction in how to accomplish what is expected of them.
- evaluation of performance and appropriate rewards.
- definition of what is or is not potentially threatening, dangerous, challenging, or harmful.
- protection against the deleterious effects of unfamiliarity and uncertainty.
- care, protection, comfort, and emotional assistance in times of need.

High social support augments the individual's strengths and past experience, and facilitates adaptive coping behavior, which in turn results in maturation and mastery of the environment.

Absence of these social supports, absence of group membership as in social isolation, or the loss of existing supports through major bereavements (death of spouse, job loss) greatly enhances susceptibility to psychophysiological responses, which in turn lead to illness or maladaptation.

*Social isolation* is a major factor in the increased risk of disease. Those individuals who live alone, who are not involved with other individuals or organizations, for this very reason, have a high vulnerability to chronic diseases. In the work environment those individuals who remain alone or isolated tend to be more accident prone than those who are involved with others in a cohesive group.

*Marginal social status* or membership in a low-status group or minority is associated with health risks including a high rate of major mental disorders (Rabkin and Struening, 1976). In any environment a smaller group of ethnically similar members will have fewer social supports available to each member. This situation results in greater manifestation of maladjustment and illness.

Cobb (1976) defines social support as information leading to the belief that an individual is cared for, loved, esteemed, and a member of a network of mutual obligations. He presents evidence to show that social support protects individuals in crisis from a wide variety of pathological states: from low birth weight to death, from arthritis through tuberculosis to depression, alcoholism, and the social breakdown syndrome. Furthermore, social support may reduce the amount of medication required, facilitate compliance with prescribed medical regimens, and accelerate recovery.

In an occupational setting, individuals' supportive social relationships with supervisors, colleagues, and/or subordinates at work have been shown to reduce known occupational stresses such as:

- role conflict and role ambiguity.
- job dissatisfaction.
- low occupational self-esteem.

Social support also mitigates the effect of potentially stressful objective situations such as:

- a boring job.
- heavy work loads.
- unemployment.

The observation that shift workers with a constant set of co-workers had considerably lower cholesterol levels (a CHD risk factor) than those whose coworkers were ever-changing is only one of an increasing number of observations of the importance of affiliation, cohesiveness, and consistency in the work team at any occupational level.

Social support is closely connected to occupational safety. Poor social support from an immediate superior or from coworkers is associated with depression, hostility, and psychological strain. These problems in turn predispose toward accidents, inefficiency, and poor performance through a variety of pathways that include irritability, inattentiveness, boredom, fatigue, poor emergency responses, and self-damaging behavior.

Compliance is associated with high social support. Compliance with recommended procedures under circumstances of danger or emergency conditions is as important to safety as it is to health. Failure to follow safety precautions among isolated, unaffiliated, or untrained and poorly prepared workers is an important cause of occupational accidents.

A review of the relationship between safety and human stress factors (Moss and Riess, 1977) indicates that the *quality of support* within coworker groups and supervisor–worker units has a critical impact on:

- the general level of safety under usual operating conditions.
- the effectiveness of personnel responses to unexpected contingencies and emergency conditions.
- the control of apprehension and panic among personnel.
- effective coping with individuals in the work setting who display disturbed behavior.

The quality of support in a work setting is indicated by such components as shared goals, group cohesiveness and affiliation, the level of mutual trust and confidence among group members, and indications from previous experience that members of the group or specific close individuals will be available to help in times of need. The quality of social support is further determined by how the group is chosen, how its members are trained to work together, and how important differences among group members are resolved.

The importance of the selection process should not be underestimated. Mutual trust and cohesiveness cannot develop properly in a group whose members do not have the basic competence required for the performance of assigned tasks. Preparation for work that emphasizes shared experiences tends to develop an important sense of support.

It seems reasonable to anticipate that if individuals working together have different expectations as to how the workplace should accommodate particular cultural patterns or different attitudes about work culture, autonomy, coping style, management style, and behavioral mores, then obstacles to cohesiveness and trust may develop. It is not uncommon in a multinational workforce, for example, for individuals to express the customary attitudes of their own work culture only to meet with disagreement or disapproval from coworkers of a different background. Social behavior related to incomplete group affiliation (disapproval of others with different attitudes, avoidance of strangers, formation of cliques) may have little apparent relevance to safety or social support during regular operations, but can be a particularly important factor in the effectiveness of group responses to unexpected contingencies and high stress.

Workforce heterogeneity can stem from *any* important difference within the work group. Variations in culture, language, and customs are, of course, factors to be considered in a large multinational industrial workforce. But differences in work background and experience, previous and present work status, role changes upon entry into a new organization, or differences in social values may prove to be even more significantly related to the effective functioning of support systems than national and ethnic differences. Work culture differences may be particularly important during the start-up of any large new undertaking where personnel enter from various backgrounds.

Effective factors that tend to counteract the potentially detrimental effects of workforce heterogeneity include proper preparation for work; opportunities for involvement, participation, and social interaction at work; and open acknowledgement and discussion of important differences in work culture. In addition, the opportunity for any individual to form a close personal relationship with a person whose specific function it is to be available for support (health professional, employee relations representative, ombudsman, mentor or godfather, selected supervisory personnel) will provide the necessary support until group cohesiveness develops.

## SOCIAL SUPPORT AND THE MANAGER

In what is now considered a definitive study of the effect of social support, NASA at the Goddard Space Flight Center measured physiological outcomes (blood pressure, serum glucose, stress hormone levels) of job stressors such as heavy workload and role ambiguity. Outcomes were compared for two groups: those who had good interpersonal relationships with superiors, coworkers, subordinates (high social support), and those whose relationships were poor (low social support). High job stress was associated with physiological changes that threatened health, but *only* for those with low social support. Those with high social support responded to all levels of job stress with no physiological changes at all, or even a slight improvement (Kiritz and Moos, 1974).

Managers with high job stress and low social support ultimately developed three times as much coronary heart disease as managers with high job stress and high social support. Fig. 12.1 shows how the relationship between job stress and social support at work influences the outcome of the stress process.

The triggering of coronary heart disease or other stress-related illness is rarely accounted for by variation either in stress levels or support levels measured independently. Only by measuring how levels of stress and support vary in relation to each other, is the role of social support in protecting against the illness consequences of stress conclusively demonstrated. Isolation of the high stress/low support group (upper right box in Fig. 12.1) is the significant step in defining the population at greatest risk.

Low stress and high support (lower left box) combine to protect against adverse consequences of stress. Generally, low stress does not trigger adverse consequences to any significant degree. However, conditions of low stress and low support (lower right box) may adversely affect vulnerable individuals.

High stress, on the other hand, can trigger adverse consequences at all levels of social support, most particularly when support is low. High stress at work rarely results from the ordinary pressures of daily work, but rather from the extraordinary pressures that arise during conditions of uncertainty, change, unfamiliarity, complexity, emergency, and overload. It is precisely such extraordinary pressure that is most effectively protected against by high social support. In short, supportive relationships are good for the

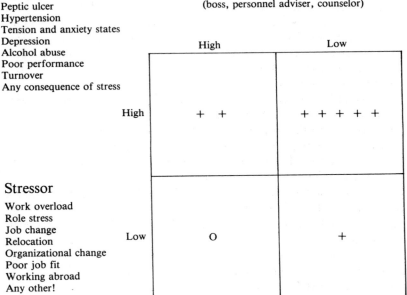

FIG. 12.1   *Social support and the outcome of management stress.*

health of managers and executives but most especially when work pressure is intense, or when they must respond to external initiatives over which they have little control, or when something goes wrong.

Viewed from the perspective of organizational coping strategies, what does this research mean in terms of actions to be taken?

Consider the case of a young forward-looking female personnel manager who is convinced by what she studied in business school that programs to improve the "supportive context" of the organization will pay off by maintaining a vital organizational resource— the health and effectiveness of managers and executives.

The young personnel manager put together an improvement program that included a management education module on "coping with executive stress, a workshop for relations managers on managing organizational change, a suggestion for counseling in career-related personal crisis, a program for second career planning and preretirement preparation for long service employees. These suggestions were then forwarded in a memo to her boss.

The older, organization-wise superior glanced at the memo. "Paternalism," he mumbled to himself, as he shuddered at the disruptions in established practices implied by such a program and the problems of justifying the costs to top management. He was irritated by a memo that presented an unsolicited solution to an unidentified problem of unknown proportion.

He summoned all his self-control and tried to behave like a gentleman to his newly appointed personnel manager. He called her into his office and asked politely, "What made you suggest such a program?"

"The program will enhance the social support systems in our organization, will help managers cope with stress, and will ultimately protect them against coronary heart disease. Scientific evidence from NASA proves that."

"Do we have a problem with coronary heart disease," he asked. "How many cases did we have last year in our office?"

"I can think of only one or two cases that I know of. But the program also protects against peptic ulcer and other stress-related illness" she replied. She could only think of one case of peptic ulcer among managers at their location. If her boss was going to continue to play the devil's advocate she could not maintain the cost effectiveness of this approach to stress reduction only on the basis of affecting the incidence of one or two well-known stress related illnesses.

She presented her last remaining argument. "This program also protects against other stressors such as the effects of organizational change." "That's interesting," answered her boss. "Are you sure?" She was startled by his change of tone. They discussed recent developments in personal and organizational stress management. Her boss made suggestions about what supportive evidence should be attached to the memo before it could be sent upstairs for review by superiors.

The personnel manager never really knew what changed her practical, level-headed, antipaternalistic, old-line superior's mind. She did not know that because of changing market conditions management was considering consolidation of two regions where there were large numbers of managers in late career. The planned reduction in head count would be anywhere from 15 percent to 25 percent. Her boss was concerned about the fate of loyal, long-service employees, some of whom would be faced with the unexpected and unwanted choices of relocation late in their career, entering the outside job market, or separation.

Morale of the survivors was also an important consideration in the mind of her boss. He was interested in protecting against what he knew from long experience would accompany sudden, unanticipated, and unwanted organization change, namely a wave of stress reactions followed by an increased incidence of long term stress-related illness. He was moved by a combination of concern, guilt, and a perceived opportunity to get help with knotty placement problems. In short, this was a proper motivational context for the serious consideration of an improvement program.

The boss knew from experience that the practical value of a preventive program to cope with the effects of management stress should be measured by the reduction of all adverse stress reactions taken together. Fig. 12.1 reflects this approach by grouping all stressors, all supports, and all adverse consequences of stress. The model implies that if all stress consequences taken together are considered as the outcome of the management stress process, then the buffering effects of social support can be demonstrated even in populations of modest size. The quality of organizational social support systems may not be apparent during everyday work when ordinary pressures do not have sufficient threat impact to underline how well the system protects against managerial stressors. This buffering effect appears only in response to extraordinary pressures and unexpected contingencies.

High social support should be thought of as a safety system that must be maintained in working order at all times although its positive effects on safety can be demonstrated only under unusual, abnormal, or emergency conditions.

Evidence for the importance of the supportive context of the work setting in buffering against the illness consequences of occupational stressors comes from epidemiological studies of CHD rates. In an effort to account for epidemiological variation in CHD rate Matsumoto (1970) hypothesized that differences between the societies in Japan and the United States could explain low CHD rates in Japan. His description of the work role and of the typical occupational career of a Japanese worker is quoted by Kasl as a comment on the influence of the social support network in a work setting.

> *It would appear that the firm one works for, the work setting, and one's co-workers truly become an extended family, which has enormous stability over time and provides an unchanging order. Work and other activities, such as leisure, become intimately intertwined and possibly a blurring of social roles takes place. I mention this . . . not to evoke nostalgia in the Western reader, but only because it points dramatically to a certain class of "social support" variables which are worth investigating. . . . Perhaps the broad social-emotional context (and its stability) of the work setting has been inadequately explored.*

> (KASL, 1978, pp. 23–24)

Social factors described throughout are interactive rather than independent, each describing the manager's interpersonal relationships at work from a slightly different perspective. Role stress, responsibility for people, interpersonal conflict, social support network, factors in the work ethic that activate predispositions in the coronary-prone individual—all have a common element. This common element is the quality of the interaction individuals have with others at work with whom they have regular contact, on-going relationships, share mutual obligations, and to whom they turn for practical and emotional assistance in time of need.

The phrase "time of need" is very important. Up to now the typical study of stress factors at work has explored the stable environment in which significant adaptations have long since taken place. At work, as in all other areas of life, even difficult relationships can be "lived with" once individuals know what to expect from them. "The devil you know is always better than the devil you don't know." Thus, the true supportive quality of existing social support systems may not be apparent during ordinary everyday work when stressors do not have sufficient impact to expose the inherent protective capacity of these systems.

It is under conditions of extraordinary pressure that the quality of social support will have its greatest effect on the outcome of the stress process set in motion by these pressures. Significant events and transitions in the gradual evolutionary growth of an organization, or more radical changes in response to threats to organizational survival (sudden changes in market conditions, takeover) are stressors that are likely to highlight the strength or weakness of support in the organization's interpersonal environment.

Intense stress may be unpredictable. Sudden changes such as deteriorating market conditions, unstable economic conditions, or radical sociopolitical changes may trigger rapid changes in workload, work pressure, internal organizational structure, and managerial roles. (Note that all of these changes are also associated with a high CHD risk.) The illness consequences of accelerating changes in business conditions depend upon the quality of support systems already in place. High management stress could not have been prepared for in advance because the changes giving rise to stressful conditions are often unforeseen, especially when these changes are organizational responses to external initiatives.

However, there is every reason to build in a social support network to buffer against the stress effects of planned organizational change by means of special procedures designed to prepare personnel for that change. As mentioned so many times here in different contexts, accurate communication of conditions (good or bad), candid discussion of the reasons for change and how personnel will be affected by it, and involving managers in the process of problem solving and planning for change are all support building factors that help buffer against the inevitable impact of change.

Remember that not all social support need come from the workplace. Realistic schedules should allow managers sufficient time to go through the process of making the necessary personal adaptations to anticipated changes. This adaptation always involves discussion with their families and a serious decision-making process that may lead the managers to conclude that such a change is not in their best interest or in the best interest of their dependents.

Realistically arrived at self-assessment and job-selection decisions should be respected by the organization. As is evident from the interviews with managers and executives presented here, making important career changes in the face of clearly identified, serious personal obstacles to that change, often ends in equally serious illness or maladjustment and a practical and financial loss to both manager and organization.

A further technique to enhance the total support available in the manager's social network is the encouragement of confidential discussion of problematic personal decisions and conflicts with professionals experienced in techniques of brief intervention in career-related life crises. An organization-supported program that provides easy access on a voluntary and confidential basis to expert advisors who are aware of the characteristic problems of managers going through the stress of major organizational change, holds out great promise as an important supplement to other organizational support systems. However, high level organizational support for such a counseling procedure is necessary to counteract the usual stigma attached to going to someone for advice and counsel about personal matters that the work ethic demands individuals must handle on their own.

Ultimately, a well-planned social support program, if effective, should appear as an anticlimax after the change has been accomplished. Ideally, the response of managers and executives planning and participating in the program should result in such comments as "I don't know why we were so careful about preparing for this move. There really weren't too many bad reactions. It really wasn't so stressful after all." The alternative to good planning—the health risks that inevitably accompany poorly planned and executed organizational change—is well known.

## REFERENCES

Caplan, R. D., S. Cobb, J. R. P. French, Jr., R. V. Harrison, and S. R. Pinneau, Jr. (1975). *Job Demands and Worker Health*. Washington, D.C.: HEW (NIOSH) Publication No. 75–160.

Cobb, S. (1976). Social support as a moderator of life stress. *Psychosomatic Medicine* **38**:300–314.

Drucker, P. F. (1971). What we can learn from Japanese management. *Harvard Business Review* (71202):110–122.

House, J. S. (1981). *Work Stress and Social Support*. Reading, Mass.: Addison-Wesley.

Kasl, S. V. (1978). Epidemiological contributions to the study of work stress. In C. L. Cooper and R. Payne (eds.) *Stress at Work*. Chichester, England: Wiley.

Kiritz, S., and R. H. Moos (1974). Review article: physiological effects of social environments. *Psychosomatic Medicine* **36**:96–114.

Matsumoto, Y. S. (1970). Social stress and coronary heart disease in Japan: a hypothesis. *Milbank Memorial Fund Quarterly* **48** (1) 9–36.

Moss, L., and B. F. Riess (1977). Human stress and platform living and working conditions on Statfjord "A." Presentation to the Norwegian Petroleum Directorate.

Rabkin, J. G., and E. L. Struening (1976). Social changes, stress and illness: a selective literature review. *Psychoanalysis and Contemporary Science* **5**:573–624.

# 13

# PERSONAL COPING STRATEGIES

This chapter focuses on strategies to help the manager, and where possible the manager's family, to cope with the more highly personal aspects of management stress. The aspects under consideration are:

- career-related crises.
- difficulties in making realistic self-assessments and career choices.
- the need for timely confrontation of characteristic career progression problems.

Organizational pressures that demand exclusive concentration on work initiatives while directing attention away from personal and private considerations all too commonly result in a denial and avoidance of personal issues. Special effort is required to counteract these organizational pressures and to help the manager maintain awareness and perspective, and to anticipate and think through the extraordinary challenges that arise in both personal and working life from time to time.

Model individual coping strategies outlined in this chapter are based on the principle that managers who are able to maintain perspective, make realistic self-assessments, and control their own situations as much as possible will also cope effectively with less than ideal conditions. They will make the hard choices and develop the creative insights necessary to master the challenges, frustrations, transitions, and crises that characterize a career at any level of management.

### CAREER-RELATED PERSONAL CRISES

Work pressures and forces in the manager's personal life often combine to precipitate career-related personal crises. A common mechanism for the genesis of such a crisis is illustrated by the equation

$$\underset{(\text{stressor})}{\underset{\begin{array}{c}\text{ordinary}\\\text{work}\\\text{pressure}\end{array}}{}} + \underset{(\text{stressor})}{\underset{\begin{array}{c}\text{added}\\\text{work}\\\text{pressure}\end{array}}{}} + \underset{}{\underset{\begin{array}{c}\text{stressful}\\\text{life}\\\text{event}\end{array}}{}} = \underset{}{\underset{\begin{array}{c}\text{career-related}\\\text{personal crisis}\end{array}}{}}$$

Under ordinary levels of work pressure the manager's capacity to cope with stress is adequate to deal with the ordinary stressful life events that arise from time to time and to maintain a satisfactory level of job performance. Added work pressure, however, requires that the manager use reserves of adaptive coping capacity to deal with the higher level of job pressure and also to continue to maintain satisfactory performance.

With a high proportion of the manager's adaptive coping capacity devoted to dealing with job pressures alone, the manager is more vulnerable to intercurrent stressful life events that also demand a coping response. When the combined stress load (work pressure of all types and stressful life events) threaten to overwhelm the manager's capacity to cope and thus adversely affect job performance, a career-related personal crisis is likely to develop.

A model showing how stress influences job performance (Fig. 13.1) is presented to clarify the relationship between work pressure and stressful life events and to help plan crisis intervention strategies. The model is based on the classic bell-shaped curve that describes the relationship between work pressure (also job complexity) and job performance (also work satisfaction). The entire area under the bell-shaped curve can be thought of as the manager's total adaptive coping capacity. Each of the five zones in the model represents a different relationship between stress and performance.

*Optimum work pressure*—the white area under the curve—In the range of work pressure perceived as optimal by managers and executives, job performance is at its peak. Note that the optimum range can include considerable work pressure. Thus a certain level of challenge or stress load is required for the manager to perform

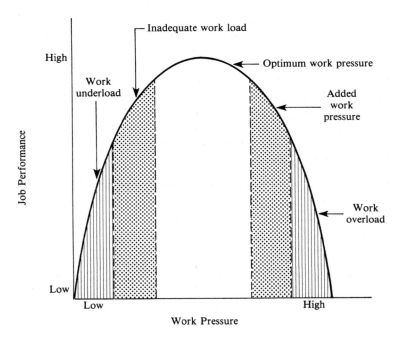

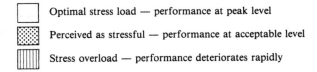

Optimal stress load — performance at peak level

Perceived as stressful — performance at acceptable level

Stress overload — performance deteriorates rapidly

FIG. 13.1 *Relationship between work pressure and job performance.*

effectively and achieve satisfaction. Note also that in this zone sufficient adaptive coping capacity remains in reserve to:

- deal with added work pressure or stressful life events and still prevent stress overload.
- develop outside interests in addition to the usual work and thereby prevent the adverse consequences of extreme work underload.

*Work underload*—striped area on the left—The model indicates that work performance (and satisfaction) deteriorates rapidly under conditions of extreme work underload. Depression and serious self-esteem problems are consequences of the absence of challenge and work pressure.

*Inadequate workload*—shaded area on the left—The manager's ability to cope is called into play under circumstances of inadequate challenge to prevent the deterioration of performance and self-esteem that accompanies extreme work underload. Coping responses will vary with the reason for the nonchallenging or inadequate workload. These might include:

- developing outside interests if the problem is one of waiting for retirement.
- efforts to establish a second career.
- looking for a better job fit in another job or with another organization.
- reinforcing sources of satisfaction outside of work if job change, job redesign, learning new skills, or changing reporting relationships are not the answer to work that lacks challenge and reward.

*Work overload*—striped area on the right—Of greater importance is the area of work overload. Under conditions of extremely high stress or overload, job performance tends to deteriorate rapidly with only small amounts of additional stress. Stress overload can come from extremes of work pressure alone or from a combination of stressors such as extraordinary work pressure plus other stressful life events.

*Added work pressure*—shaded area on the right—The buffer zone between optimum stress levels and the area of stress overload is of special interest. In a practical sense this buffer zone represents the manager's reserve capacity to cope with or adapt to additional stress from any source.

At these stress levels the manager can cope with added ordinary work pressure, or with extraordinary pressure, or with the complexities of stressful life events and still experience only a modest decline in productivity. The manager may be tense, anxious, or irritable with a high pulse rate and increased blood pressure. But job performance remains at levels that are acceptable to both manager and management.

Managers and executives generally operate in this buffer zone using some reserve coping capacity to perform their ordinary day-to-day work. Evidence for this comes from Mintzberg's (1973) survey of the manager's usual work and roles and from the American Management Associations' (Kiev and Kohn, 1979) findings that middle and top managers often work under heavy workload, intense time pressures, and unrealistic deadlines. Furthermore, striving is a basic element of the conventional organization personality. Facing challenges that strain capacities to cope with them is the very cornerstone of the manager's self-image as a successful manager and an important contributor to the goals and survival of the organization.

Objective measures of performance fall off from peak levels as individuals move from the area of optimum pressure to the shaded area of added work pressure. Subjectively, however, this shift is not perceived as a decline in effectiveness but rather as an ego-enhancing struggle with challenging work.

Generally, the difference between peak performance and lowered productivity under conditions of added work pressure is not a cause for alarm. Management is more concerned that extraordinary problems requiring immediate attention are taken care of, that the manager gets the job done, and that nothing important "falls between the cracks."

Furthermore, the manager's work is usually organized around critical decision points such as annual budget reviews, departmental meetings to assign objectives for the next year, and intense marketing and sales campaigns. Peaks of work pressure cluster naturally around critical decision points.

Under conditions of predictable peak work loads the manager is not at all unhappy. Getting the job done provides a psychic income that far outweighs the discomfort of stress reactions (anxiety, tension, irritability) or any possible concern about loss of efficiency at these levels of work pressure. Certainly, managers lose no self-esteem when they devote their undivided attention to preparing the annual budget or finishing a review of objectives for the next year that will be presented at the upcoming departmental meeting at a secluded resort hotel.

What is most important about managers' responses to these added work pressures is that at first they are usually unaware of them. The fact that they function at these stress levels (work overload, time pressure, unrealistic deadlines) consumes their adaptive coping capacity and moves them closer to the area of work overload where small increments of stress produce large and noticeable decrements of job performance.

As pressure mounts, stress reactions appear and managers become aware that *there is a cost to coping with increasing work pressure.* Managers whose reserves are consumed by the need to respond to peak workloads will feel less interested than usual in other life events. Even minor sources of stress external to work will be perceived as unwanted distractions. Managers will respond with irritability to personal and family demands for time and attention—time and attention that home or personal affairs may require at that moment.

Family members will remember that they did not receive the necessary support from the manager who appears distracted or disinterested in them, yet at the same time is absorbed with the interesting task of working out the departmental budget or objectives for the next year. During periods of intense preoccupation the manager may not notice the growing distance, even alienation, that may develop in personal and family relations. Or the manager may be unsympathetic toward claims made by others on time and attention. After all, doesn't the family benefit if the manager performs well and is rewarded both financially and through career advancement?

At this point organizational supports help sustain the manager's momentum and motivation. Work is given special importance by the group. The annual departmental meeting is regarded as critical. Superiors are vitally interested in the manager's product. This is a time when performance is noted, evaluated, and rewarded. Hopes are high. Career progression is at risk. At that moment the work product to be displayed at the meeting is the manager's highest priority and exclusive concern.

This point is also one of greatest vulnerability to life stress for overworked and preoccupied managers. Virtually all of their capacity to cope with stress (the total area under the bell-shaped curve in Fig. 13.1) is consumed by the need to cope with ordinary work pressure plus added work pressure (a stressor). Additional stress from still greater work pressure, from other life events, or from any source threatens to throw managers into the area where job performance may deteriorate rapidly (striped area on the right) and threaten career progression.

The type and timing of additional stress, and the perspective from which it is perceived at this point by the manager are critical factors in precipitating stress overload.

• With regard to work, more work pressure in the same area is not as stressful as less pressure from other work roles, or from other factors that add to job complexity.

• With regard to events external to work, sources of stress are usually seen out of perspective by the manager who is temporarily preoccupied with other higher priority concerns. Any unfamiliar or unwanted stressor is perceived as highly threatening or frustrating. Even small problems from sources other than work that demand time, attention, interest, and distract from the primary focus of coping with work pressure will be highly disturbing. A personal problem whose outcome at that moment is uncertain can be exceptionally stressful even though the manager is quite capable of resolving the problem once free to give it the coping effort it requires.

Timing in life is everything. The manager whose adaptive efforts are consumed by preparing for a meeting will undoubtedly cope much more effectively with the same intercurrent stressful life events once the work pressure is over and adaptive coping reserves have been restored. But during the preparation for the meeting, stressful life events threaten to precipitate rapidly deteriorating performance through the mechanism of stress overload. Therefore, when the manager's wife becomes depressed and reaches out for support, or when a teenaged youngster gets into trouble for the first time because of drug abuse, or when a tree falls on the house during a severe storm causing considerable damage and there is some doubt about the reimbursement because the insurance policy was inadvertently allowed to lapse in the crush of intense work pressure, then job performance is likely to suffer as a consequence of the overload caused by any one of these events.

Characteristically managers blame the intercurrent life event rather than the intense work pressure that monopolizes adaptability for the ensuing performance problems and their consequences. It is not uncommon for managers to comment under such circumstances and for colleagues to agree, "I can handle the big problems at work, it's the nagging small problems of everyday life that cause all the trouble."

But a personal problem waiting to be solved is not the same as a personal crisis. A crisis has a developmental history. It arises from a present context that has broader implications than are apparent from the precipitating problem alone. Managers' past relationships with spouses and/or teenaged youngsters will determine whether the problem is perceived as an isolated issue to be dealt with or whether the event becomes a turning point in the relationship.

The performance problem can remain an isolated though unfortunate occurrence or can become a factor that triggers more far-reaching consequences:

- disappointment, defeat, self-esteem problems.

- a compulsive need to restore lost work gratification by working even harder (for factors leading to individual burnout, see Chapter 5).

- blaming personal relationships or external stressors for the loss of work satisfaction and ego gratification leading to permanent distortions in these relationships.

### ANATOMY OF A CRISIS

The origins of a personal crisis lie in the attitudes and perspectives of the individuals involved. The stressfulness of triggering events is usually of secondary importance. An episode in the life of a newly promoted general manager illustrates this point. The scenario is a composite of many similar episodes reported during stress interviews, clinical consultations, and psychotherapy. It provides a source for the understanding of many of the individually initiated and organization supported intervention strategies suggested here.

### INTERVIEW 12 – The Newly Promoted General Manager

Tom Johnson, age forty-two, has been recently promoted to General Manager of a large metropolitan office. Originally when he discussed the possibility of such a move his wife expressed reluctance to relocate for the ninth time in their marriage. The Johnsons have four children ages fifteen, twelve, nine, and five. Their oldest child, a daughter, has begun to show signs of adolescent rebellion. Because of this Mrs. Johnson thought it might be unwise to require the youngster to make a new social adjustment in a community where she had no friends or associations.

Tom's wife was also concerned about her own ability to adjust to a sophisticated suburban community, where she knew no one to turn to for support. Tom prevailed upon her to relocate with the argument that this was an exceptionally fine opportunity to display his talents to the right people.

The scenario begins after Tom Johnson has been working nights and weekends for a month to prepare a five-year plan for presentation at a meeting of all general managers and top executives of the division. The meeting is to take place at a resort hotel that is somewhat inaccessible, the theory being that isolation from everyday activities and obligations during planning helps concentration and promotes creativity.

This is Tom's first divisional meeting as general manager. Because he does not know what to expect he is overpreparing. As general manager Tom finds that he must rely heavily on the input of subordinates. The problems of integrating their input into his five-year plan are greater than he had anticipated.

Three days before the divisional meeting Tom's boss unexpectedly summons his managers to an emergency meeting to review their reports. They are told to drop whatever they are doing a day early, for a practice run through. He does not want to be taken by surprise by what his managers will present at the actual meeting.

The only way Tom will be able to make the emergency meeting on time is to ask his wife to change her car pooling and child sitting arrangements for the day, pack his things, pick him up at the office, and drive him to the airport. This situation precipitates a crises. The critical event takes place in the car on the way to the airport. His wife begins to tell him something but he doesn't hear what she says. Tom, who has been preoccupied for weeks preparing for the meeting, is preoccupied once again.

Early the next morning, Tom receives a call from his wife. Speaking very slowly in a low, sad voice she tells him that things at home have become too much for her. She can no longer cope. She informs him that their fifteen-year-old daughter has become involved with a gang of kids who leave school to hang out and take drugs. She has not wanted to tell him about this because of the importance of his preparation for the meeting. On the previous morning their daughter was arrested along with others in a neighboring community. The police suspect the youngsters of dealing in drugs. Tomorrow they are scheduled to appear in court. It was this that she was trying to tell him on the way to the airport but he was too preoccupied and never heard a word she said. "Or maybe you were not interested."

After a short pause she asks for the name and telephone number of a lawyer to represent their daughter. As Tom looks through his wallet for a card he has been given recently by a local lawyer whom they met socially, his wife says very deliberately and in an ominous tone, "Don't bother to look for me at the train station when you come home. I will never again be there to pick you up when you finish your bridge game and emerge from the bar car."

At this point she hangs up. Tom calls back immediately but she does not answer. Tom is distressed. His wife has called him at work like this before. Calls usually cluster around important transitions, such as the move to a new community. But this time her voice seemed different. Again he calls back and again no answer. Now he becomes angry. Why does she have to put this on me just before the most important event of my entire career? If she kept it from me for so long why couldn't she handle the problem herself for a few more days until I was free from distractions and could participate? She is always making me feel guilty about being more interested in my work than I am in her and the children.

Like a good manager who gets things done through the efforts of others, Tom calls his young, attractive, eager-to-be-of-help secretary. He asks her to contact his lawyer, whose telephone number he has found by this time, and also to call his wife's sister and ask her to fly out and visit his family that day.

When he hangs up Tom weighs whether he should go home himself. What explanation can he give—"personal reasons"? If he tells the truth, his boss will probably think, "What kind of general manager will he make if he can't even manage his family life." It would have been better if a tree had fallen and collapsed the roof of his house during a storm and he had to rush home to take care of a natural catastrophe rather than one of his own making.

Tom decides to go to the "emergency" run-through knowing that he can rely on his secretary to take care of things and to call him if there are any problems. "For a young woman, she copes very well," he thinks.

At the run-through the presentation is lackluster. His material is good but is presented without enthusiasm. The boss wonders how much he will be able to rely on this newly appointed general manager to make the region look good to top management. Tom fears his image has been tarnished in the eyes of his boss.

That night, he calls home to ask how everything has worked out. His wife answers coldly, "Everything is taken care of." She does not wish to speak further on the telephone.

The next day the presentation before the larger group goes somewhat better, but again Tom appears to his listeners to be somewhat lacking in drive and enthusiasm. On the way home Tom is concerned about the adequacy of his performance. The more he thinks about it the more irritated he becomes. His wife could have delayed confronting him with family problems until after he had put his best foot forward. By contrast his willing and helpful secretary appears more attractive to him than ever.

When his train pulls into the station Tom is not sure his wife will be there to meet him. She is there and greets him with apologies for bothering him with the phone call. "I feel so foolish. I know I should have coped better, but I was so upset about what might happen to our daughter."

Recovering somewhat from her self-depreciation she informs Tom that she contacted a lawyer retained by others in the community under similar circumstances. Their daughter was not involved in the selling of drugs as it turned out and has promised not to associate with that group of youngsters and to stay out of trouble. At the moment she appears to be keeping her promise.

Then his wife adds, "In the future I can do without any interference from that young secretary of yours, thank you, and from my sister also, for that matter."

Tom accepts her apology for the phone calls. They agree to drop the subject and let bygones be bygones.

### Outcome of a crisis

This episode appears to end well, but it actually ends badly. The appearance of a crisis is an indication that there is a problem to be solved. In this instance, although peace prevails at the moment, the attitudes and perspectives that shaped the crisis remain unchanged, and the conflicts that emerged are neither relieved nor resolved. As long as the dynamics of the crisis remain unaltered by new understandings the problem is likely to reappear. Only next time the strain and consequences may be more severe.

The potential for future conflict is apparent when the perspectives of the three participants in the crisis, the manager, his wife, and his superior are compared. None of the participants has broadened personal perspectives or achieved a greater understanding of the perspectives of the others.

**1** The *manager* sees himself as coping well with an intense workload at a critical point in his career only to be thwarted in an effort to impress superiors by his wife's inability to handle a family problem that surfaced at an unfortunate time. He accepts her apology but remains inwardly resentful that she is not fulfilling his image of the supportive household, family, community, and social manager required by an executive on the way up. By contrast other sources of help appear more attractive to him than his wife who demands his time and attention when he must concentrate on work priorities. He fails to recognize the role of his own career anxieties in increasing his workload and in rendering him far less available than usual to his family. Career anxieties include:

- making the transition to a new and challenging role as general manager.

- intense career expectations surrounding this role.

- uncertainty about what to expect at a type of meeting with which he has no prior experience.

- suppressed criticism of his superior's management style.

He also fails to perceive that from his wife's point of view she is going through a similar overload in her own work with "career" anxieties comparable to his:

- making the transition to a new lifestyle in a new community without established social supports.

- concerns about social role, adequacy, and issues of self-realization appropriate to a woman in the midlife transition of the early forties.

- practical problems with scheduling school and other activities for four children in various stages of development requiring involvement in different social groups.

- the irritations and self-doubts usually aroused when mothers cope with daughters in adolescent turmoil.

2   The *wife* sees herself as coping with an overload of family transitions and adjustments without help from her husband. She feels it was not asking too much of him in an emergency to give her the name of a lawyer to represent their daughter whose trouble may be related to their frequent relocations. Her resentment of her husband's failure to provide support is mixed with doubts about her own adequacy as a high level executive's wife, doubts stemming from deeper concerns about her adequacy and attractiveness. As a result, she apologizes for her behavior, suppresses her anger, and feels foolish. She fails to perceive that her husband is unable to show interest not because of her lack of attractiveness and adequacy as a woman (chronic psychological themes in her personality) but because his coping capacity is monopolized by career pressures.

3   The *superior* sees himself as less than ideally represented by a newly chosen general manager. He fails to realize that the added pressure on his managers created by his own need for reassurance is partly responsible for the disappointing contrast in their performance during regular daily work and at critical meetings of divisional staff. He also fails to realize that he is sending clear messages that his managers are expected to drop everything else to respond to *his* emergency priorities. The possibility that his management style adversely affects his managers' job performance, by restricting their options to cope with an overload of work pressure plus stressful life events, has never convincingly been brought to his attention.

Each participant has increased the possibility of self-defeat during subsequent crises by reinforcing the very behavior that caused the problem. Tom doubts that he can rely on his wife at times of intense work pressure and wonders if she is adequate to the role of an executive's wife. True to his training as a manager, he make a difficult business decision. In the future he will devote even more time and attention to work in an effort to regain his boss's approval at the risk of coping poorly with future stressful life events or personal relations at home.

His wife manages family affairs very well with no support from her husband. Instead of a feeling of accomplishment she comes away from the experience feeling even more self-depreciatory. She blames herself for the unfortunate outcome of her reasonable request for support. She anticipates that her husband will be less interested in her in the future. True to character she resolves to keep her concerns to herself from then on.

His superior faces the greatest problem with self-defeat. Because of doubts about being able to rely on his manager he will probably maintain an even higher level of surveillance using a management style that perpetuates the superior–subordinate support/confidence problem.

Top management has much to gain from feedback about the effect of work pressure, management practices, mores, and coping style on the adaptive capacity of key personnel.

The higher up the organizational ladder a manager goes, the more that manager becomes dependent on subordinates for the information necessary to make crucial decisions. Ultimately the key executive must make decisions based on brief summaries only, or incomplete first-hand knowledge of technical matters. *A great deal of trust must be placed in the accuracy, effectiveness, and judgment of subordinates.*

Key executives must manage and guide subordinates so that their effectiveness is not adversely affected by the stresses of the management process or by any of the characteristic work-related personnel crises that may arise from time to time. Managers who report to them should feel free to indicate when and through what mechanisms, work pressures and personnel stressors threaten to overload capacities to maintain desired levels of job performance.

## COPING WITH CRISIS

Techniques for coping with career-related personal crises are aimed at maintaining perspective, avoiding distress, and offering support in times of need. These techniques should provide the manager and where possible the significant others in the manager's life with the tools and opportunities to cope with their own situations, by preventing the occurrence of crises or by successfully resolving the crises that do occur.

Maintaining perspective is the key issue. There are several action points at which perspective can be achieved. Returning to the scenario of the newly appointed general manager preparing for his first divisional meeting: Would a similar crisis have developed if he had an awareness of how career anxieties, heightened by the uncertainties of a new and challenging work role consumed his capacity to cope, increased his need for support, and rendered him far less available to his family than ever before? And what would have been the outcome if he had a sympathetic awareness that his wife was going through a similar overload and needed his support in exactly the same way he felt he needed support from her?

Or what might the outcome have been if, following his return from the meeting, husband and wife had agreed to discuss a family plan of action to cope with perceived stressfulness of new roles, new demands, new commitments, and a new lifestyle? Would they have agreed to better communication and cooperation so that important issues (their daughter's welfare) would not "fall between the cracks" and be overlooked as they responded to the initiatives of the organization as interpreted by his boss? And would they have agreed to live with the present situation for a while longer before making any decisions about whether this was indeed the lifestyle they wished for their future together?

Would the crisis have developed in the first place if both husband and wife had been prepared for the stressfulness of combined work and life transitions, or if they had learned through experience or training to expect that, during times of mutual overload, one might not be available to support the other as desired?

If preparation had modified the wife's self-depreciatory response to feeling unsupported and/or the husband's resentful response to a perceived lack of support, would they then have cooperated better? Would the job performance of the general manager on the way up have been different?

As has been emphasized many times, realistic anticipation of and preparation for career stressors and their impact on personal life should modify their adverse effects by helping the manager and the manager's family to cooperate better during emergencies, or at least tolerate each other's point of view and postpone resolving differences until the peak overload has passed.

Perspective can be achieved in many ways through:

- individual self-assessment.
- management training that highlights the personal and family issues related to management stress.
- outside discussions of personal stress management.

- internal discussions of the effects of peaks of extraordinary stress and periodic career-related personal crises that characterize the manager's role.
- discussions with peers going through similar crises.
- personal supportive discussions with mentors, godfathers, or other personnel at work.
- counseling with professionals who have special expertise in the area of intervention in career-related crises.

Some techniques to achieve or maintain perspective are individually initiated, while others are initiated by the organization or can be sponsored by the organization and made available to managers and their families for participation on a voluntary and confidential basis.

### REFERENCES

Kiev, A., and V. Kohn (1979). *Executive Stress.* An AMA Survey Report. New York: American Management Associations.

Mintzberg, H. (1973). *The Nature of Managerial Work.* New York: Harper & Row.

# 14

# COUNSELING FOR STRESS

The opportunity to seek advice and exchange ideas and opinions under timely and appropriate circumstances can be very helpful to managers as they cope with a wide variety of managerial stressors. Standard organizational practices provide many such opportunities. Discussions of job choice, evaluations of performance, career development planning sessions and workshops in management skills are components of a broad and continuing job counseling program to help managers perform effectively and maintain a role in the organizational hierarchy.

Opportunities to help managers cope with the personal and interpersonal aspects of management stress, however, are provided rarely, and then only under special circumstances. Counseling to help managers cope with the stressfulness of office politics, or with the distressing consequences of troubled relationships with superiors is not a component of standard job counseling programs. Even when personality clashes in top management threaten to paralyze effective decision making (a problem not uncommon in smaller organizations) counseling is not given high priority on the list of remedial actions to be taken.

Programs to cope with maladaptive managers, once their handicaps become apparent, receive more attention than preventive programs to deal with the underlying causes of their maladaptation. For example, management is likely to support an out-placement counseling service for managers who are being separated because they no longer fit into the organization. But preventive programs to improve the circumstances of managers before the misfit develops are rarely considered.

The special problem arising from interacting and often conflicting career and personal demands and responsibilities are generally thought to be outside the realm of job counseling. Thus, managers who are working mothers, or parents without partners, or managers who must cope with an alcoholic spouse, or an addicted teenaged child, or a chronically ill dependent parent are left to deal with their problems on their own. Management may assure a sympathetic role, but remains essentially uninvolved in the process of easing such personal burdens even though these burdens may interfere with managers' ability to deal with the pressures of the job.

Stress management programs initiated by the employer usually have a physical fitness component, teach the use of relaxation techniques, and provide referral for professional counseling at the request of troubled employees. But employer-initiated programs rarely have personal stress counseling components to deal specifically with the employee's disturbed well-being and the reduced effectiveness that arises periodically as a consequence of extraordinary pressures at work or career-related personal crises.

Counseling refers to a process of consultation, deliberation or interchange of opinions and ideas in which

- the purpose of the interchange is to direct the judgment and behavior of the individual seeking counsel.

- the person giving counsel has special competence to give advice.

- the individual seeking counsel expects to benefit from the exchange.

Thus counseling is more than just a casual contact, or a conversation, or a rap session. It is an interchange with a structure and a purpose, one in which the participants have clearly defined roles.

This chapter suggests various approaches to personal stress counseling, whereby counselors may be experienced senior managers, peers who share common stressful experiences, and medical personnel, as well as outside professional counselors. The ultimate goal of this broad approach to counseling for stress is the strengthening of organizational social support systems.

Suggestions are presented for:

- the use of experienced senior managers as mentors to younger managers.
- the use of peer groups to provide mutual social support through discussion of shared stressful experiences.
- a periodic stress review as part of a comprehensive health examination.
- a program of counseling for stress that includes outside professional counseling and a feedback system to management as an aid for planning personnel policies.

## OBSTACLES TO COUNSELING PROGRAMS

There are several reasons why management does not take a more active role in developing personal stress counseling programs for their managers.

1 Conventional coping style reinforces managers' fear of exposure, thereby discouraging their interest in and demand for employer-supported personal stress counseling.

2 Management tends to misperceive personal counseling programs as mental health programs rather than as components of social support systems.

3 Management fears that the costs of counseling programs will get out of control.

4 There is no accepted conceptual framework for counseling for stress in an occupational setting.

### Fear of exposure

Conventional coping style discussed in Chapter 6 attaches a stigma to being troubled, distressed, or in need of help. Coping with personal problems is viewed as a private concern. These attitudes reinforce the fear of exposure that is usually associated with the awareness and recognition of personal problems.

The stigma that may be associated with a personal stress counseling program at its inception is likely to disappear as the benefits of the program become apparent. But the fear of exposure that presently exists among managers cannot be underestimated as an obstacle to the start-up of such a program, especially when it is linked to management. Thus, issues of voluntary participation, confidentiality, and appropriate routes of access to counseling are important factors to be considered in program design.

### Fear of mental illness

The process of counseling is often misperceived as psychotherapy, which in turn is misperceived as treatment for mental illness. Thus management's reaction to the suggestion of a personal stress counseling program is likely to be a negative one. "We're not in the business of providing for the mental health of our employees and their families." And managers may have a similar reaction to the suggestion that they use the counseling program. "Why should I go for counseling? I'm not mentally ill!"

Actually, counseling as presented here is a program of prevention rather than intervention. It is not intended as treatment for established maladjustment, disorder or illness, but as an aid to coping with adverse effects on well-being and effectiveness as managers cope with the crises, transitions and problems of life, including work stressors.

The 1980 American Psychiatric Association manual for coding reasons why individuals seek consultation reflects this perspective. Reasons for each consultation are described along five axes:

- a diagnosis of a behavior or nervous or mental disorder, if any.
- the underlying personality structure of the individual seeking consultation.
- physical symptoms and conditions associated with the present problem or reaction.
- psychosocial stressors, including quality of social supports, that contribute to the present problem or reaction.
- an assessment of the degree to which usual functioning is affected by the present problem or reaction.

The new diagnostic system closely parallels the stress process model (stressors—individual characteristics—social support systems—stress reactions—maladjustment and disorder) used in this book as a framework for the discussion of management stress.

It is my experience that managers who seek counseling have been active, functioning members of their organizations, their families and their communities. They are not likely to present with severe and disabling disorders (with the occasional exception of serious depression, severe mood disorders, and alcohol or drug abuse). Most often they are seeking relief of tension, anxiety, depression or other symptoms commonly associated with distress. The most frequent reason for consultation can be described as an adjustment reaction to problems of adult life. Such adjustment reactions include

- marital problems.
- personality clashes with peers and superiors.
- suppressed emotional reactions to peers and superiors.
- problems with the control of hostility.
- difficulty asserting or responding to authority.
- hidden conflicts over dependency, disappointed ambition.
- unconscious fear of success, or a success phobia, with an associated tendency toward self-defeat, often triggered by problems relating to career choices or relations with superiors.

## THE COST OF RELIEVING DISTRESS

Recent research indicates there are substantial benefits to be gained from counseling programs that focus on the relief of distress. A comprehensive analytic review of twenty-two programs by Jones and Vischi (1979) concludes that these studies were almost unanimous in finding a reduction in utilization of general health care services subsequent to treatment for stress related health problems. A recent study also indicates significant therapeutic value as well as surprising cost benefits that resulted from a personal and family counseling program conducted by outside resources but actively supported by the organization.

Dr. Nicholas A. Cummings (1977) summarizes two decades of prepaid health plan experience at the San Francisco Kaiser-Permanente Medical Center with the finding that persons in emotional distress were significantly higher users of both inpatient (hospitalization) and outpatient medical facilities as compared to the health plan average.

Almost 68% of physician visits were from sufferers of emotional distress rather than organic illness. The impact of a brief crisis intervention counseling program by professionals trained in this mode of service delivery is dramatically indicated by their results. One session only, with no repeat visits, reduced utilization of medical benefits by 60% over the following five years. In those patients initially receiving two to eight visits (brief therapy) there was a 75% reduction in medical utilization over a five-year period.

A subsequent eight year follow-up indicated that improvement was maintained. Results suggest that the reduction in medical utilization over such a long period of time was the consequence of 1) resolving the emotional distress that had been expressed in symptoms presented to the physician, and 2) remaining symptom-free through coping more effectively with the real problems.

The cost effectiveness of direct access to counseling for emotional distress as contrasted with visits to a physician to rule out physical illness is apparent. Direct, confidential, low cost counseling for relief of distress accompanying career-related personal crises should improve coping and avoid the expense of negative medical diagnoses.

The service delivery system is considered critical to both the therapeutic and cost effectiveness of counseling (Cummings and Follette, 1976). The success of the Kaiser-Permanente approach was attributed by the authors to a team of therapists with specific expertise in intervention in crises and problems of living and in alleviating emotional distress by means of a brief course of active counseling.

It is important to note that the conventional executive coping style encourages the use of the medical route for all types of complaints including disturbed well-being, and discourages seeking professional counseling and support for signs of anything but obvious mental illness or serious depression. Managers and executives will be sympathetic to a colleague who goes to the doctor for stomach pains. "I don't feel well. I must have a serious physical illness" is an approved scenario for taking time off from work to seek medical advice. However, "I don't feel well, I must be troubled, in distress or in crises" is not an approved route to help and support unless the stomach pains (a common symptom of "masked" depression) give way to severe depression with obvious suffering or self-destructive trends.

## Problems of program development

Inasmuch as there is no accepted model for counseling for stress in an organizational setting, many issues remain to be resolved by any organization interested in undertaking such a program. The question of whether or not personal counseling for managers is the proper responsibility of the employer is the fundamental issue. If so, where does the function belong in the organizational structure? In personnel, medical, training, management? Or should the program be the responsibility of an outside professional group?

If employees are to be used as counselors (mentors, for example, or leaders of group meetings) is special training in counseling required? If professional counselors are to be used, should they be required to have specific expertise in counseling in an occupational setting? Should they be given specific background information about the organization so their observations of the employees counseled can be abstracted and fed back to management for use in planning personnel policies?

My opinion that management is responsible for the resolution of its managers' personal crises is based on two considerations. First, although coping with crisis often appears to be a personal and private matter, when managerial stressors or organizational practices play a role in the genesis of the crises or obstruct the process of coping, then management can and should take an enabling position with regard to crisis resolution. Second, management has a vested interest in the outcome of personal crises because of the association between crisis and declining job performance. Thus, the manager and management share responsibility for the establishment of organizationally supported and approved channels to counseling for problems in living, career-related personal crises and other illness that are consequences of stress. There are indications from many sources that such programs can be both therapeutically and cost effective.

## SUGGESTIONS FOR COUNSELING

### Senior managers as advisors

A system of career counseling for younger managers by experienced senior managers is suggested as a means of easing extraordinary pressures on young managers and executives.

Senior managers have special competence in dealing with some of the more problematical aspects of life in a hierarchical system. They have learned how to survive the politics and informal power structures that exist in every organization. They know how to cope with competition from peers, or with superiors who resist younger competitors and jealously guard their turf. Through wisdom and perspective they have achieved the ability to realistically assess the career prospects of younger managers and help them plan accordingly. Finally, senior managers find personal satisfaction in the coaching role. Younger managers seek advisors.

For the suggested counseling system to be effective, certain guidelines must exist. There should not be a reporting relationship between coach and player, but an advisory one with senior managers available to give counsel on request. The relationship should not be one of advocacy in which the coach intervenes on behalf of the player. And finally, the coach should avoid the very human tendency to gain a sense of personal accomplishment through the accomplishments of the player.

Such advisory relationships are limited in duration. At some point the younger manager is likely to break away and develop an independent management style. This may be a disappointment to the coach. But while the relationship lasts it can be an effective means of using internal resources to counsel a population of managers at risk of executive stress.

### Peer group counseling

The formation of self-help groups of individuals sharing the stressful experiences of organizational life should be encouraged as an important internal source of counseling for stress. Group process can contribute to constructive thinking through of problems and encourage the synthesis and testing of new approaches.

Organized and ongoing group discussion of issues of common concern provides valuable reassurance to the participants that others were able to resolve similar problems. There are currently in existence a number of groups of managers (including in some instances their spouses) that find discussion of the following issues to be very helpful:

- the problems of living abroad.
- the problems of managers who are parents without partners.
- the problems of two-career couples.
- the problems of the "corporate wife."
- the problems of a heavy travel schedule.

In-house groups of recovered alcoholics have been shown to provide an important source of peer support, leading to continued recovery and successful functioning in sobriety.

### Periodic stress review

A periodic physical examination for managers and executives is now standard practice in many organizations. It is suggested that a structured dialogue focused on how the manager is coping with work and personal pressures be added as part of a comprehensive health review.

Many health examinations include an adjustment component but the relevance of the interaction varies considerably. Physicians interested in psychological issues who have time to listen and the ability to respond to personal communications can be very helpful. If the examining physician is aware of the types of work and life stress managers face, the review is likely to be timely and relevant. The problem with most reviews is that inquiry into how the patient is coping with work or personal relationships receives cursory treatment from the examiner, and perfunctory response from the manager.

The standard dialogue during a periodic health examination is likely to be:

Physician: "How are you feeling?"

Manager: "Fine."

Physician: "Are you under stress?"

Manager: "No more than usual."

Physician: "Do you have any specific problems?"

Manager: "Not really."

Many managers acknowledge that they allow themselves too little time for reflection. "I have no time to think. I just react. And that worries me," is a common complaint of managers.

Generally the manager who just reacts at work will just react in personal life as well. The periodic health examination provides an opportunity for personal reflection if the review is conducted by a physician or health professional with special competence to counsel for stress. The map of executive stress and the questions suggested for its use in the Appendix can function as a check list of pertinent issues for discussion.

## A PERSONAL STRESS COUNSELING PROGRAM

A model program is presented here to illustrate an approach to personal stress counseling. The program is also applicable to other health maintenance and counseling activities ordinarily carried out by the organization:

• counseling for health-related performance problems including, but not confined to, substance abuse.

• counseling in connection with determining medical fitness of employees and dependents for expatriate assignment.

• counseling for employees in personal crisis to be offered on the same basis as intervention in any acute medical crisis.

• pre-retirement counseling.

• preparation for relocation and/or job change.

The relevance of each program component to the specific organization, population at risk or manager group must be designed to meet the identified needs of each individual organization. There is no alternative to the thinking through of "improvement programs" before committing individual and organizational resources to strategies designed to cope with management stress.

### Features of the program

**1**  Services: services are to be offered to all employees and dependents on a voluntary, confidential, no-cost basis as a supplement to, but not a replacement for, outpatient services available under existing medical benefit plans. Providers are to be contacted directly by the employee. Services include:

• orientation workshops in personal stress management for employees and dependents conducted off the premises in groups of up to twenty participants, and

• brief crisis-oriented counseling services suited to individual and/or family needs up to a limit of five sessions per employee (including services to dependents).

a) *Workshops* aid in the assessment of personal crises and effective decision-making, and orient participants to constructive ways of coping with stress. The workshop concludes with a discussion of further steps to be taken and the variety of counseling services available under the program for those who seek personal consultation or counseling.

b) *A single consultation session* with a professional counselor is offered to employees (with or without other family members) to evaluate personal problems, reduce distress and determine the need, if any, for further brief crises-oriented services.

c) *Brief counseling suited to individual and family needs* is offered up to a total of five sessions per family (including the consultation session). Individual, group, family and marital counseling will take place in the private offices of professional counselors. The identity of participants will be kept strictly confidential and no records will be sent to the employer.

2   Providers: services are to be provided off the premises by an outside group of health professionals with special expertise in the areas of occupational stress and career-related personal crises.

•   Members of the professional group understand that services must be made immediately available to employees.

•   Professional services are intended to be brief and crises-oriented. Every effort will be made to accomplish counseling goals within the five session limit. Any recommendation for further counseling must be reviewed by the professional group.

•   If counseling is recommended beyond the program entitlement referral will be made to outside treatment resources. Further treatment will be at employee expense utilizing applicable medical coverage. Continuing with a member of the professional counseling group is also available at the option of the employee.

3   Feedback to Management: before the program is offered to employees the professional counselors will meet as a group and formulate a plan to evaluate their findings (while maintaining the confidentiality of client communications). Management will be provided with periodic and timely reports on occupational stress factors and internal organizational social support systems to be used for planning purposes.

4   Program Evaluation: all steps in this special counseling program (workshop, consultation session, subsequent counseling services) as well as the "professionalism" of the program will be evaluated by the participants and the evaluation reported to management.

## LOOKING AHEAD

Managers should become aware of developments in two areas that will undoubtedly influence their future stress management efforts: 1) the responsibility of the employer for helping employees to cope with the stressfulness of the workplace and 2) the effect of social change on the manager's roles.

Like exposure to toxic substances, the stressfulness of the workplace is now regarded as an occupational hazard. This development raises two as yet unresolved issues: the extent of employer liability for employee's stress related illnesses; and the employers' responsibility for providing programs to help employees cope with these illnesses.

Government health agencies recommend that the most effective approach is to provide employees with the means to cope with work stress and its consequences through social support systems at work and employee assistance programs, rather than attempt to change the work environment. Present policy indicates that the government is likely to take the initiative in shaping the direction of employers' stress management programs to help employees cope with the most common of stress-related health problems—alcoholism, depression and marital maladjustment. Difficulties arise when employers follow such regulations without realizing that each organization requires a stress management program tailored to internal needs. Managers should therefore be prepared to shape programs according to the constellation of stressors found within their organizations.

The interaction between business and the changing values of society today will profoundly influence the managers' roles, but in as yet unknown ways (Lodge, 1974). According to Lodge, changing social values will call into question the authority of management unless large organizations become responsive to public demands.

It can be anticipated that management will be required to respond more and more to external and community initiatives that use the organization to bring about social change (greater employment of minority workers, for example). Employees, as a matter of entitlement, will seek to gain self-esteem from their work, to become masters of their immediate environments and to feel that their work is important.

Alternatives to management authority are emerging. Decision

by consensus, somewhat like the Japanese system of management, self-managed work teams, and participative management provide a sense of fulfillment at the expense of conventional authority structure. The success of these alternatives implies that some levels of the management hierarchy may not be necessary.

Counseling for the stress of changing roles requires programs to broaden the manager's vision and develop an awareness of challenges to accustomed practices and roles.

> *It requires courage (for the manager) to rinse out the mind and inspect all the assumptions (especially those that underlie his power and legitimize it); to consider the interests of the whole and not merely his own momentary bureaucratic status and prerogatives; to think the unthinkable and discuss it.*
>
> (LODGE, p. 69)

The managers' need to think through current challenges to familiar roles emphasizes the principal theme of this book. Knowing what to anticipate and how to prepare for it helps managers achieve the benefits of successful coping with stress.

## REFERENCES

Cummings, N. A. (1977). Prolonged (ideal) versus short-term (realistic) psychotherapy. *Professional Psychology* (8):491.

Cummings, N. A., and W. T. Follette (1976). Brief psychotherapy and medical utilization. In H. Dorken (ed.) *The Professional Psychologist Today: New Developments in Law, Health Insurance, and Health Practice.* San Francisco, Jossey-Bass: pp. 165–174.

Jones, K. R., and T. R. Vischi (1979). Impact of alcohol, drug abuse and mental health treatment on medical care utilization: a review of the research literature. Supplement to *Medical Care* (17) No. 12.

Lodge, G. C. (1974). Business and the changing society. *Harvard Business Review:* 59–72.

# APPENDIX:
# AN EXECUTIVE'S MAP OF MANAGEMENT STRESS

Every manager or executive will face a series of challenging personal and career crises, transitions and stressful events during a career in an organizational setting. To cope effectively choices and decisions must be made.

The executive's map of management stress (Figs. A and B) is a guide to the realistic self-assessment so essential to effective problem solving. It is designed to increase awareness, provide perspective and channel concerns and introspection. At best, an awareness of how hopes, ambition and personality interact with opportunity, personal relations and work environment will lead to creative problem solving. At worse, realistic self-assessment will lead to constructive worrying.

Ideally, the aspiring young executive is aware that not every high potential performer will become chief executive officer but that it is possible, after overcoming disappointment, to function happily in a lesser role. Ideally, every manager in mid-career will yield gracefully to the forces of the life cycle that shift one's capacities from inspired, driving, competitive solo performer to older and wiser leader, mentor, developer of the talents of others. Ideally, each manager will anticipate challenges to the fit between skills and personal goals and organizational requirements and opportunities, and will prepare accordingly, by seeking alternative career channels or retraining, and by assuring viable external job options at all times to avoid becoming boxed-in, obsolete or dependent on the status quo for survival. And last but not least, ideally managers will realize that pursuing career goals and responding to work

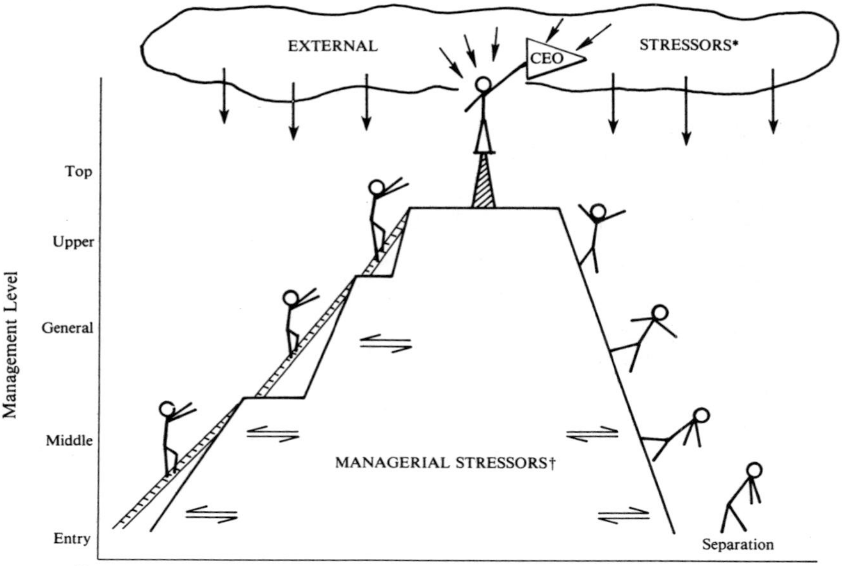

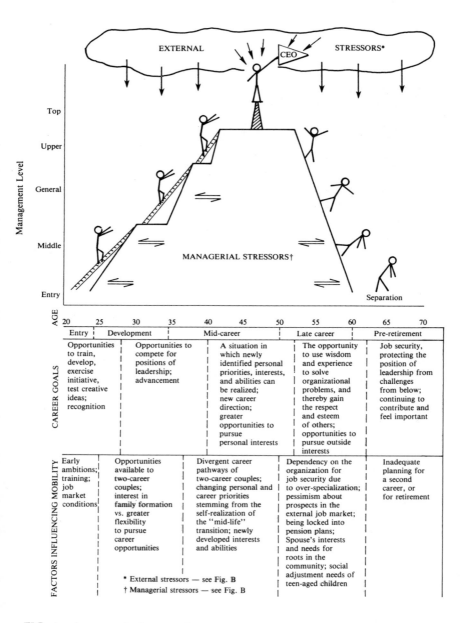

EXTERNAL
STRESSORS*
CEO
Management Level
Top
Upper
General
Middle
Entry
MANAGERIAL STRESSORS†
Separation


| AGE | 20 25 | 25 30 35 | 35 40 45 50 | 50 55 60 | 60 65 70 |
|---|---|---|---|---|---|
| | Entry | Development | Mid-career | Late career | Pre-retirement |
| CAREER GOALS | Opportunities to train, develop, exercise initiative, test creative ideas; recognition | Opportunities to compete for positions of leadership; advancement | A situation in which newly identified personal priorities, interests, and abilities can be realized; new career direction; greater opportunities to pursue personal interests | The opportunity to use wisdom and experience to solve organizational problems, and thereby gain the respect and esteem of others; opportunities to pursue outside interests | Job security, protecting the position of leadership from challenges from below; continuing to contribute and feel important |
| FACTORS INFLUENCING MOBILITY | Early ambitions; training; job market conditions | Opportunities available to two-career couples; interest in family formation vs. greater flexibility to pursue career opportunities | Divergent career pathways of two-career couples; changing personal and career priorities stemming from the self-realization of the "mid-life" transition; newly developed interests and abilities | Dependency on the organization for job security due to over-specialization; pessimism about prospects in the external job market; being locked into pension plans; Spouse's interests and needs for roots in the community; social adjustment needs of teen-aged children | Inadequate planning for a second career, or for retirement |

* External stressors — see Fig. B
† Managerial stressors — see Fig. B

FIG. A *An executive's map of management stress.*

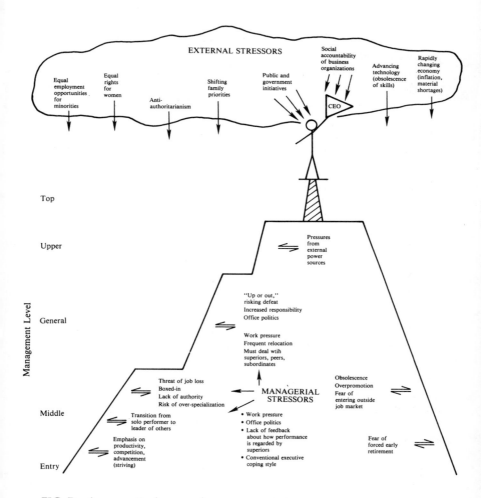

FIG. B  *An executive's map of management stress.*

247

pressures are not all there is to life; that it is also satisfying and a source of self-esteem to pursue personal interests, respond to family demands and fulfill responsibilities to others. But ideally adjusted managers are rare, as are ideally adjusted individuals in other occupations or professions that involve survival in an ever-changing atmosphere that cannot be personally controlled.

Managers or executives need help with the common psychosocial dilemmas relating to management stress, such as:

- organizational mores that stimulate competitive striving for advancement within a pyramidal structure that predisposes to dissatisfaction, disappointment, and defeat.

- management practices that promise advancement for competent performance but fail to follow through with career planning or training to deal with known mid- and late-career progression problems.

- job demands that invade all aspects of personal life and predispose to crises, and an executive style of coping with crisis that requires the appearance of control at all times achieved by denying conflict and suppressing distress.

The map sketches career transitions (vertical axis) and life transitions (horizontal axis), indicates how forces acting on the individual and the organization may affect compatibility over time (arrows within and around the organizational pyramid), and reminds us of the ever-present challenges of external conditions (dark cloud threatening overhead.) It is meant for the private use of the manager at any level. The goal is to think through the more "personal and private" issues that one tends to deny, avoid or simply overlook as less important than immediate work pressures and striving to get ahead. The manager is asked to answer *hard* questions about the stressful work and life events he or she has just been through or is going through at the moment, or that may be in prospect in the foreseeable future.

After answering the checklist of "stressful events in the life of a manager" and answering the "hard questions," the manager decides on the coping strategies that are required *now*. The reader is encouraged to review the principles for individual coping strategies listed below and then plan for the future.

## HOW TO USE THE EXECUTIVE'S MAP
## OF MANAGEMENT STRESS

Managers must anticipate challenging conditions and plan accordingly if they are to cope successfully with management stress. This requires a realistic assessment of interacting influences both at their work and in their personal lives that may lead to significant changes, transitions, crises and disappointments.

The Executive's Map of Management Stress (FIG. A) is intended to heighten the user's awareness of some of these influences. It sketches the interaction of such factors as age, organizational structure, career progression patterns, changing personal goals, conditions that influence mobility, and external stressors that threaten accustomed organizational practices.

Review the map, then think of your own situation. If possible, find your place on the map. Then answer the hard questions listed below. It is hard to think through the issues raised here without encountering problems and concerns. But remember, the reward for thinking through of worrisome issues is the stimulation of creative problem solving.

Each series of questions below ends with a principle for personal strategies to cope with stress. At the conclusion of this exercise you may have identified challenges that must be dealt with. You may or may not have a ready plan to cope with these challenges. Remember that the goal of heightened awareness is to counteract the denial or avoidance of troublesome issues and to reduce resistance to change. The most important question to be answered is, "Do I have a problem?" Once the problem is defined constructive solutions will follow.

### Hard questions

*Issue 1: career goals*

What were your career goals when you entered the organization?

What are your goals now?

How have your goals changed to reflect:

- available opportunities?
- how your potential is regarded by superiors?

- what you have come to realize are your special talents and interests?
- your evolving family responsibilities?

Are you advancing your career goals in your present position?

*Principle 1:* unrealistic goals or ambitions that are not altered by experience and an increasing awareness of self may lead to severe and disabling disappointment when these goals are not fulfilled.

*Issue 2: present job*
What are the satisfactions of your present job?

What are the stresses?

How do your superiors regard your performance? Your potential for advancement?

How secure is your present job?

What are your alternatives to your present job?

How will you feel if you are in the same job three years from now? What actions will you take then?

*Principle 2:* be prepared for unexpected challenges to your job security. Have a realistic alternative to your present job available at all times. Continue to learn new skills and to find new applications of old skills. You should not depend on the organization exclusively to assure your job security, or to fill your career development needs.

*Issue 3: job change*
What job changes are you facing now? In the near future?

Do these changes involve:

- the need to learn new skills?
- important career transitions (such as assuming a leadership position, shifting from specialist to generalist, winding down an active career)?

How will these changes affect your lifestyle? Members of your family?

What preparations are you making to cope with changes in life-style? Or to accommodate the interests of members of your family?

*Principle 3:* successful adjustment to previous job change by you or your family does not guarantee adjustment to the next change. Each job choice and each transition must be thought through anew. Sufficient information should be available to make a realistic job choice or commitment. Realistic assessments require the involvement of family members in the decision making process.

*Issue 4: mobility*
How do you assess your mobility in the event you may be required to:

- relocate?
- take a new job?
- join a new organization?
- develop a new career?

What factors (family, lifestyle, personal interests, skills) will enhance your mobility? What factors will restrict your mobility?

*Principle 4:* impending changes and transitions tend to strain fragile personal relationships and to expose latent conflicts. Decisions regarding important changes that will affect your lifestyle and the interests and adjustment of members of your family should be made in consultation with those who will be affected by the change. Resolving conflicts and personal problems in advance of an important change enhances mobility and avoids career-related crises later on.

*Issue 5: stressful life events*
What were the stressful events in your life during the past year?

What are the stresses in your life today?

What stresses do you anticipate in the near future?

What is the impact of these life stresses on your well-being, effectiveness, and health?

Do you feel overloaded?

How are stressful life events affecting your capacity to cope with work pressures? Personal pressures?

What are you doing to cope with the stressful events in your life?

*Principle 5:* all stressors have a cumulative effect. Coping with one stressor will decrease the total pressure you are under and increase your capacity to deal more effectively with other stressful life events. Therefore, decide where your coping efforts will yield the greatest results and concentrate on that area of your life (job pressure, family problems). Other areas of your life will benefit from successful coping with the major (or most manageable) pressure.

*Issue 6: health*
What is the state of your health? Your physical fitness?

Is your health adversely affected by such avoidable habits as overeating? Smoking? Excessive striving?

*Principle 6:* poor health is a major stressor as well as a consequence of stress. Maintain good health and avoid excessive striving through effective time management, delegation of responsibilities where appropriate, and the establishment of realistic work and personal priorities.

*Issue 7: a personal plan*
What problems and concerns have emerged as a result of the issues raised here?

What are your plans and strategies to cope with them?

*Principle 7:* it is not a sign of weakness or dependence if, while formulating a personal plan to cope with challenges, you seek the advice and counsel of others.

# INDEX